Anna May Wong

Anna May Wong

A Complete Guide to Her Film, Stage, Radio and Television Work

Philip Leibfried *and* Chei Mi Lane

McFarland & Company, Inc., Publishers
Jefferson, North Carolina, and London

ALSO BY PHILIP LEIBFRIED
AND FROM MCFARLAND

*Rudyard Kipling and Sir Henry Rider Haggard on
Screen, Stage, Radio and Television* (2000; paperback 2008)

Frontispiece: Anna May Wong circa 1935

The present work is a reprint of the illustrated case bound edition of Anna May Wong: A Complete Guide to Her Film, Stage, Radio and Television Work, *first published in 2004 by McFarland.*

LIBRARY OF CONGRESS CATALOGUING-IN-PUBLICATION DATA

Leibfried, Philip, 1948–
Anna May Wong : a complete guide to her film, stage, radio and television work / Philip Leibfried and Chei Mi Lane.
p.   cm.
Includes bibliographical references and index.

ISBN 978-0-7864-4696-4
softcover : 50# alkaline paper ∞

1. Wong, Anna May, 1905–1961.   I. Lane, Chei Mi, 1957–
II. Title
PN2287.W56L45   2010   791.4302'8'092 — dc22   2003020314

British Library cataloguing data are available

©2004 Philip Leibfried and Chei Mi Lane. All rights reserved

*No part of this book may be reproduced or transmitted in any form
or by any means, electronic or mechanical, including photocopying
or recording, or by any information storage and retrieval system,
without permission in writing from the publisher.*

Cover photographs: *(foreground)* Anna May Wong from the 1934 Paramount
film *Limehouse Blues; (background)* shadow detail from the 1931
Paramount film *Daughter of the Dragon*

Manufactured in the United States of America

*McFarland & Company, Inc., Publishers
Box 611, Jefferson, North Carolina 28640
www.mcfarlandpub.com*

To the memory of the one and only
Anna May Wong
(1905–1961)

Two Acknowledgments

[P.L.] With a career far more diverse and often more obscure than many performers, Anna May Wong proved a tough subject to research. Such a project required as much assistance as possible. Fortunately, I had an indefatigable and enthusiastic collaborator in Chei Mi Lane, whose unflagging zeal was inspiring. Thanks, Chei Mi. I was also blessed with the assistance of a fellow New Yorker, my friend John Cocchi, "The Researcher's Researcher," who discovered some of the more obscure items found in the following pages. My longtime contact at the Library of Congress, Madeline Matz, was again a major force in sending me much needed material. To Vincent Sneed goes my profound gratitude for suggesting the idea of this book way back when. Special thanks also to Elaine Mae Woo, who took time from her own Anna May project to help out.

To Michael Dixon, Archivist of the British Puppet and Model Theatre Guild, Tony Freeman of the London branch of The Sherlock Holmes Society, Douglas Hayward of the National Directory of Puppets and Related Material in Staffordshire and David Barraclough, who all helped with the single most obscure entry herein, goes my sincere gratitude.

To Fabian Cepeda of Argentina goes my sincere thanks for sending some obscure data. To the world's greatest film-buff, Pierre Guinle, my thanks for your assistance and continued support.

To all of the following who gave of their time in sending information and material, my sincerest thanks: Haris Balic of the Osterreiches Theater Museum, Vienna; Hans Berggreen of Det Kongelige Bibliotek, Copenhagen; Elizabeth Bernard, Research Assistant, Performing Arts Museum, Melbourne, Australia; George Biderman; Stephen Bourne; Matthew W. Buff, Reference Assistant, San Francisco Performing Arts Library and Museum; Melanie T. Christoudia, Curatorial Assistant, Theatre Museum, London; Annette Fern, Research and Reference Librarian of the Nathan Marsh Pusey Library, Harvard University; Chris Gampel; Jay Hickerson; Ed Hurley; Bruce Kellner; Claus Kjer of Det Danske Filmmuseum, Copenhagen, Denmark; Roberto Landazuri, Librarian at the San Francisco Public Library; Marguerite Lavin of the Museum of the City of New York; Kristen Maier, Librarian of the Deutsches Filmmuseum in Frankfort/Main, Germany; Thomas Mauch, Chair of the English Dept. at Colorado College, Colorado Springs; Merrill T. McCord; Verena Nickel of the State Library of Berlin; Michael Ravnitzky; John Riley, Library Services, British Film Institute; Ray Schnitzer, Brian Taves of the Library of Congress; John Yau; the staff of the Shubert Archive in New York; the staff of the Library for the Performing Arts in New York.

Special thanks to Hugh O'Brian, TV's Wyatt Earp, for taking time from his busy schedule to answer my letter.

A hearty "Vielen dank!" to my German e-mail pal Verena Hartmann, whose translation skills were a big help with Anna May's German films. To Pat Battle I extend much gratitude for sending me some fascinating photos. Thanks also to Sue Terry for her generous assistance.

My late friend and fellow historian Gene Vazzana deserves my eternal gratitude for his support and enthusiasm for this project, being as eager as I was to see this project reach fruition and doing all he could to help.

And, of course, my usual support crew: Ellen Aug-Lytle, Catherine Beck, Michael F. Blake, Kelly Brown, Ann Chase, John DeBartolo, Sally Dumaux, Ellen Flanagan, Katie Harris, Larry Ivie, Estella Johnson, Annette D'Agostino Lloyd, Tsuyoshi Minamoto, Jannine Petska, George Rackus, Franklin Santana, Thom Sciacca, Frances Whalen, Michael Whalen, Richard Whalen, Fred Yannantuono and Gary Zaboly — thanks to all of you for your continued interest in my projects.

Philip Leibfried
New York, Summer 2003

[C.M.L.] To Phil, I owe this whole book. He has never wavered in his support for my part in this work. He patiently waited while I took almost three years to heal from a broken neck, never putting pressure on me until I was able to handle it. He has been a true friend, and also a real pro.

Annette D'Agostino Lloyd introduced me to Phil during the early days of mass Internet service, when the Usenet Newsgroups were the best way to get a message out there. That was six years ago, but I have never forgotten her and what she caused to happen. Thanks, Annette. Without you, my name is not on this work.

For setting me straight about the Chinese Characters pertaining to Anna May Wong's name and for a lifetime of support, my wife Xuan Busch has a lifetime of love ahead from me.

Larry Ching, Dale Choy, and Wellman Wong have not only befriended me, they have given me valuable details and historical information. In researching Anna May Wong, their knowledge has helped make people and events come alive. I literally walked through the scenes of some of Anna's movies and life. They have my eternal gratitude.

Michael Sullivan helped me dig up information on Anna May long before the book became a project. Thanks for all the times we shared.

Vince Sneed started the ball rolling with the first fan magazine devoted to Anna May Wong. He is to be commended. Thanks also to Lillian Spencer and William Song.

Chei Mi Lane
St. Louis, Summer 2003

Contents

Two Acknowledgments vii
Prologue 1
Introduction 7
Chronology 9

I. American Silent Films 11
II. European Silent Films 65
III. European Sound Films 73
IV. American Sound Films 88
V. Stage Work 148
VI. Radio and Television 161

Epilogue 173
Bibliography 175
Index 177

Prologue

With the passage of the Chinese Exclusion Act in 1882, life suddenly became markedly more difficult for those adventurous souls who had journeyed across the vast Pacific Ocean from Asia to make their fortunes in the United States, or "Gold Mountain," as they referred to it. The act instituted a ten-year ban against the immigration of laborers from China. While the door was still open to merchants, officials, teachers, students and travelers, it was the men who worked with their hands who formed the bulk of the immigrants from that ancient land. An earlier piece of legislation, the Alien Land Act of 1870, had forbidden any Chinese from owning real estate, and an 1879 Supreme Court decision disallowed them from becoming naturalized citizens.

The Chinese first arrived in appreciable numbers during the 1848 gold rush at Sutter's Mill in California. Those pioneer immigrants all came from Canton in Kwangtung province, the only Chinese port open to foreign merchants at the time. Immediately they were persecuted for being "too different," far "too exotic" to be acceptable in American society, with their "slanted" eyes, strange language and even stranger habits. Their purpose in coming to the United States was simply to make a quick strike in the gold fields and return to their homeland to retire in comfort. It was only natural that they should live together, establish their own organizations, and attempt to retain their ethnic identity. As in every society, there were mavericks who tried to assimilate, but they were very few among the Cantonese.

Added to these conspicuous differences were the writings of Americans visiting China, who seemed to have eyes only for the corruption in the government there. Their books and articles further fanned the flames of a bias which was already growing out of hand.

Both the national and local legal systems worked against the Chinese; besides being prohibited from attaining citizenship, they were criticized for handling criminal matters in their own fashion. In 1879 the state constitution of California was rewritten, banning Chinese labor in public works. Never mind that the railroad linking California to the rest of the nation had been built mainly by Chinese laborers replacing whites who left that task to try their luck at various gold and silver strikes. Those "dang furinners" were still stealing jobs from Americans, so they had to be stopped.

With the completion of the railroads and the decline in mining, the Chinese who had lost or failed to make their fortunes moved to some of the larger cities, where they formed their own communities, known as "Chinatowns." Many were employed in different types of manufacture. Others went into the laundry business. Such a venture took little capital to start, required a meager knowledge of English to run, filled a ubiquitous need, and, most importantly, was non-competitive with whites, who considered it "woman's work." Some gravitated to farming, that having been their occupation in the old country. They helped inexperienced American fruit growers cultivate new strains, such as the Bing cherry, which was developed by an individual named Ah Bing.

Still others became domestic servants in the homes of the wealthy. This did nothing to ingratiate them to the vast American public, who were always envious of the rich. It seemed the newcomers just could not win. Anti-Chinese bias soon turned to violence, reaching a peak in 1885. One of the most egregious incidents was the Rock Springs Massacre which occurred in September of that dark year in Rock Springs, Wyoming Territory. Chinatown was burned to the ground and at least twenty-eight residents of that district lost their lives.

Even language was affected by their situation. The expression "He didn't stand a Chinaman's chance" meant utter hopelessness.

Passed in 1888, the Scott Act outdid the earlier law in unfairness. It expressly forbade Chinese laborers from entering the United States, including those who owned valid re-entry permits. This piece of legislation also included a more narrow definition of the five groups which *were* allowed to immigrate.

A mere four years later, yet another anti–Chinese measure, the Geary Act, was passed. This one disallowed resident Chinese writs of *habeas corpus* in cases of arrest. It also required them to register with the government and obtain a certificate attesting to their eligibility to remain in the United States. Chinese community leaders advised their people not to comply with this blatantly biased law. When two men lacking this bit of paper brought suit against the government, the Supreme Court ruled against them and marked them for deportation. This meant that all those non-compliant with the law stood a chance of being deported. Having been discredited, the community leaders were faced with challenges to the right to hold their positions. The result was a series of "*tong* wars" (a *tong* was a secret society) erupting chiefly in San Francisco, and to a smaller degree in other major cities in the 1890s, as the *tongs* sought control of their communities. From these conflicts emerged the most vicious stereotype of the Chinese—cunning, cowardly, violence-prone criminals who prowled about carrying hatchets or with daggers hidden in their sleeves in search of white victims. This inaccurate and unfortunate representation would linger in the Anglo-American consciousness for generations to come, perpetuated and abetted by such fictional creations as the evil Dr. Fu Manchu, Ming the Merciless and the Dragon Lady.

Meanwhile, anti–Chinese legislation became anti–*Asian* legislation as immigrants from Japan and Korea also arrived on American soil. Quotas on immigration were set, and with the National Origins Act of 1924, which lowered percentages allowed from each nation, *all* Asian immigration was banned except for Filipinos, who were allowed in only by virtue of their having lived in an American protectorate.

Assimilation of another type was dealt a severe blow by the passage of anti–Asian miscegenation laws in thirteen states, California among them. It was December 1943 before the original exclusion act was repealed, at which time the Chinese were brought under the quota of the National Origins Act and naturalization granted to all resident Chinese. In October 1948 the California State Supreme Court ruled that miscegenation laws were illegal. Those of most of the other states, however, remained on the books until

1967, when they were finally declared unconstitutional by the United States Supreme Court.

On the literary front, the term "Yellow Peril" was coined when Caucasian novelists and historians depicted the Chinese as a serious menace to the white race and the United States in particular. These representations were very inaccurate, since the authors did not bother researching their subjects. Sadly, historical events were soon to fortify this fear.

With the increasing influx of Christian missionaries and the threat of control of China's economy by several western nations, matters were brought to a head in the Celestial Kingdom in June 1900. A Chinese peasant movement known as the Fists of Righteous Harmony ("Boxers" in western parlance, due to their use of martial arts) sought to drive the whites from their country by any means, including murder. When they laid siege to the foreign legations in China's capital, Peking (now Beijing), with the support of the government, the term "Yellow Peril" received worldwide attention. An international force lifted the siege after eight weeks, but the threat of Asian dominance persisted in the west. More fuel was added to this phobia with tiny Japan's startling victory over mighty Russia in the Russo-Japanese War of 1904–05.

All of the aforementioned events impacted upon the efforts of both immigrant Chinese and their descendants to better their situation. Many were able to find some acceptance by creating or supplying products or services sought by Caucasians, like the aforementioned farmers and launderers. Others were content to deal only with their own people. A paltry few ventured into show business, but were unable to advance beyond vaudeville, where they were regarded as oddities.

In the 1910s and 1920s several "all-Chinese" film companies sprang up, of which Marion E. Wong's Mandarin Film Company of Oakland was the first. Their purpose was to provide motion pictures with authentic Chinese actors and actresses in stories featuring accurate portrayals of the Chinese people. Unlike the related "race movies" produced by African-American outfits, they quickly withered and died, like unwatered flowers, due to a lack of outlets for exhibiting them.

A few entertainers did manage to make names for themselves. A Japanese dancer by the name of Tokuko Nogai Takagi (1891–1919) came to the United States and appeared in four films for the Thanhouser Company in 1911 and 1912, all unfortunately lost. In 1914 a native-born Japanese actor named Sessue Hayakawa (1889–1973) entered films in the U.S. and became an immediate star. His wife, Tsuru Aoki (1892–1961), also a native Japanese, appeared in many of his films. By the mid-twenties he had departed for Europe, making pictures in France and England. (Hayakawa did appear in one Hollywood film in the 1930s—*Daughter of the Dragon* (1931). He later returned to his native Japan where he appeared in only one film; after that it was back to France until 1949, when Hollywood again beckoned. The busy actor made two more films in his homeland in the early 1950s before returning to the west. He died in Tokyo. A popular vaudeville singer known as "The Chinese Nightingale," the Cantonese-born Lady Tsen Mei (1888–1985), starred in a film for the Lubin Company of Philadelphia in 1918 entitled *For the Freedom of the East*. She made at least two subsequent film appearances in the 1920s, then returned to vaudeville before changing her name to Josephine Kramer and opening a booking agency with her American husband in the early 1940s.

These were the exceptions and all Asian-born; other Asians and Asian-Americans toiled for years as movie extras while Caucasians made up to look Asian, a technique known as "yellowface," were given the important roles and the credits. It would take an extremely precocious and determined second-generation Chinese-American girl, who early in life became enamored of motion pictures, to attain more than a modicum of success in the industry and to break down the barriers allowing others of Asian extraction to receive real recognition on the silver screen in the United States.

It was in the shadow of the Geary Act that Anna May Wong was born as Wong Liu Tsong (the Chinese place the surname first) in Los Angeles on January 3, 1905, the second of seven children. The ebullient Theodore Roosevelt lived in the White House and life in America reflected his ambitious spirit. Within the previous fifteen years, motorcars and motion pictures had made their appearances, and just a little over a year before, the Wright brothers had shown man how to fly. The United States had joined the imperialist nations of Europe when it acquired several possessions of Spain after a brief war with that weakening country in 1898. This exciting period also saw the arrival of millions of immigrants from all over the globe, albeit chiefly from Europe, each group bringing its distinctive culture to the Land of the Free. Each group also felt the sting of discrimination, but not to the extent of its being made legal, as in the case of the Chinese.

Lee Gon Toy, Wong Liu Tsong, Wong Liu Ying, Wong Sam Sing

Even though both of Liu Tsong's parents, Wong Sam Sing and Lee Gon Toy, had also been born in California, they retained the customs of their ancestors. Sam Sing's father had made and kept a small fortune working in the mines.

He later settled in San Francisco, where his son was born. When he reached manhood, Sam Sing traveled to China, where he married and sired a son. Returning to California, he wed Liu Tsong's mother and operated a laundry on Flower Street outside the crowded confines of Los Angeles' Chinatown. It was above this establishment that the future film star received her initial impressions of life.

Although well cared for at home, Liu Tsong and her older sister, Liu Ying, suffered the taunts and gibes of their schoolmates for being the only Asians in the public school they attended. Eventually their parents transferred them to the Chinese Mission school where all the children were Chinese. Later they also attended Chinese school in the evenings.

Miss Wong wrote of her childhood in a two-part article published in *Pictures* magazine in 1926. The manner in which her fellow students would bully her and her sister and shout ethnic slurs at them, she described as "…the knife stab which, even today, has left a scar on my heart." This was her introduction to anti–Asian racism, the spectre which would haunt the multi-talented actress throughout her life, as it had countless others. Her response to this obstacle can be seen in the following pages.

Introduction

She was truly one-of-a-kind, the first and only Asian-American actress to achieve stardom during Hollywood's Golden Age, in a career that spanned more than four decades. She later became the first Asian-American to have her own television series. Anna May Wong's very uniqueness proved to be a double-edged sword, however, making her climb to the top a tortuous one. First and foremost was her family's opposition to her becoming an actress, an occupation seriously frowned upon by traditional Chinese. When they saw the money Anna May was earning from it and the modeling work she was also doing, they eased up a bit, however. While lacking any real competition among her fellow Asian-American performers, Anna May had to withstand the discrimination against her race, which remained a potent force throughout most of her life, looming like an invisible great wall between her and both truly significant film roles and marital happiness. To wed one of her own race would have meant giving up the career for which she had worked so hard and becoming subservient to her husband; to wed a non-Asian was impossible due to California's miscegenation laws. Either way, Anna May would have had to abandon her lifelong dream. She therefore remained single.

With all the grace and delicacy implied by her Chinese name of "Frosted Yellow Willow," Anna May Wong won the hearts of connoisseurs of female beauty wherever she traveled. Redefining the term "class act," filmdom's first Asian-American star became living proof that one can realize one's dreams by remaining steadfastly focused on them. This she did with a passionate determination. Despite having only a tenth grade education, Anna May taught herself all she needed to know for her chosen profession by religiously attending motion pictures and carefully studying the styles of its pioneer actors and actresses.

Although her frequent hooky playing from her lessons incurred the indignation of her tradition-bound father, Anna May persisted and eventually had her day in the sun, most notably in Europe. There the actress attained true stardom and blossomed into an enchantingly beautiful example of Chinese womanhood. Her natural grace of movement was the stuff of legend; her hands especially, with their long lissome fingers, gave promise of an exceptionally sensual touch. With large, mesmerizing, almond-shaped eyes, her raven hair in bangs, and a complexion described as "a rose blushing through old ivory," she became the darling of the intelligentsia, who responded to her beauty, talent and elegance with poems, songs and other artistic tributes. Sophisticated, witty and multi-lingual, Anna May Wong more than held her own in their company.

In addition to films, the entertainer appeared on the stage and on radio, performing throughout the British Isles and on the continent. After an extended visit to her ancestral homeland of China in 1936, she returned to the United States, where she resumed her film career and appeared on stage twice more in summer stock. With China being ravaged by Japanese forces, Miss Wong became devoted to Chinese War Relief, a cause which took her heart's priority for the years up until the end of World War II. Forsaking films in 1942, she worked tirelessly in this effort, also doing her bit by entertaining American troops in Alaska and Canada.

Having attained middle age at the end of the war, Anna May played her first character role in a drama for United Artists in 1949. Then it was on to the burgeoning medium of television, where she had her own short-lived series in 1951, which was canceled due to poor scripts and low ratings. Once bitten, twice shy, the veteran actress did not return to television work until 1956, making several guest appearances on various dramatic series in the next few years. In 1960 she had a supporting role in a Lana Turner vehicle for Universal. Producer Ross Hunter then signed her for a role in the film version of the immensely popular all-Asian Broadway musical, *Flower Drum Song*. But it was not to be. On February 3, 1961, Anna May Wong, filmdom's pre-eminent Asian-American performer, passed away in her sleep of a heart attack at her brother's home in Santa Monica at the too-young age of fifty-six. One might say that she died of a broken heart due to the many sacrifices that she made over the years.

Leaving a legacy of some sixty film appearances, numerous stage and television shows and several radio spots, Anna May Wong remains an outstanding role model for all Asian-American performers. That none of her followers has even approached her career for either longevity or variety is proof positive of her importance in show business history, while her graceful figure and haunting beauty endures as an image for the ages.

Chronology

1905	Born Wong Liu Tsong January 3 in Los Angeles.	1936	Visits China for first and only time. Returns to U.S. in September.
1919	First film appearance as extra in *The Red Lantern*.	1937	Signs with Paramount.
1921	First on-screen credit in *Bits of Life*.	1939	Travels to Australia and New Zealand on behalf of Chinese war relief.
1922	Stars in first true Technicolor film made in Hollywood, *The Toll of the Sea*.	1942	Signs three-picture deal with PRC; only two are made. Retires from screen.
1923	Selected by Douglas Fairbanks for role of the Mongol Slave in *The Thief of Bagdad*, released in 1924.	1944	Entertains troops for USO in Canada and Alaska and works for China Relief Fund.
1928	Leaves U.S. for Germany. Stars in her first European film, *Song*.	1949	Returns to screen in *Impact* for United Artists, her first character role. Father dies in October.
1929	Goes to England. Appears on stage for the first time in London in *The Circle of Chalk*.	1951	Stars in TV series, *The Gallery of Mme. Liu-Tsong*, on Dumont network. Show canceled after 13 episodes.
1930	Stars in and produces *Tschun-Tschi* in Vienna. Appears on Broadway on Edgar Wallace play *On the Spot*. Mother dies as result of car accident in November.	1957	Narrates episode of *Bold Journey* (ABC), which consists of footage from her Chinese trip.
1933	Back in England. Tours British Isles with stage act.	1960	Final film appearance in *Portrait in Black*.
1934–5	Tours Europe with stage act. Appears in final British film, *Java Head*.	1961	Dies of a heart attack in Santa Monica, California, February 3.

Wandering Up Lo-Fu Creek on a Spring Day

At the canyon's mouth I am singing. Soon
 the path ends. People do not go any higher.
I scramble up cliffs into impossible valleys
 and follow the creek back toward its source.
Up where newborn clouds rise over open rock,
 a guest come into wildflower confusions,
I am still lingering on, my climb unfinished,
 as the sun sinks away, west of peaks galore.

—Li Po (c. 750)

I

American Silent Films

The year was 1919; the great guns of the First World War finally lay mute across the remains of Europe after four horrific years of slaughter which had left the nations of that small continent reeling. Turmoil still reigned in Russia in the wake of the shattering revolution of 1917; the countries on the losing side, Germany, Turkey and Austria-Hungary, experienced everything from runaway inflation to toppled governments. Among the victors, France and Great Britain licked their wounds with the loss of a generation of young men. Only the United States remained relatively unscathed. Physically untouched by the conflict, it stood on the brink of an unparalleled period of excitement and prosperity. In the following year women would become enfranchised, and liquor would be forbidden to be sold or consumed when the Volstead Act, the greatest mistake ever made law, went into effect.

In the world of entertainment, a new form of music called "jazz" was sweeping the nation like a prairie fire, while the preeminence in film attained by the European countries prior to 1914 shifted to America. During the war, American filmmakers had learned new ways of story-telling from their counterparts across the Atlantic, producing longer pictures which signaled the end of the nickelodeon and the rise of the movie palace. The sphere of filmmaking in the United States also changed, from eastern cities such as New York City and Fort Lee to a sleepy suburb of Los Angeles, California, known as Hollywood. The consistently fine weather and variety of locales nearby led to Hollywood's becoming the center of filmmaking in America and eventually the world. It was the dawn of the mega-star era, when names like Chaney, Keaton, Lloyd, Swanson and Valentino would be added to the holdovers from the teens—Chaplin, Fairbanks, Gish and Pickford. Individuals from every walk of life came to try their luck in the Baghdad of the West. Failed stage actors became directors; ambitious salesman became studio heads; cowboys turned into stuntmen and stars; beauty contest winners were transformed, Cinderella-like, into leading ladies. As in the gold rushes of the previous century, the failures far outnumbered the successes. Those who could not make the grade either returned home or took menial jobs in the film capital. The survivors went on to earn enviable salaries and the adulation of millions.

During the teens, studios had sprung up like mushrooms in the Los Angeles area; young Wong Liu Tsong would often skip her lessons to watch the filming that was done on the local streets. She finally yielded to the siren song in 1919 when she westernized her given name to "Anna May" and approached James Wang, an agent who handled much of the Asian talent utilized by the film industry. He sent her over to the Metro lot, where a film with a Chinese setting was in production.

Metro Pictures had been incorporated in March 1915 by Richard Rowland with studios at 6300 Romaine St. With popular stars such as Francis X. Bushman and Edith Storey under contract, they began spending more and more money on their productions, especially on acquiring film rights to literary properties. By 1920 they were in dire financial straits; their stock was bought by Loew's Inc., which was seeking someone to supply films for its ever-expanding chain of theatres. Within the next four years, independent producer Louis B. Mayer would be brought in and the Goldwyn Pictures Corp. acquired to form Metro-Goldwyn-Mayer, the wealthiest and most prestigious Hollywood studio for the following four decades.

The film in which Anna May found herself appearing was called *The Red Lantern*, and was based on a novel about the Boxer Rebellion of 1900. (The women who supported the Boxers were called "Red Lanterns" because they carried those objects when assisting the Boxers in burning missionary buildings.) The fourteen-year-old became one of three hundred lantern bearers in a nocturnal procession. The film's star was Russian emigré Alla Nazimova (1879–1945), a stage actress noted for her portrayals of Ibsen heroines, who had made a very successful switch to motion pictures.

Following her baptism on celluloid, Anna May Wong continued to be a presence in films containing Chinese characters. She had to wait over two years before seeing her name on screen, however. Just over a year after that hurdle, Anna May became a leading lady when she headed the cast of the first Technicolor film made in Hollywood, *The Toll of the Sea* (1922). Although only five reels in length, this picture provided a showcase for Miss Wong's talents which did not go unnoticed by film critics or her peers. This part, along with her work in a Tod Browning melodrama released the following year, caught the eye of Douglas Fairbanks (1883–1939), by then producing lavish costume films starring himself. He picked her for the important role of the Mongol Slave in his grand fantasy *The Thief of Bagdad*, which began production in 1923 and was released in early 1924. Again she received much praise for her portrayal, but no roles of substance were offered her, though two of her other 1924 films were also major hits.

For a brief period in early 1925, Anna May Wong was one of 14 film celebrities comprising "The Cosmics," a group led by leading man Bryant Washburn (1884?–1963), also known as "Bryant Washburn and His Hollywooders." With a bankroll of $10,000, the company started out from Hollywood on February 14. Among the other players were Cullen Landis (1895–1975), Wanda Hawley (1895–1963), Helen Holmes (1892–1950), Ena Gregory (1905–1993), Carl Miller (1893–1979), Ruth Stonehouse (1892–1941), Jack Daugherty (1895–1938), Kathryn McGuire (1903–1978) and Joe Murphy (1877–1961). Washburn was a matinee idol who had begun his career with Essanay in 1911 and was noted for playing "Skinner" in a series of films based on that character.

From the beginning the group experienced problems; there was dissension among the members and several legal actions were brought against them due to overdue bills.

Among the venues at which they performed were Chicago and an auditorium in Berwyn, Illinois, both in late March 1925. They presented a fifty minute program at the latter site, with *Variety*'s reviewer remarking: "Anna May Wong scored the individual hit of the of the turn with two pop numbers, utilizing the Oriental garb. She possesses a good delivery and would survive in the varieties." On March 2 the group appeared at the Tangier Temple of the Shriners in Omaha, Nebraska.

The April 29, 1925 issue of *Variety* announced: "Hollywooders Disband Over Draw and Credit; Detroit Week Brought Other Time, Also Bickering—$3,500 weekly. (Bryant Washburn and his "Hollywooders" disbanded their stage act. Anna May Wong is anticipating continuing as a single attraction in picture theatres.)"

That Anna May was selected to be a member of this otherwise Caucasian company is a tribute to either her status or possibly her friendship with Washburn; most of the performers in the group had appeared in at least one of Washburn's films. He and Anna May were both in *Mary of the Movies* [q.v.] playing themselves, though not in the same scene.

At the groundbreaking of Sid Graumann's world-renowned Chinese Theatre on January 5, 1926, Anna May helped turn the first shovelful of earth with movie queen Norma Talmadge (1895–1957). On April 15, 1927, a tradition of having film personalities place their hand and footprints in cement in the theatre's forecourt was begun. While Talmadge was among the first so honored, Anna May was never invited to participate in this custom. It should be noted that there are but two Asian actors among the over 200 celebrity names embedded there; however, there are three horses and one cartoon character.

In September 1926, Anna May signed with the Roach Studio, home of some of the finest comedy talent around. Hal Roach (1892–1992) was a former actor and stuntman who found his true calling in the production (and sometimes direction) of comedy shorts. While the Asian-American actress was announced as appearing in several films, she made only one during her tenure at the studio. Apparently Roach found it more lucrative to loan her out to other studios, for 1927 was her busiest year; she had roles in six features at studios ranging from Chadwick to MGM.

The following year was to be a pivotal one for Anna May Wong. Of the four American features in which she appeared, two gave her very little screen time, and her footage was completely cut from one. In the remaining film she played in support of Caucasian Myrna Loy (1905–1993) in yellowface. Since Loy's features easily lent themselves to Asian interpretation, she became Hollywood's reigning exotic, despite Anna May's presence. That was the final indignity for Miss Wong; like African-American singer/dancer Josephine Baker (1906–1975) and other non-whites before her, she left America for the more tolerant atmosphere of Europe.

(Anna May Wong may very likely have appeared in a number of other uncredited parts, but with incomplete listings and so many lost films, the only way of determining them would be exhaustive searches of stills. The following filmography contains all her certified appearances. Cited reviews include Miss Wong's name when mentioned, which was sporadically during the silent era. All derogatory terminology, a common occurrence in those days, has been excluded.)

The Red Lantern

Metro Pictures/Nazimova Productions; Released May 4, 1919; 7 reels

Director: Albert Capellani; *Photography*: Eugene Gaudio; *Scenario*: June Mathis and Albert Capellani, adapted from the novel by Edith Wherry; *Art Direction*: Henri Menessier

Cast: Nazimova (Blanche Sackville/Mah Lee), Mrs. McWade (Mme. Ling), Virginia Ross (Huang-Ma), Frank Currier (Sir Philip Sackville), Winter Hall (Rev. Alexander Templeton), Amy Van Ness (Mrs. Templeton), Darrell Foss (Andrew Templeton), Noah Beery (Sam Wang), Harry Mann (Chung), Yukio Ao Yamo (Sing), Edward J. Connelly (Jung-Lu). Anna May is an extra.

The New York Times May 5, 1919: "'The Red Lantern' is rich in detail and ensemble ... despite its splendor and the genuine quality of its characters, is not convincing."

Variety May 9, 1919: "No film production could

be more perfect in the matter of creating the atmosphere of a locale ... far and away the biggest thing Nazimova has ever done in pictures and many times the finest Metro has ever turned out."

The Moving Picture World May 10, 1919: "...the production is a revelation. The Temple of Buddha is a wonderful setting and in the reincarnation of the fictitious goddess the illusion is so striking that one might almost imagine the gorgeous colorings which alone are lacking to complete the effect."

Synopsis: Mahlee is an Eurasian — an outcast among the Chinese and ostracized by the whites. At the death of her grandmother, who had raised her since her mother died in childbirth, she goes to the Christian Mission in Peking, where she is converted to Protestantism. She becomes a sincere and active mission worker.

She meets and falls in love with Andrew Templeton, son of the American minister who heads the mission. Templeton's admiration is constrained by his knowledge of her ethnic background. Sam Wang, a Boxer who professes Christianity, also lives at the mission. He covets Mahlee, but she spurns him in favor of Andrew.

One day Blanche Sackville visits the mission and is recognized by Mahlee as the daughter of the Englishman of whom Mahlee's grandmother had told her.

Templeton becomes attracted to Blanche and Mahlee becomes jealous, especially when she realizes that Blanche's father, who is also her father, favors Templeton's suit.

Sam Wang notes this and convinces Mahlee to join him — to become the Goddess of the Red Lantern. Mahlee still feels the call of both bloods, and though serving the Boxers' cause she cannot bear to have her loved ones become victims of the Boxers. She goes to the mission to warn them of their danger.

There she meets Sir Phillip Sackville and begs him to acknowledge her as his daughter and take her out of China.

Sackville refuses. Mahlee returns to Sam Wang and celebrates the Feast of the Lanterns. The Boxers distrust Mahlee and want her dead, but Wang saves her. A battle between the Boxers and western forces ends in victory for the latter.

Mahlee flees to the Boxers' palace and drinks poison. She is found dead on the throne by Sir Philip, Blanche and Andrew Templeton.

Print status: Only known copy in fragile condition at the Cinematheque Royale in Brussels, Belgium.

Anna May Wong's first appearance in a film was rather inauspicious; she was one of 300 lantern bearers in a night scene. When she took some friends to see the picture, she was unable to identify herself in the crowd.

This was Nazimova's most lavish production and her most popular. Though its cost was high, every cent showed on the screen. The final scene was shot at night on Metro's back lot. Over one hundred members of the press were invited to watch the filming of the coronation procession by six cameramen.

At one point during filming author Edith Wherry visited the Metro set. Among her comments was: "I can see that some alterations have been made in my story in the course of adapting it to the camera, but the changes have in nowise affected the main incidents, nor the general trend of the narrative. The changes, if anything, have made the story more compact."

Dinty

First National/Neilan Productions; Released November 29, 1920; 6 reels
Directed and Produced by: Marshall Neilan; *Story*: Marshall Neilan; *Scenario*: Marion Fairfax; *Photography*: David Kesson; *Assistant Director*: Tom Held
Cast: Wesley Barry (Dinty O'Sullivan), Colleen Moore (Doreen O'Sullivan), Tom Gallery

(Danny O'Sullivan), J. Barney Sherry (Judge Whitely), Marjorie Daw (Ruth Whitely), Pat O'Malley (Jack North), Noah Beery ("King" Dorkh), Walter Chung (Sui Lung), Kate Price (Mrs. O'Toole), Tom Wilson (Barry Flynn), Aaron Mitchell (Alexander Horatius Jones), Newton Hall (The Tough One), Young Hipp ("King" Dorkh's son). Anna May is an extra.

The New York Times November 22, 1920: "...one of those deliberately funny, sad and touching motion pictures that does not conceal its deliberateness ... an accompanying plot ... brings Chinatown villains, an honest Judge [sic], his lovely daughter, an horrific den, subterranean passages, seaplanes, submarines, wireless telautography, opium smuggling, abduction, murder, torture and about everything else conceivable...."

Variety November 26, 1920: "...a lot of human interest stuff, a number of Chinatown shots with the under the surface life ... which all goes to make an interesting picture."

Synopsis: "Dinty" is but an infant when his mother, Doreen O'Sullivan, comes to America to meet her young husband, who awaits her in San Francisco. No one appears to meet them. After waiting all day, a kindly woman appears and tells Doreen that her husband has been killed in an accident. For many years Doreen works hard to support herself and her son and is bed-ridden by the time he is able to work.

He becomes a newsboy, fighting with other newsboys while trying to observe his mother's moral teachings. One day he returns a pocket book and makes a staunch friend of the owner, a district attorney. Dinty kindly attends to his ailing mother up until her death. Meanwhile, in the underworld, a son of a leader of Chinese criminals is indicted for murder. The boy's father menaces the judge and finally kidnaps his daughter. It is decided to let the murderer escape temporarily in order to recover the girl, but Dinty, who has become familiar with the city, discovers the criminals' hideout.

They escape in a fast schooner, but sea planes are sent in pursuit and they are soon captured. It is learned that the girl has been left in a torture chamber. An attack on the place fails. Dinty attaches a rope to the door and fastens the other end to a passing car. The door is torn off its hinges, revealing the girl bound to a table beneath a swinging blade which gradually lowers. She is saved in time to join the man she loves. Dinty is made a hero and finds a home for himself and his friends for life.

Print status: No known copies extant.

The New York Times review also mentions that the dozens of boys in the picture were well selected, adding that one unbilled Chinese child (no gender given) or one unidentifiable among the other Chinese kids, stands out. This could very likely be Anna May, but without the film to view, one cannot be sure.

Colleen Moore (1900–1988) achieved stardom with this production, later becoming the quintessential "flapper" of the silver screen in such films as *Flaming Youth* (1923) and *The Perfect Flapper* (1924).

Outside the Law

Universal-Jewel; Released January 6, 1921; 8 reels

Director: Tod Browning; *Producer*: Carl Laemmle; *Scenario*: Lucien Hubbard, from a story by Tod Browning; *Photography*: William Fildew; *Titles*: Lewis Lipton and Fred Archer; *Art Director*: E.E. Sheeley; *Assistant Director*: Leo McCarey

Cast: Priscilla Dean (Molly "Silky Moll" Madden), Wheeler Oakman ("Dapper Bill" Ballard), Lon Chaney ("Black Mike" Sylva/Ah Wing), Ralph Lewis ("Silent" Madden), E. Alyn Warren (Chang Low), Stanley Goethals ("That Kid Across the Hall"), Melbourne McDowell (Morgan Spencer), Wilton Taylor (Inspector), John George (Humpy). Anna May appears in one scene with some other Chinese girls and E. Alyn Warren.

Re-issued May 1926. Remade by Universal in 1930 with Browning again as director.

Variety January 21, 1921: "Mr. Browning did the

job well ... in all particulars ... the picture is exceptionally cast...."

The New York Times May 12, 1926: (the *Times* did not review the film upon its original release) "It is almost impossible to keep track of all the killings in 'Outside the Law' a production of the vintage of 1921.... 'Outside the Law' is entertaining in much the same way as 'Nellie the Beautiful Cloak Model.' You are more amused than grieved at the many mortal coils that are severed."

Synopsis: "Silent" Madden, former gang leader, comes under the influence of Chang Low, a Chinese sage. His daughter, Molly, goes along with his reformation. Meanwhile, "Black Mike" Sylva and his cronies plot to frame Madden so that Molly will revert to crime.

Madden is shot in an ambush, but is saved by Ah Wing, a disciple of Chang Low. Ah Wing takes him to Chang Low's home, where he is tended to by Molly.

A cop is also shot by the gang, one of whom tells the police he saw Madden do it.

When her father is arrested, Molly becomes angry at Low. Madden gets eight months in jail due to lack of evidence.

Sylva convinces Molly to steal some jewels for him while planning a double-cross out of hatred for her. The man sent to work with Molly reveals Sylva's duplicity, however. After the jewels are stolen during a reception at a mansion, he is to take them, leaving her to be caught by the police. Molly decides to turn the tables on Sylva. After the robbery she and Sylva's man, "Dapper Bill" Ballard, hole up in an apartment on Nob Hill. There Bill becomes friendly with the kid in the apartment across the hall. He gets cabin fever and wants to give up. When he goes out for some air, he is spotted by one of Sylva's gang. While in the apartment, Molly learns to like the kid, too.

Meanwhile, Chang Low is negotiating with the police chief to go easy on Molly if she returns the jewels.

Bill returns to the apartment and the kid's mother comes for him; Bill and Molly learn that his father is a police detective. Bill insists on returning the jewels then. Molly informs him that they are a nest egg for them when they go straight. After seeing the shadow of a cross on the floor (caused by the kid's kite stuck on a pole) she agrees with Bill.

Sylva arrives just as Bill and Molly are leaving to return the jewels. Bill takes him to a room across the hall. Sylva asks about the gems and is told that Molly has them, but hid them somewhere before she moved here. Sylva's gang awaits outside; Bill is afraid they'll be seen by the cops, so Sylva goes to tell them to lay low. Instead, he picks Molly's lock, unaware that Bill is watching. Bill jumps him and a fight ensues. As Sylva gains the upper hand, Molly intervenes. Sylva asks which one is lying about the jewels. Sylva pretends to hear cops at the door; Bill goes for the gems, fooled by Sylva's trick. An inspector appears at the door with a gun, not knowing that Molly is behind the door. He tells Sylva to drop his gun; Molly signals to him to do so and gets the drop on him as Dan covers Sylva. Bill and Molly leave; Sylva battles with the inspector and wins; he then goes after the couple.

"Silent" Madden has been released from prison and goes to Chang Low. Molly and Bill show up and the woman tells her father of Sylva's plot and that she is returning the stolen jewels.

Sylva and his gang show up at Low's place and are spotted by Ah Wing, who alerts his companions. As Sylva grabs the gems from Molly, Ah Wing and his men attack Sylva's gang. Sylva is killed just before the cops arrive to break up the fight. Chang Low informs the police chief of Molly's reformation so the former does not bring any charges against her.

Print status: Available on video.

Though appearing in but one scene,

Anna May is the beneficiary of two close-ups, courtesy of director Browning, with whom she was allegedly having an affair. *Outside the Law* marked star character actor Lon Chaney's (1883–1930) initial use of yellowface. The film had a special one-day premiere in New York on January 16, 1921, where it was shown at four different theatres. Prior to that, it had an advance screening during Christmas week in 1920 in Los Angeles at the Superba Theatre.

The First Born

Hayakawa Feature Play Co./Robertson-Cole; Released January 30, 1921; 5 reels
Director: Colin Campbell; *Scenario*: Fred Stowes, from a play by Francis Powers;
Photography: Frank D. Williams
Cast: Sessue Hayakawa (Chan Wang), Helen Jerome Eddy (Loey Tsing), "Sonny Boy" Warde (Chan Toy), Goro Kino (Man Low Tek), Marie Pavis (Chan Lee), Wilson Hummel (Kuey Lar), Frank M. Seki (Hop Lee). Anna May is an extra.
The New York Times January 31, 1921: "A rather unpleasant and not exceptionally well-made melodrama ... its stereotyped arrangement, and its unglossed improbabilities [are against them]...."
Variety February 4, 1921: "The production is atmospheric and most artistic ... a very high class feature."
Moving Picture World February 12, 1921: "A startling revelation at times ... typing Chinese characters with people no makeup art could transform to Orientals."

Synopsis: The first born of Chan Wang, a son named Chan Toy, comes to him from an unloved wife. Long before he gave his heart to a young girl sold into slavery as a mandarin's daughter. When his son reached the age of five, Chan Wang had no use for any woman. At that time he is eking out a living as the proprietor of a small lumber yard in San Francisco. This employment brings him into the house of the wealthy Chinese man who bought and enslaved his childhood sweetheart.

The two meet and rouse the jealousy of the girl's master. He learns the girl is not really a mandarin's daughter and plots revenge. He lures Chan's wife and little son to his home. The man and woman struggle; the boy is pushed through a window and falls to the street below. By the time Chan Wang reaches him, the boy is dead. Crazed with grief, Chan Wang carries the boy's body to where he has prepared a birthday cake and many little presents. He tries reviving the boy by every art his simple mind can devise.

Finally realizing the boy is gone, Chan Wang becomes embittered. His only thought is for revenge. Through subtle means, he kills both the abductor of his sweetheart and the destroyer of his first born. He and the girl return to China. He sits on a river bank, dreaming of the past, while his lady consoles him. She assures him that heaven will send a replacement for his beloved "first born."

Print status: Copy at the National Film Archive, England.

Anna May can be seen serving tea to Hayakawa in one scene.

The source play, by Francis Powers, was first performed in 1897 in New York at the Manhattan Theatre, with the author in the role later essayed by Hayakawa. The critic for *The New York Times* wrote on Oct. 6, 1897: "'The First Born' is a novel blend of realism and poetry. The performance is all thoroughly artistic...."

Bits of Life

Marshall Neilan Prod./Associated First National Pictures; Released September 4, 1921; 6 reels
Produced and Directed by: Marshall Neilan; *Scenario*: Lucita Squier, additional story by Marshall Neilan; *Camera*: David Kesson; *Assistant Directors*: James Flood and William Scully
Cast: Wesley Barry (Tom Levitt, as a boy), Rockliffe Fellows (Tom Levitt), Lon Chaney (Chin Gow), Noah Beery (Hindoo), Anna May Wong (Toy Sing), John Bowers (Reginald

18 • Bits of Life (1921)

Vanderbrooks), Teddy Sampson, Dorothy Mackaill, Edythe Chapman, Frederick Burton, James Bradbury, Jr., Tammany Young, Harriet Hammond, James Neill, Scott Welsh.

The New York Times October 17, 1921: "Although without any particular cinematographic quality, all of the pictures are well made, as animated photographs and the acting is above the average. [Others] in the different casts are ... Anna May Wong...."

Variety October 21, 1921: (reviewed each segment separately) Chinese story: "Here are six reels of picture drama that fairly vibrate with action, suspense and surprise. A Chinese story from *The Saturday Evening Post* that most producers would never have been contented to let go inside of six reels of elaboration."

Synopsis: Chin Gow's father was very happy to have a son, for boy babies bring good luck. Three of his sisters had been thrown into the Canton river, for girl children are considered unlucky in China. When he attained manhood, Chin Gow ran away from home. He journeyed to San Francisco, where he became the owner of a dozen opium dens. He falls in love with Toy Sing, and by pretending he has reformed and sold his illegal businesses, wins her. He leaves for New York and on his return discovers that his wife has given birth to a girl. Reverting to the traditions of his ancestors, he beats his wife mercilessly and vows to kill the baby. As he leaves the room, a friend of Toy Sing's enters with a crucifix, sent by a priest as protection. The friend nails it to the wall with a long spike. When blood begins running down the wall, the women discover that the spike has penetrated the skull of

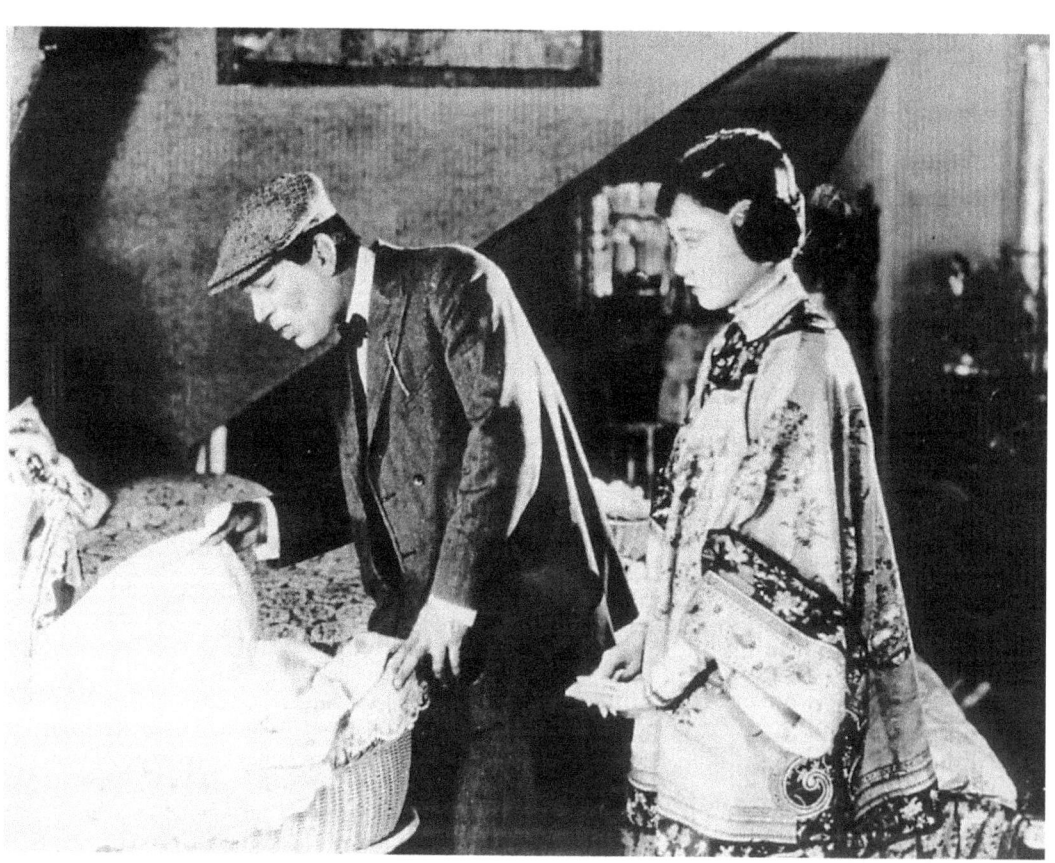

Bits of Life (Marshall Neilan/Assoc. First National, 1921): Lon Chaney, Anna May Wong

Chin Gow, who lay in an opium stupor in the next room.

Print status: No known copies extant.

With the release of *Bits of Life*, the name Anna May Wong was finally seen on theater screens. It had taken a little over two years of work as an extra to reach this plateau. From here on, the Asian-American actress found herself more in demand than ever.

The world premiere was held at the Raymond Theater in Pasadena on August 9, 1921. Unfortunately, it was not a money-maker.

Shame

Fox Film Corp.; Released October 16, 1921; 9 reels
Director: Emmett J. Flynn; *Scenario*: Emmett J. Flynn, Bernard McConville, based on the story *Clung*, by Max Brand; *Camera*: Lucien Andriot
Cast: John Gilbert (William Fielding/David Fielding, his son), Mickey Moore (David at 5), Frankie Lee (David at 10), George Siegmann (Foo Chang), William V. Mong (Li Clung), George Nichols (Jonathan Fielding), Anna May Wong (The Lotus Blossom), Rosemary Theby (The Weaver of Dreams), Doris Pawn (Winifred Wellington), "Red" Kirby ("Once-over" Jake).
Re-issued in 1927.
Variety August 5, 1921: "Is no knockout and is open to serious criticism as it stands ... it never scores as it should."
Harrison's Reports August 6, 1921: "A Chinese melodrama, consisting of a lot of 'claptrap' that will not stand scrutinizing."
Motion Picture News August 13, 1921: "One of the best performances is that of Anna May Wong as 'The Lotus Blossom.'"

Bits of Life (Marshall Neilan/Assoc. First National, 1921): Lon Chaney, Anna May Wong

New York Review November 5, 1921: "...in places it is exceedingly well done and at other times it is exceedingly overdone."

Synopsis: William Fielding, a missionary in China, loses his wife shortly after she gives birth to a son. He then marries a Chinese woman, who treats the child as if it were her own. Charged by one Loo Fong that the child is hers, she does not deny it. Foo Chang, who is in love with the woman, later kills the father and brands the child. Fielding's Chinese wife commits suicide. Li Clung, aware of the child's true parentage, takes the boy, named David, to the home of his wealthy grandfather in San Francisco. There the boy befriends Li Clung and inherits his grandfather's business upon reaching manhood. He marries Winifred Wellington, an American woman. One day Foo Chang appears. Now head of an opium ring, he demands the use of David's ships for smuggling. When David refuses, Foo Chang informs David that he is a half-breed. Although he has no proof other than the brand on David's arm, that is enough for David. He goes to pieces, than flees with his infant son to Alaska. His wife goes to Li Clung, who promises to take her to David, without revealing her husband's ethnicity. She travels to Alaska under the impression that her husband is half–Chinese; only when she is with him does Li Clung reveal the truth. They return to San Francisco apparently to live happily ever after.

Print status: No known copies extant.

Shame was a Fox "Special" and had a top ticket price of $2.00 when it opened in New York on July 31, 1921.

This picture marked Anna May Wong's first "suicide" on screen, something for which she would become noted. In the press notice, she is called "the pretty and talented little Chinese actress." The same notice also suggests that "Lobby displays with *Japanese* lanterns and other Oriental knick knacks is recommended." Some things never change. Add this to the fact the title of the film refers to the protagonist's feeling on learning of his Chinese heritage and you have a typical anti–Asian statement clearly reflecting the mood of the era. One of the film's highlights is John Gilbert's bare-handed fight with a wolf.

The Toll of the Sea

Technicolor Motion Picture Corp./Metro Pictures; Released November 26, 1922; 5 reels
Director: Chester M. Franklin; *Scenario*: Frances Marion; *Photography*: J. A. Ball
Cast: Anna May Wong (Lotus Flower), Kenneth Harlan (Allen Carver), Beatrice Bentley (Barbara Carver), Baby Moran (Little Allen), Etta Lee, Ming Young (Gossips).

The New York Times November 27, 1922: "As a photoplay in colors ... 'The Toll of the Sea' may be counted a distinct achievement. Miss Wong stirs in the spectator all the sympathy her part calls for, and she never repels one by an excess of theatrical feeling ... with a fine sense of proportion and remarkable pantomimic accuracy, she makes the deserted little Lotus Flower a genuinely appealing understandable figure. She should be seen again and often on the screen."

Variety December 1, 1922: "...the extraordinarily fine playing of Anna May Wong, who is an exquisite crier without glycerine ... the natural colors ... in this Technicolor product are attractive...."

Synopsis: Somewhere in China, Lotus Flower finds a Caucasian man washed up onto the rocks. With the aid of some fishermen, she has him carried to her home where she nurses him back to health. One of the fishermen warns her: "Beware of this stranger! The sea is treacherous. His coming bodes no good!"

The man is taken with Lotus Flower and decides to linger. He asks the girl if she would like to go to America. The local gossips tell her that he will forget her once he leaves since he only married her "Chinese style." One says she has already been forgotten by four faithful American husbands. Lotus Flower refuses to heed them, but the idea has been planted in her mind. Meanwhile, the man meets with some American friends at a club and receives a telegram from his parents calling him home immediately. His friends ask him if he is serious about Lotus Flower. "Why not? She's sweet and charming—and different." "That's just it, she *is* different." replies one, as he points to a Caucasian woman and then a Chinese woman sitting nearby.

The man shows the telegram to Lotus Flower; she thinks she is finally going to America. She runs inside and dons a dress that is thirty years out of date. She models it for him, then learns that he cannot take her with him. "Oh, my husband, I

The Toll of the Sea (Technicolor Motion Picture Corp./Metro, 1922): Title card

love you so. If you no come back to me, you make my heart go dead." He just walks away then, leaving her sobbing. Looking up, she flings out her arms, then slowly drops to the ground.

After her husband's departure, Lotus Flower gives birth to a son. She continually goes to the shore and watches for a ship. The forlorn girl also waits for a letter that never arrives. To quiet the gossips, she writes one herself, pretending each day that it is one just arrived, but the women know better and pity her. She carries on the charade with her son, pretending to read a letter to him.

Finally she receives word that her husband has returned. She hurries and puts on her bridal robe and has her son bathed and dressed. The man breaks her heart anew by explaining that they are not truly married, and that he has brought his real wife with him. He introduces her and says that she asks for his forgiveness. Lotus Flower graciously states that there is nothing to forgive and invites the couple to join her for tea. When her son is brought to her, she explains to the wife that he is the child of the American family next door. She whispers to him that he can have candy and gum if he runs and hides. Later, when the wife returns, Lotus Flower reveals everything. She tells the woman that she named the boy after his father and asks her to take him and be a mother to him. She explains to the boy that she is not really his mother, just his little Chinese nurse, adding that his real mother has come for him. As she hands the child to the wife, he clings to her before allowing the woman to take him.

22 • The Toll of the Sea (1922)

The Toll of the Sea (Technicolor Motion Picture Corp./Metro, 1922): Kenneth Harlan, Beatrice Bentley, Anna May Wong

Having nothing to live for, Lotus Flower pays her debt to the waiting sea; the intertitle shows her in its grasp.

Print status: Available on video.

Anna May Wong's first starring role occurred in an historically important film, the first true Technicolor feature made in Hollywood. The brainchild of two graduates of M.I.T., Herbert T. Kalmus and Daniel F. Comstock, the Technicolor Motion Picture Corporation set up operation in 1915. The first release of the Technicolor Motion Picture Corp. was *The Gulf Between*, a short feature made in 1917. The color effect was achieved by a special projector fitted with lenses and aperture plates. Proving too unwieldy, it was abandoned after a singularly embarrassing showing in Buffalo, New York. The negative to this film has been lost and there are no prints extant.

With the aid of Dr. Leonard T. Troland, one of Dr. Kalmus' staff, an imbibition process was devised, wherein the red-orange and blue-green images were etched in relief on two strips of film. The strips were then cemented back-to-back and "floated" over two baths of dye. The gelatin coating of the film soaked up the dye, allowing the film to be shown by any standard theater projector. While the colors lack the richness of the later three-strip Technicolor, they possess all the charm of early 1900s hand-tinted postcards.

Metro gave the film national distribution, which resulted in a $250,000 gross by the end of 1923.

Anna May displays remarkable

restraint in portraying a young woman who twice goes from ecstasy to despair. At seventeen she shows unusual maturity in her acting, using both body and facial expressions equally well. Perhaps she was recalling her unhappy struggle to make a success in her chosen profession; in any case, her performance is memorable.

Kenneth Harlan (1895–1967) is a rather bland leading man who underplays his part to the point of listlessness. Lotus Flower must have been extremely bored to hook up with him, no matter the circumstances.

Frances Marion's (1887–1973) scenario, a variation of *Madame Butterfly*, is frequently poetic: "The garden knew she loved him, for her laughter stirred the rose leaves." It is also rather vague, as no reason is given for Carver floundering unconscious in the water and his occupation is never mentioned, though he seems to be of some means. More direct versions of *Madame Butterfly*, utilizing that title, were made in 1915 by Famous Players-Lasky with Mary Pickford, and by Paramount in 1932 with Sylvia Sidney.

Technicolor supplied the original camera negative to YCM Laboratories, where, in collaboration with Robert Gitt of the UCLA Film, Television and Radio Archives, it was restored on 1985. The American Film Institute Endowment for the Arts Preservation Grants Program furnished the funds. The final sequence was missing, however; new footage of the Pacific Ocean was shot with an authentic two-color Technicolor camera in October 1985, minus Miss Wong. The new titles created from Frances Marion's script implied that Lotus Flower leaped into the sea; now there are only empty waves.

Mary of the Movies

Columbia Pictures/C.B.C.; Released May 1923; 57 minutes

Director: John McDermott; *Producer*: Jack Cohn; *Scenario*: Louis Lewyn; *Photography*: George Meehan and Vernon Walker *Titles*: Joseph W. Farnham

Cast: Marion Mack (Mary), Harry Cornelli ("Lait" Mayle), John Geough (Reel S. Tate), Raymond Cannon (Oswald Tate), Rosemary Cooper (Jane), Francis McDonald (James Seiler), Jack Perrin (Jack), Creighton Hale, Zasu Pitts, Anna May Wong, Rex Ingram, Florence Lee, Mary Kane, Ray Hanford, John MacDermott, Stuart Holmes, J. Frank Glendon, Herbert Rawlinson, Maurice Tourneur, Dorothy Phillips, Alan Holubar, Bessie Love, Bryant Washburn, Anita Stewart, Estelle Taylor, Rosemary Theby, Alec B. Francis, Tom Moore, Carmel Myers, George O'Hara, David Butler, Douglas MacLean, Miss Dupont (Themselves).

Variety June 21, 1923: "The production is an ingenious routine of travelog, 'behind scenes' stuff and fiction to make it appeal to film fans generally."

Synopsis: In the hamlet of Barston, Arizona, lives Mary Mack, one of the prettiest girls in town and an avowed movie fan. She spends most of her spare time either sending photos to film stars to be autographed, or acting out her own scenarios. Everyone in town admits that Mary has talent.

She is the object of affection of Oswald Tate, son of Reel S. Tate, the richest man in town. He frequently threatens to propose to Mary, of whom his father does not approve.

Forced by the necessity to secure funds for an operation for her lame son, Mary's mother asks Tate for a loan. The request is refused and even Oswald's loyalty wavers when his father gives him the choice of Mary or a Ford. He opts for the latter, and Mary begs her mother to let her try her luck in Hollywood. Mrs. Mack consents because the money Mary may earn would mean so much to Jack's recovery.

Arriving at Hollywood Station, she mistakes a private car for the Hollywood bus and fails to recognize the car's owner as Bryant Washburn. Entering into the fun,

Washburn drives her to Hollywood; along the way she spots a film star and is introduced to several more by her "chauffeur" when they arrive at the Hollywood Hotel. At the desk she learns that the rates are $12 per day; she has but a total of $27.70.

Friendless and alone, Mary is taken under the wing of Jane, an extra girl, who allows the waif to live with her. That night, Jane's upstairs neighbor, actor Creighton Hale, shows Mary many of the stars' homes. Next day she begins looking for work. George O'Hara, Johnnie Walker and Barbara LaMarr direct her to the casting offices, where she meets Craig Biddle, the young Philadelphia millionaire. She is given a good idea of how tough it is to break into the movies, but does not land an engagement.

That night she meets more celebrities as Hale takes her around to some of the studios.

The following day she gets work in a mob scene directed by Rex Ingram, but the studio burns down and the production is indefinitely postponed. Depressed, she nonetheless sends five dollars to her folks without reference to her ill luck.

While wandering about a studio lot, Mary's likeness to a reigning screen favorite is noted by two directors, who place her name and address on file. Unable to obtain immediate film work, Mary takes a waitress job in a studio restaurant. There she waits on many screen personalities. She writes her parents that she "had lunch" with these stars.

Back home, Oswald Tate begins to think he made a mistake in picking a Ford over Mary, so he heads for Hollywood. By coincidence he enters the restaurant where Mary is working. Miss Dupont, however, helps Mary to pose as a star. Tate later returns to the restaurant and learns Mary's true status.

The star whom Mary resembles becomes gravely ill, and with large sums of money tied up in her current production, the directors decide to take a chance with Mary in the part. With a little training by director John MacDermott and some help from Stuart Holmes, J. Frank Glendon and Malcolm MacGregor, she makes good and goes with the company on location in the desert.

Her sole regret is that she ran away from Creighton, with whom she was in love. That is remedied when he is sent for. In the meantime he had inherited some money, but realized that without Mary it was meaningless, so he heads for the film site upon learning of it.

At the same time in Barston, a stranger has arrived and tells Reel S. Tate that there is oil under the Mack homestead. Tate makes an offer for the place, but is told by Mrs. Mack that she has put it up for auction. At first it seems that Tate will get the property for a price too low to help the Macks. But Lait Mayle, the old postman, also discovers signs of oil in the family ground and the bidding becomes fast and furious.

At the desert filming site, a terrific sandstorm arises, endangering the company. Terrified, Mary turns toward Barston on her horse, but is thrown and partially buried in the sand. She is found by Creighton and taken to Barston, arriving at the height of the auction. Hale begins bidding against Tate, driving the price up. Just as Tate outbids Hale again and Creighton is about to bid yet higher, word comes that the "stranger" has been working a game, and that the only oil on the property was put there by him. The auctioneer, who dislikes Tate as much as anyone, closes the bidding then, forcing Tate to pay several times the true value of the property.

At this point, the film director, who had been trailing Mary, arrives with word that she will soon be one of the biggest stars in pictures. The entire Mack family goes to Hollywood, their future happiness assured.

Print status: No known copies extant.

While not mentioned in the synopsis, Anna May Wong must have been one of the stars spotted by "Mary," or maybe she was just visiting the lot, as she was between films at Universal at the time.

Drifting

Universal Film Manufacturing Company; A Universal-Jewel DeLuxe Production; Released August 26, 1923; 7 reels

Director: Tod Browning; *Producer*: Carl Laemmle; *Scenario*: A.P. Younger, based on the stage play by John Colton and Daisy N. Andrews; *Camera*: William Fildew; *Editor*: Errol Taggart; *Titles*: Gardner Bradford; *Assistant Director*: Leo McCarey

Cast: Priscilla Dean (Cassie Cook, alias Lucille Preston), Matt Moore (Capt. Arthur Jarvis), Wallace Beery (Jules Repin), J. Farrell MacDonald (Burke), Rose Dione (Madame Polly Voo), Edna Tichenor (Molly Norton), William V. Mong (Dr. Li), Anna May Wong (Rose Li, his daughter), Bruce Guerin (Billy Hepburn), Marie DeAlbert (Mrs. Hepburn), William Moran (Mr. Hepburn), Frank Lanning (Chang Wang).

Re-made by Universal as *Shanghai Lady* in 1929.

The New York Times August 20, 1923: "...interesting and in spots quite thrilling. The little Chinese maiden, who was about to plunge a carving knife into herself, thinks twice, and decides to give the weapon to Jarvis."

Variety August 23, 1923: "...the real star of the performance is the little Chinese girl who walked away with all the honors and who handled a death scene magnificently."

Moving Picture World September 1, 1923: "Anna May Wong gives a skillful and touching portrayal of the Chinese girl."

Synopsis: An American woman named Cassie Cook is involved in the opium trade in China with a confederate, Jules Repin. They are in need of cash after failing to bring in a large shipment of opium from Hang Chow, a village in the interior. Cook is anxious to return to the U.S. with her friend Molly Norton, who has become an opium addict. She and Repin lose their remaining money on a horse race. Cook goes to Hang Chow to check out an American miner named Jarvis, whom she suspects of being a government agent. In the village, she and

Drifting (Universal, 1923): Anna May Wong

26 • Thundering Dawn (1923)

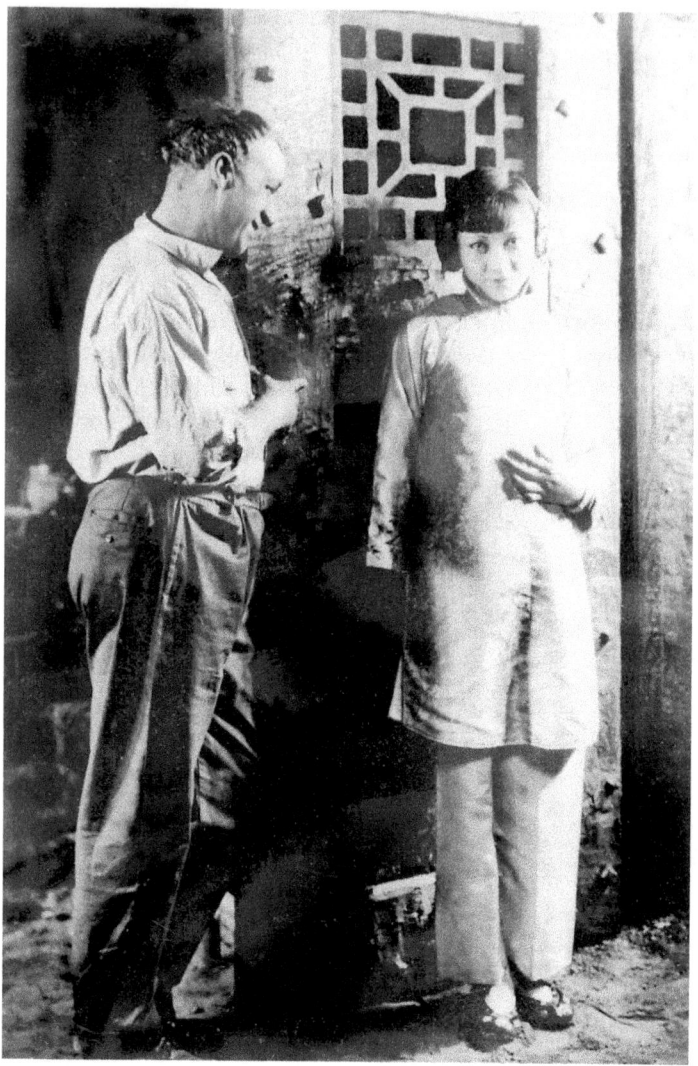

Drifting (Universal, 1923): J. Farrell McDonald, Anna May Wong

Repin consult with Dr. Li, whose daughter, Rose, is in love with Jarvis. Cook poses as a novelist and wins Jarvis' confidence. Cook steals a government report from Jarvis, who is threatened by Dr. Li and Repin with a revolt of the hill tribes. Rose sees her doing this, but fails to convince Jarvis of the theft.

Cook soon falls for Jarvis and looks upon her occupation with disgust. Jarvis denounces her and sends his subordinate to the nearest cavalry post for aid in fighting the hill tribes. He then rallies the villagers to fight the invaders.

Cook persuades Repin that she will smuggle opium, but takes it to Burke's cabin instead. The Hepburns, a missionary couple, are killed by bandits, but their son Billy escapes and seeks refuge with Cook. She holds off the bandits with a rifle until the cabin is set afire.

Meanwhile, Jarvis and Repin engage in a knife fight; as Repin gains the upper hand, he is shot by Rose Li. Jarvis rescues Cook and Billy from the cabin. Jarvis is now certain of Cook's loyalty and admits his love for her.

Print status: Copies at Filmovy Archiv in Prague, Czech Republic; Filmarchivum Magyar Filmtudomanyi Intezet in Budapest, Hungary; Gosfilmofond, Moscow, Russia.

The synopses and reviews for this film are very confusing regarding Anna May's fate in this film. According to at least one review, her character commits suicide; others have her alive at the end, but forgotten. One early synopsis has her in Burke's arms at the end.

Thundering Dawn

Universal Super-Jewel Production; Released August 19, 1923; 7 reels
Director: Harry Garson; *Scenario*: Lenore Coffee, John Goodrich; *Story*: John Blackwood; *Adaptation*: Raymond L. Schrock; *Photography*: Charles Richardson and others

Cast: Winter Hall (The Elder Standish), J. Warren Kerrigan (Jack Standish), Anna Q. Nilsson (Mary Rogers), Tom Santschi (Gordon Van Brock), Charles Clary (Lawyer Sprott), Georgia Woodthorpe (Mrs. Standish), Richard Kean (Hotel Keeper), Edward Burns (Michael Carmichael), Winifred Bryson (Lullaby Lou), Anna May Wong (Honky Tonk Girl).

Moving Picture World October 6, 1923: "...the manner in which Director Harry Garson has handled the production, the effective and realistic storm scenes, the excellent atmospheric effects in reproducing life on the island of Java which makes you feel that you are looking at the real thing, the closely knit story ... makes this an attraction that should appeal to audiences that like frankly melodramatic entertainment."

Variety November 29, 1923: "...suffers from the plaint of so many of our program pictures—sameness; sameness not only in story, but in directorial touch, in Thespian work and in the all-important bits that lend color and individuality to a film. The plot is subsidiary to the physical and technical side of the film."

Synopsis: The Standishes of Boston, whose forbears arrived on the *Mayflower*, enjoy a spotless reputation. The elder Standishes are about to celebrate their thirtieth wedding anniversary and their son, Jack, is engaged to their ward, Mary Rogers.

On the night of the celebration, the elder Standish receives word that his lawyer, without authorization, has involved him in an unscrupulous deal that means disgrace and failure. Jack protects

Thundering Dawn (Universal, 1923): Anna May Wong, unidentified actor, Winifred Bryson, J. Warren Kerrigan, Charles Clary, unidentified actor

his father's and the firm's name by assuming the guilt and then disappearing. He journeys to Java, where he rapidly degenerates into a drunkard.

Back in Boston, his father recovers from a stroke, the crooked lawyer confesses and Mary sets out to find Jack. Arriving in Java, she finds her fiancé in the grasp of a notorious adventuress. Mary is nearly driven mad by the driving rain and the attentions of one of Jack's acquaintances. Her struggle to redeem Jack also appears hopeless. During a typhoon the village and the adventuress are swept away. Mary horsewhips the villain and succeeds in nursing Jack back to manhood and happiness. Together they return to Boston.

Print status: Trailer only at the Library of Congress, Washington, D.C.

This would appear to be the first film in which Anna May's character supplied some of the local color without doing anything to advance the plot. Unmentioned in the synopsis, she is also at the bottom of the cast list.

The Thief of Bagdad

Douglas Fairbanks Pictures/United Artists; Released March 18, 1924; 12 reels
Director: Raoul Walsh; *Scenario*: Elton Thomas [Douglas Fairbanks] after a story by Edward Knobloch; *Camera*: Arthur Edeson; *Script Editor*: Lotta Woods; *Art Direction*: William Cameron Menzies, Irvin J. Martin; *Cos-*

The Thief of Bagdad (Fairbanks/United Artists, 1924): Julanne Johnston, Douglas Fairbanks, Anna May Wong

tumes: Mitchell Leisen; *Assistant Cameramen*: P.H. Whitman and Kenneth MacLean; *Technical Direction*: Robert Fairbanks; *Editor*: William Nolan; *Assistant Director*: James T. O'Donohoe; *Music*: Mortimer Wilson; *Director of mechanical effects*: Hampton Del Ruth; *Associate Artists*: Anton Grot, Paul Youngblood, H. R. Hopps, Harold Grieve, Park French, William Utwich, Edward M. Langley

Cast: Douglas Fairbanks (The Thief), Julanne Johnston (The Princess), Anna May Wong (The Mongol Slave), Snitz Edwards (Evil Associate of the Thief), Charles Belcher (The Holy Man), Winter-Blossom (Slave of the Lute), Sojin (The Mongol Prince), K. Nambu (His Councilor), Sadakichi Hartmann (His Court Magician), Etta Lee (Slave of the Sand Board), Brandon Hurst (The Caliph), Tote Du Crow (The Soothsayer), Noble Johnson (Indian Prince), Mathilde Comont (Persian Prince), Charles Stevens (His Awaker), Sam Baker (The Sworder), Jess Weldon, Scotty Matraw, Charles Sylvester (Eunuchs).

Remade by London Films in 1940; by Titanus-CCF/Lux (Italy) in 1960 and by MTV in 1978.

The New York Times March 18, 1924: "...remarkable sets and costumes ... are a feast for the eye. This film is filled with brilliant ideas ... a feat of motion picture art which has never been equaled ... Anna May Wong as the Mongol Slave...."

Variety March 26, 1924: "Anna May Wong as the little slave girl who is a spy for the Mongol Prince proved herself a fine actress ... a magical tale brilliantly picturized ... the picture carries its audience along in the spirit of the depiction."

Synopsis: A lowly Thief plies his trade very successfully in Bagdad with the aid of a cohort. One day as he is fleeing from some angry victims, he hides in a mosque. There he argues with the *imam* over the afterlife and storms out. He stops to watch a man work the magic rope trick and steals the rope. He next witnesses the flogging of a thief. The official in charge shows the gem he stole to the onlookers with a warning against stealing. The Thief trips him as he walks past; as he helps him up, he pockets the stone.

In another land, a Mongol prince is shown a model of the Bagdad palace. "It shall be mine. What I want — I take." He

The Thief of Bagdad (Fairbanks/United Artists, 1924): Anna May Wong

is told of the suitors for the Princess' hand going to Bagdad in the following month and makes plans to be a suitor.

As the suitors begin arriving, the Thief tries to disguise himself as a bearer, but is stopped by the guards before he can pass the gate. That night he uses the magic rope to scale the palace wall. The Nubian guard and eunuchs all doze off; the Thief steals a key from a eunuch and opens a large chest. As he admires the contents, he hears soft music. Following the sound, he finds himself in the bedchamber of the Princess and is immediately smitten by her beauty. He touches her hand, awakening her; she throws off a coverlet, which covers the Thief. Her screams rouse the palace. A search for the intruder is begun. When all have left the chamber, the Mongol Slave picks up the coverlet to put on the Princess and feels a knife in her back. The Thief forces her to a wall and puts a pillow between the wall and knife to make her think he is still there. She discovers the ruse as he takes one of the princess' slippers. Seeing the slave, the Thief leaps through a window and lands on a tree which lowers him to the ground.

The next day the Slave of the Sand Board reads the Princess' fate in the sand. "This is the meaning: Thou wilt wed the suitor who first toucheth the rose tree in thy garden." The Mongol Slave hears this and slips away. The Princess watches the suitors as they arrive and likes none of them.

Outside the gate, the Thief's associate tells him he can procure princely raiment in the bazaar. He does so and enters as "Ahmed, Prince of the Isles, of the Seas, and of the Seven Palaces." The Princess is impressed; "See how he rides—a Prince indeed!" The Mongol Slave tells the Mongol Prince about the rose; as he approaches the tree, a bee scares him off. The same bee frightens Ahmed's horse, which bucks, sending Ahmed flying onto the tree. The Princess is overjoyed. The Thief later climbs up to the Princess' chamber and returns her slipper. After he leaves, he is met in the garden by court officials, who escort him to the Caliph. He announces the Princess' choice by having a ring placed on his finger. Ahmed is chosen. Meanwhile, the Mongol Slave has recognized him as the thief who robbed the palace on the previous night; she tells the Mongol Prince's councilor, who informs his master. He in turn tells the Caliph. At the same time, Ahmed is admitting to the Princess his true station. She weeps, then hears the guards and tells Ahmed to hide. She gives him a ring and admits her love for him. She hides while guards take Ahmed to the Caliph. He orders the Thief to be flogged, then thrown to an ape to be torn apart. The Princess gives pearls to her handmaiden and tells her to bribe the guards into letting Ahmed go free. He is thrown into the street outside the palace.

The Caliph calms the suitors by having the Princess choose again. She refuses, advised by the Slave of the Sand Board to stall for time. She asks her father: "Send them to distant lands to seek some rare treasure. At the seventh moon let them return. Who brings the rarest treasure I will wed." The Caliph agrees to this.

The next morning the Thief's associate informs him that he has found a way into the palace through the tunnel of the tigers so the Thief can enter and steal the Princess. When the Thief shows no interest, he tells about the treasure quest. The Thief goes to the mosque and tells the *imam* of his love for the princess. The *imam* replies, "Make yourself a prince." He adds that happiness must be earned. He also offers to help the Thief, for he knows of a magical silver chest. The Thief cuts in half the ring given him by the Princess and asks the *imam* to give one half to her, and sets off to find the chest.

Before departing, the Mongol Prince

orders his councilor to remain in Bagdad and build an army from within from the soldiers disguised as porters he will send.

At a desert inn, the princes part, agreeing to meet there at the end of the sixth moon. The Mongol Prince tells his Captain of the Guard to have spies follow the other two princes.

In Bagdad, the *imam* gives the ring half to the Princess and tells her to pray for the Thief.

First Moon — The Thief makes his way through the Valley of Fire. Second Moon — The Persian Prince acquires a flying carpet. Third Moon — The Thief defeats a dragon, then at the Cavern of Enchanted Trees gets a chart to guide him to the Old Man of the Midnight Sea. Fourth Moon — The Prince of the Indies steals a gem from the eye of a forgotten idol near Kandahar and discovers it to be a magic crystal. Fifth Moon — The Old Man of the Midnight Sea takes the Thief out in a boat, informing him that he will find a star-shaped key in an iron box at the bottom of the sea. The Thief dives in, finds the key, but is attacked by a giant spider, which he quickly dispatches. A beautiful maiden lures him into an underwater palace, where two other maidens try to tempt him to remain. He looks at the ring half on his finger and remembering the Princess, returns to the Old Man's boat. The Old Man says the key will give the Thief entrance to the Abode of the Winged Horse. There the Thief rides off into the night on the Winged Horse. Sixth Moon — The Mongol Prince comes to the Island of Wak. He is told by his Court Magician of a secret shrine. The Magician enters and steals a magic apple. Ordered by the Prince to test it on a fisherman, he kills the man with a poisoned snake, then passes the apple up and down the man's body. He is restored to life and runs away in fear. The Mongol Prince orders his Captain of the Guard to proceed to Bagdad, and at the end of the sixth moon, have the Princess poisoned.

The Thief finally locates the magic chest at the Citadel of the Moon, only to learn it is wrapped in a cloak of invisibility. He manages to acquire both without difficulty.

In Bagdad at the end of the sixth moon, the Mongol Slave fans some fumes toward the Princess in her bedchamber, causing her to pass out. She then forces some poison pills down her throat.

The princes meet again at the inn, each showing off his gift. As they are about to leave for Bagdad, the Mongol Prince suggests they look into the magic crystal to see if the Princess is waiting for them, as she had pledged. Seeing the Princess lying gravely ill, the Persian Prince orders his flying carpet spread. The princes climb aboard and set off for Bagdad. They arrive there in short order, and the Mongol Prince saves the Princess with the magic apple.

Meanwhile, the Thief learns the secret of the magic chest — it contains a powder which can create anything he wishes. He creates a horse and some regal clothing (as well as a loaf of bread) and heads for Bagdad.

In the city, the Princess marvels at her recovery and learns of the magic apple used by the Mongol Prince. The other princes insist their gifts were equally important, and begin bickering. The Caliph is about to decide who shall marry his daughter when the Slave of the Sand Board shows the Princess the crystal; the Thief is on his way! The Princess remarks that each gift was useless without the other two. Seeing the wisdom in this, the Caliph decides that it is best to deliberate. The Mongol Prince's councilor advises his master: "Bide your time. You have 20,000 troops within the walls." The Mongol Prince goes along with the Caliph's suggestion to deliberate.

That night the Mongol soldiers quickly take over the city. The next morning, the Mongol Prince orders the wedding to be held immediately. Fleeing citizens encounter the Thief at a desert well and inform him of the situation. He sets out for Bagdad posthaste. Arriving at the city gate, the Thief is denied entrance, and creates his own army from the magic powder; thousands upon thousands of troops magically appear. Seeing this, the Mongols flee in panic. Informed of this, the Mongol Prince orders guards to be set at the palace gates. Someone opens the city gate for the Thief and his forces. Told there is no escape now, the Mongol Prince commands a soldier to behead him. He is stopped by the Mongol Slave, who reminds her master, "The flying carpet — and the Princess." The Slave of the Sand Board overhears her and runs to tell the Thief. He dons the cloak of invisibility to get by the Mongol guards, arriving inside just in time to save the Princess from being kidnapped. The Mongol Prince and his councilor suffer the indignity of having their queues tied together and being suspended from a pole. The Caliph gratefully gives his daughter to the Thief. Annoyed by a surfeit of attention, the Thief again puts on the cloak of invisibility and slips away with the Princess to the flying carpet. They climb aboard it and fly away above the city.

Print status: Available on video.

Budgeted at two million dollars, *The Thief of Bagdad* failed to make the profit of Fairbanks' previous feature, *Robin Hood* (1922), mainly due to its cost. Although heavily influenced by contemporary German productions, the film stands on its own with its highly imaginative costumes, magnificent sets and wondrous special effects. Only some of the creatures encountered by the thief are disappointing. The flying horse, the magic carpet and the cloak of invisibility are all quite convincing. It won first prize at an international film exposition held in Warsaw, Poland, in October 1927 as well as several other international awards. The best known of Anna May Wong's silent features, it is still being shown at retrospectives.

For the film's New York opening, Fairbanks created a special distribution unit to conjure up the proper atmosphere at the Liberty Theatre. Enlargements of famed artist Willy Pogany's Arabian Nights illustrations adorned the walls and incense, silks and tapestries filled the lobby. Turkish coffee was served and Oriental singers sang songs of welcome.

Anna May fit right in to the surroundings, with her hair in looped braids and clad in a revealing two-piece outfit for much of the picture. Her natural grace was well in evidence and in her one scene with the irrepressible Fairbanks, it is she who grabs the viewer's attention.

This was the first pairing of Anna May with Japanese actor Sojin Kamiyama (1874–1954), billed by his first name. He would appear with her eight more times, all in the silent era, making him her most frequent co-player.

The Fortieth Door

Pathé Exchange; Released May 25, 1924; 10-chapter serial; Feature version released August 17, 1924; 6 reels

Director: George B. Seitz; *Scenario*: Frank Leon Smith

Cast: Allene Ray (Aimee), Bruce Gordon (Jack Ryder), David Dunbar (Andy McClean), Anna May Wong (Zira), Frances Mann (Jimmy Jeffries), Frank Lackteen (Hamid Bey), Lillian Gale (Miriam), Bernard Siegel (Tew Fick Pasha), Whitehorse (Sheik Hassan), Omar Whitehead (Paul Delcarte), Scott McGee (Police Commissioner), Eli Stanton (Ali).

Chapters: 1. The Secret Portal 2. Two Lockets 3. The Wedding 4. Buried Alive 5. Desert Trails 6. The Tomb of a King 7. Claws of the Vulture 8. Held for Hostage 9. The Rack 10. The Temple of the Forty Doors

Harrison's Reports, August 22, 1924: "The picture has been produced well, direction and acting being good ... a satisfactory program attraction."

Moving Picture World, August 23, 1924: "Another corking serial story from the house of the red rooster trademark ... holds the interest...."

Synopsis: Hamid Bey, a high Cairo official, holds proof that Tewfick Pasha is a smuggler of hashish. He promises to destroy the evidence if Tewfick's daughter, Aimee, is married to him.

Jack Ryder, an archaeologist excavating the tomb of a pharaoh, attends a masked ball in Cairo. There he meets and falls in love with Aimee, who has stolen away from her father's palace. It is a great indiscretion, and she is frightened by her own daring. She tells Jack that he can never see her again. In an unfortunate encounter with Hamid Bey, Jack incurs his wrath. While pleading with Aimee in a hotel garden, Jack is attacked by one of Hamid's servants.

Returning home from the ball, Aimee is informed that she must marry Hamid Bey within the week. Horrified but helpless, she returns to the gate in the garden wall to say good-bye forever to Jack.

At the tomb in the desert, Jack is visited by a Frenchman seeking news of the heir to the Delcarte fortune. Paul Delcarte, with his wife and baby daughter, had disappeared in the desert fifteen years earlier. Later, in the tomb, Jack finds a locket bearing a picture that is the image of Aimee. Convinced that the girl he loves is French and not Arabic, he hurries to Cairo, but on the way is beset by two of Hamid Bey's men, who attack him with sabres.

Tewfick Pasha admits to Jack that he married Delcarte's widow and that Aimee is their child. It is the day of Aimee's wedding. Disguised as a native woman, Jack attends the wedding reception and hides in the palace until all the guests are gone. He covers Hamid with an automatic and grabs Aimee, but Hamid resists and cleverly gets Aimee between himself and Jack's gun. He blows a whistle to summon his servants.

Jack is walled up with bricks in a niche, but Aimee has hidden Jack's gun and uses it to compel Hamid to take her to Jack. He tricks her and has her in his power. Zira, queen of Hamid's household, is jealous of the new bride. She frees Jack before he suffocates and directs him about the palace. As he is climbing an outer wall, Hamid spots him and calls his guards.

To distract attention from their escape, Aimee sets fire to some curtains. She and Jack get as far as the stables. Jack saddles a horse while Aimee checks to see if their way is clear. She is spotted by Sheik Hassan, who recognizes her as Aimee Delcarte and calls out her name. Jack rides past and scoops her up behind him and they flee into the desert. They hide from their pursuers in the tent of a Bedouin, who Jack fears will betray them.

Hamid Bey, along with Sheik Hassan and some servants, go to the tomb in the desert with search warrants. Ryder disguises Aimee in wrappings from a mummy and places her in a sarcophagus in an inner tomb. Feeling sure that Aimee is somewhere in the dig, Hamid decides to wait one hour. Ten more minutes in that air and the bindings and Aimee will suffocate.

When Aimee is not found, Hassan and Bey depart. Tewfick Pasha arrives and warns Jack against Hassan, who is a notorious tomb robber. Meanwhile, Hamid Bey is holding Jinny Jeffries, an American girl, hostage until Aimee is returned to him. Hassan and his bandits attack the tomb site, killing Tewfick and rendering Jack unconscious. They ride off with the tomb's treasures and Aimee.

Aimee is taken up the Nile to Hassan's stronghold. Andy McLean, Jinny Jeffries' boyfriend, enlists the aid of the police in trying to locate her. Along with Jack, Andy follows Zira and locates the place where Jinny is hidden. Hamid hears them coming and draws his knife. If they find Jinny, it will be too late!

Among Hassan's stolen treasure is the Index Stone, bearing in two ancient languages the key to the location of the Temple of the Forty Doors. Only the Silent Man can translate it and he refuses. The Silent Man is Paul Delcarte, who has been Hassan's prisoner for fifteen years. Hassan has Aimee tortured in order to make Delcarte talk.

Jack, Andy and a troop of soldiers attack Hassan's stronghold. After a terrific battle, Hassan escapes with the Index Stone. Led by Delcarte, Jack pursues him to "where the shadow of the pyramid of Ahra touches the mountains of the sun." There they find the fabled Temple of the Forty Doors. Hassan pries open the huge stone door, but it is balanced in such a manner that it falls and crushes the robber chief to death. Hamid Bey is forced into exile. Jack and Aimee and Andy and Jinny have a double wedding.

Print status: No known copies extant.

In the silent era, it was the ladies who were the serial stars and Allene Ray (1901–1979) was one of the best. Born in San Antonio, Texas, she grew up on a ranch and learned to ride early. She made her first film appearance in 1919 and starred in her first serial in 1924; *The Fortieth Door* was her second. She appeared in a total of 16 serials, all but the last for Pathé.

With this film, Anna May Wong added an Arabic woman to her list of varied ethnic roles for the only time.

The October 1924 number of *Art and Archaeology* magazine ran an article on the spate of recent motion pictures with Egyptian settings, *The Fortieth Door* among them. Authored by Bruce Bryan and entitled "Movie Realism and Archaeological Fact," it pointed out the numerous inaccuracies in the details of the sets and included three stills from the film.

The Alaskan

Famous Players-Lasky/Paramount Pictures; Released September 22, 1924; 7 reels
Produced and Directed by: Herbert Brenon; *Scenario*: Willis Goldbeck, from the novel by James Oliver Curwood; *Camera*: James Wong Howe; *Titles*: H. H. Caldwell
Cast: Thomas Meighan (Alan Holt), Estelle Taylor (Mary Standish), John Sainpolis (Rossland), Frank Campeau (Stampede Smith), Anna May Wong (Keok), Alphonse Ethier (John Graham), Maurice Cannon (Tautuk), Charles Ogle (The Lawyer).
The New York Times September 15, 1924: "Scenically it is a beautiful production ... The narrative ... is one of those tangled affairs difficult for the ordinary mortal to unravel...."
Variety September 17, 1924: "It's a whale of a tale for action, mystery and an over-mastering love, crammed full of pep and go ... Anna May Wong as an Indian girl scored nicely."

Synopsis: The father of Alan Holt is killed after amassing a fortune in the Alaskan wilds. Alan suspects the big business interests out to despoil the territory as being responsible. Deciding to fight the combine run by John Graham, he goes to Washington, but is unable to secure help from the government.

Returning home aboard a ship, he befriends a girl named Mary Standish who is watched by Graham's lieutenant, Rossland. Mary jumps off the ship as it nears port. Realizing his love for her, Alan searches for her, finding her in the home of one of his men. She reveals the fact that she is Graham's wife and had left him because of his ill treatment of her. Graham discovers their whereabouts and demands that Alan give her up. He attacks the house when Holt refuses. As Holt and Mary try to escape through a tunnel, they encounter Graham. He and Alan struggle; one of Graham's men tries to shoot Holt, but hits Graham instead and he falls to his death over a precipice. The environment is saved and Alan and Mary are free to marry.

The Alaskan (Paramount, 1924): Thomas Meighan, Anna May Wong

Print status: No known copies extant.

Thomas Meighan (1879–1936) was a popular leading man in silents who is almost totally forgotten today. He appeared in eighty features during his career, many of them for Paramount, and many made at the Astoria, Queens studio, as Meighan had an aversion to Hollywood. The film that put him over was *The Miracle Man* (1920), which also made stars of Lon Chaney and Betty Compson.

This was Anna May Wong's first portrayal of a Native American.

Peter Pan

Famous Players-Lasky/Paramount Pictures; Released December 29, 1924; 10 reels
Produced and Directed by: Herbert Brenon; *Scenario*: Willis Goldbeck, from the play by James M. Barrie; *Camera*: James Wong Howe; *Special Effects*: Roy Pomeroy; *Fencing Supervisor*: Henri Uytennhove
Cast: Betty Bronson (Peter Pan), Ernest Torrence (Captain Hook), Cyril Chadwick (Mr. Darling), Virginia Brown Faire (Tinkerbell), Esther Ralston (Mrs. Darling), Anna May Wong (Tiger Lily), George Ali (Nana the Dog), Mary Brian (Wendy), Phillipe DeLacey (Michael), Jack Murphy (John), Richard Frazier (Giant Black Man), Maurice Cannon (Cookson), Charles A. Stephenson (Jukes), Percy Barbat (Noodles), Ralph Yearley (Italian Cecco), Terence McMillan (Nibs), Lewis Morrison (Gentleman Starkey), Edward Kipling (Smee), Maurice Murphy (Tootles), Mickey McBan (Slightly), George Crane, Jr. (Curly), Winston Daly (First Twin), Weston Daly (Second Twin), Ed. Jones (Mullins).

Remade by Disney in 1953 as an animated feature.

The New York Times December 29, 1924: "...Mr. Brenon has fashioned a brilliant and entrancing production of this fantasy....

36 • Peter Pan (1924)

Peter Pan (Paramount, 1924): Betty Bronson, Anna May Wong

Betty Bronson is a graceful, vivacious and alert Peter Pan."

Variety December 31, 1924: "The production is remarkable for its beauty.... 'Peter Pan' is a picture that will go down the years as a delightful fantasy...."

Synopsis: It is bedtime in the Darling nursery and Nana the dog is preparing the children's beds. As Mrs. Darling enters, she spots a figure at the window, one which immediately disappears. She tells her husband that she saw the face of a little boy at the window, one that she had seen before. Nana jumped at him but he escaped. As she closed the window, Mrs. Darling inadvertently cut off the boy's shadow, which she placed in a dresser drawer. She adds that a little ball of light accompanied the boy. As the Darlings prepare to leave for a party at a neighbor's home, Mr. Darling ties Nana to his doghouse in the yard. Nana starts to howl; Mrs. Darling recognizes the cry, which signifies that the dog senses danger.

After the children are asleep, their window is opened and a ball of light flies into the room. A boy flies in as well and asks the ball of light if she's seen his shadow. She points to the dresser and the boy pulls it out of a drawer. He is unable to re-attach it; finding a sewing kit, he tries sewing it back on with no luck, so he begins to cry. The oldest child, Wendy, awakes, and the boy introduces himself as Peter Pan. Wendy asks Peter where he lives; "Second to the right and then straight on till morning." When Wendy learns that Peter has no mother, she sews on his shadow. He is so happy he begins to dance about in the center of the room. He explains to Wendy that he never wants to grow up and introduces her to the fairy Tinker Bell, so named because she mends the fairies' pots and kettles. He also tells the girl about the Lost Boys and asks if she will come and be a mother to them. She explains that she could not leave her brothers, John and Michael, so Peter teaches all of them how to fly—by thinking beautiful thoughts. This does not work; Peter then remembers that he must also sprinkle fairy dust over them.

Outside, Nana breaks his leash and runs across the street to the Darlings' neighbors to alert them to what is happening. The couple looks through the window and sees their children flying about their room. They rush over, but are too late; the children are flying over London, on their way to Never Never Land.

Meanwhile, in Never Never Land, Capt. Hook is feeding a clock to a crocodile so he will know of its approach. It seems the reptile developed a taste for the good captain after biting off his hand.

On another part of the island, the Lost Boys spot Wendy flying overhead. Tinker Bell, who is jealous of her, tells them that Peter wants them to shoot the "Wendy bird," and they do, before discovering that Wendy is not a bird. Peter then arrives and informs the boys that he has brought them a mother. The boys, full of remorse, show Wendy to Peter, who is angry. Wendy stirs then; the pendant she wore about her neck saved her life, though she was rendered unconscious. Tinker Bell is upset that Wendy is alive. The boys tell Peter that Tinker Bell ordered them to shoot Wendy, so Peter banishes the fairy for one week. The boys build a cottage around Wendy. She agrees to be their mother if Peter will be the father.

On his ship, Capt. Hook plans to attack the Lost Boys in their underground home that night. Meanwhile, Peter is meeting with the Indians and is made an honorary member of their tribe. They pledge to aid the Lost Boys, taking up sentinel positions on the ground outside the tree leading to their home.

Inside, Wendy tells the Lost Boys that her parents will adopt all of them and they arrange to return to London with her, except for Peter. He steadfastly refuses to grow up.

Just then, up above, the pirates surprise the sleeping Indians. Peter hears the sounds of the fight, wondering about the outcome. The Indians are defeated and run off. Hook removes the cap of a large mushroom which serves as a chimney for the boys and listens as Peter tells the others that a beaten tom-tom is a signal that the Indians are victorious. Hook grabs a tom-tom and beats it as his men give a war whoop.

Feeling safe, the boys emerge from the tree trunk one by one and are grabbed by the pirates. Not seeing Peter, Hook climbs down through the tree trunk and surreptitiously puts poison in Peter's medicine.

Tinker Bell flies in and tells Peter of the Indians' defeat and about the poison. Peter does not believe her about the poison, so she drinks the medicine and flies to her room, where she collapses on the floor. Peter becomes distraught as her light dims and her voice weakens. She tells Peter she would get better if people would show their belief in fairies. Peter turns to the camera and urges viewers to clap, indicating their belief in fairies. Tinker Bell's light waxes and Peter thanks the audience.

Peter flies to a cove where mermaids live and asks their queen if she knows where the crocodile is. He finds the beast and removes the clock from its gullet.

On board his ship, Hook says that six of the eight boys will walk the plank; the other two will become cabin boys. Two agree to be cabin boys, but refuse when they learn that Hook is not loyal to the Stars and Stripes. Wendy is tied to a mast as the boys are made ready to walk the plank. Peter arrives and alights on a mast. He goes to the upper deck holding a clock aloft; Hook stops in his tracks and Peter throws the clock into the ocean. The boys laugh at his discomfiture, so he orders Jukes to bring his cat-o-nine-tails from his cabin. Peter sneaks into the cabin after him. Inside, he stabs the pirate and crows triumphantly. This sound frightens the pirates. Another is sent in; seeing the body, he reports to Hook and is sent in again. Peter kills him and the others run, so Hook goes into the cabin. Inside, he shoots at a figure who merely laughs. Hook flees the cabin and again becomes the object of the boys' mirth, so he orders them into the cabin.

The crew runs to the rail as Peter and the boys emerge from the cabin fully armed. Peter frees Wendy and takes her place, so that when Hook lifts the cowl on his robe he finds Peter instead. The battle is joined; five boys gang up on Hook, but Peter wants the captain, so the two are left to fight each other. "Proud and insolent youth, prepare to meet thy fate!" "Dark and sinister man, have at thee!" cries Peter. The others watch from above as Peter outduels Hook, who runs down into the powder magazine and fires it. Peter goes in and brings up the lit keg, which he tosses over the side of the ship, where it explodes harmlessly. Hook is made to walk the plank by Peter, who then replaces the Jolly Roger with the American flag. Peter takes the wheel of the ship, which soon becomes airborne.

Back in London the Darlings are still mourning their children, though they keep the window open for them. Peter and Tinker Bell fly into the nursery and close the window so that Wendy will think she is not wanted and return with Peter to Never Never Land. Peter hears Mrs. Darling playing "Home, Sweet Home" on the piano and takes a look. He says to himself that she is fond of Wendy, too, but they both cannot have her. Deciding in Mrs. Darling's favor, he and Tinker Bell depart, leaving the window open behind them. The children arrive and climb into their beds. Their mother enters and sees them, but does not believe they are real. She sits; the kids get up and speak, but Mrs. Darling is still not convinced. When her children gather around her, she finally realizes that they are back. Mr. Darling and Nana come in and join the joyful reunion. Wendy then brings in the Lost Boys and asks her parents if they can stay. The Darlings agree to raise the boys. Peter appears at the window; Mrs. Darling says she will raise him as her own. When he learns that staying means going to school, Peter declines and asks if Wendy will be his mother. Mrs. Darling offers a compromise — she will let Wendy visit Peter once each year to do his spring cleaning. Peter Pan agrees and returns to Never Never Land.

Print status: Available on video.

The character of Peter Pan first appeared in J. M. Barrie's 1902 novel *The Little White Bird*. He proved so popular that the author concocted a play with him as the protagonist. A perennial on the stage in both England and the United States, *Peter Pan* was first performed in London on December 27, 1904, with Nina Boucicault portraying Peter. Barrie (1860–1937) sold the film rights to Paramount in 1921 with the stipulation that he choose the actress for the title role, and that she must be an unknown. (For many years, Peter was played by an actress.) Betty Bronson (1907–1971) had but a few extra parts and one credit to that point. Following *Peter Pan*, she starred in the equally charming *A Kiss for Cinderella* (1926), another Barrie work, but did little of consequence after that, especially after being dropped by Paramount in 1927.

Barrie himself wrote a very detailed scenario, but the producers decided not to use it, although some ideas were retained. Paramount utilized all their top talent in the creation of this work, including Herbert Brenon (1880–1958) as director and James Wong Howe (1899–1976) behind the camera. Filming began in September and was finished in time for a late December opening. An immediate hit, *Peter Pan* made *The New York Times* Ten Best Films list for 1924.

Anna May has but four scenes in this sparkling production, but performs enthusiastically in all of them. She would have made an equally fine Tinker Bell, but her ethnicity kept her from any consideration for that role. It must be noted that in Barrie's 1911 novelization of the play, *Peter and Wendy*, the only episode featuring Tiger Lily not used in the film was that in which she is captured by Hook. Bound hand and foot, she is left atop Marooner's Rock to drown in the rising tide. She is rescued by Peter and becomes his ally.

Scottish-born Ernest Torrence (1878–1933) was a well-known operatic baritone before switching to films. He became a leading heavy of the silent screen following his memorable performance as Luke Hatburn in *Tol'able David* in 1921.

Blonde beauty Esther Ralston (1902–1994) celebrated her 22nd birthday during filming. She was chosen to portray Mrs. Darling because it was felt that children see their mothers as young. In her autobiography, *Some Day We'll Laugh*, she tells of being summoned by Paramount executives while working on a Tom Mix western. Her appearance, wearing a pair of six-guns, a large cowboy hat and boots, somewhat startled Jesse Lasky and Walter Wanger. They sent her to wardrobe, where she was fitted in a wool dress with a lace collar, and her hair upbraided. When director Herbert Brenon saw the transformed actress, he hired her on the spot. She went on to become Paramount's leading and highest paid actress. She became known as "The American Venus" after starring in the film of that name in 1926.

In 1991, an abomination entitled *Hook* was produced. Completely antithetical to Barrie's highly original and whimsical concept of a boy "who wouldn't grow up," it showed Peter as a grumpy middle-aged lawyer who has blocked out his childhood memories. Rumblings were reported from the vicinity of Barrie's grave.

Screen Snapshots

Columbia c. 1925; unidentified no. 3; 1 reel (862 feet)

Featuring: D.W. Griffith, Erich von Stroheim, Anna May Wong, Douglas Fairbanks, Carmel Myers, Lew Cody, Harry Rapf, Clarence Brown, Estelle Taylor, René Adorée, Fred Niblo, Claire Windsor, Pauline Starke, Antonio Moreno, Reginald Barker, William Seiter, Chester Conklin, Laura LaPlante, Sid Grauman, Hedda Hopper.

Columbia's Screen Snapshot series introduced each entry with: "Offer a glimpse into the Heart of the Movie World revealing intimate and Unusual Views of Your favorite Stars 'On Location' and in the Privacy of their Homes."

Anna May Wong's segment ran about one minute.

East Is West

Out in the garden of sunshine and flowers we found a real Chinese blossom.

Anna May Wong, our only Chinese movie star, spends her spare time with many other beautiful heirlooms.

INTERTITLE: Would you like to see a peppy Chinese dance?

Presto! Chango!

Anna changes from her Chinese outfit to western dress.

INTERTITLE: "This is enough to make Li Hueng Chang turn over in his grave!"

Anna does a spirited Charleston, then sits on a swing lounge.

INTERTITLE: "Whew! That's work but I like it."

She wipes her brow in a medium close shot.

Print status: Copy at the Library of Congress, Washington, D.C.

This long running series was begun in 1920 in New York by C.B.C. Film Sales, Harry Cohn's (1891–1958) original company. (The initials stood for Harry Cohn, Joe Brandt and Jack Cohn, Harry's brother.) When he founded Columbia Pictures four years later, it was decided to continue the popular and profitable series. The final one was released in 1958.

Forty Winks

Famous Players-Lasky/Paramount Pictures; Released February 2, 1925; 7 reels
Directors: Frank Urson, Paul Iribe; *Screenplay*: Bertram Millhauser, based upon the play *Lord Chumley*, by David Belasco and Cecil B. DeMille; *Photography*: Peverell Marley
Cast: Raymond Griffith (Lord Chumley), Viola Dana (Eleanor Butterworth), Theodore Roberts (Adam Butterworth), Cyril Chadwick (Gaspar La Sage), Anna May Wong (Annabelle Wu), William Boyd (Lt. Gerald Hugh Butterworth).
Working title: *Lord Chumley*.
The New York Times February 3, 1925: "Anna May Wong is splendid as the vampire.... She has specially doped cigarettes.... This is one of the most brilliant farces that has ever been picturized."
Variety February 4, 1925: "Corking melodramatic farce giving Raymond Griffith one of the best roles he has had in some time.... Anna May Wong, Cyril Chadwick and William Boyd rounded out the cast of principals giving adequate delineations of their respective roles."
Moving Picture World February 14, 1925: "...a farce without a single lagging moment. Anna May Wong, as an adventuress, is very good indeed...."

Synopsis: A young naval lieutenant awakens in a hotel room with a hangover and a dim recollection of a beautiful Oriental girl in a roadhouse. His keys are missing and the only clue is a lady's jeweled garter lying on the floor.

Later he finds his office safe has been opened and priceless defense plans stolen.

It develops that the plans were stolen under the direction of his father's attorney, who had his Oriental fiancée do the deed. The attorney attempts to force a marriage with the lieutenant's sister, telling her that with his wealth he can buy back the plans, thus saving the young man's honor. He adds that he could better do so as a member of the family. The sister agrees to the marriage providing he secures the plans.

A British dandy known as Lord Chumley blunders into the family library in time to prevent the lieutenant from committing suicide. That night he takes the garter from the library safe, although trailed by detectives. During his escape, Chumley discovers a dog wearing the mate to the garter as a collar. He follows the dog to the apartment of the Oriental woman and through a ruse secures the documents.

When the lawyer hears of this he determines to kidnap the lieutenant's sister. He tells her the documents are on a yacht and they take a speed boat. Lord Chumley follows them and all end up on a naval target. Chumley and the lawyer fight; the lawyer is knocked into the water. The couple discovers that the target is being fired upon; they are rescued by a German submarine which had been waiting at the bottom of the sea for the war to end. Realizing they are safe, Chumley takes the girl in his arms.

Print status: No known copies extant.

The work of Raymond Griffith (1887?–1957) has only recently been rediscovered by film fans when some of his once lost films resurfaced. He later became a producer. Ironically, his final and best-known role gave him no dialogue, though it was in a sound film. He played the French soldier stabbed by Lew Ayres in a foxhole in *All Quiet on the Western Front* (1930).

His Supreme Moment

Samuel Goldwyn Prod./First National Pictures; Released May 3, 1925; 8 reels; Technicolor sequences.
Director: George Fitzmaurice; *Screenplay*: Frances Marion (from the novel *World Without End* by May Edginton); *Cinematography*: Arthur Miller; *Art Director*: Ben Carré; *Editor*: Stuart Heisler
Cast: Ronald Colman (John Douglas), Blanche Sweet (Carla King), Kathleen Myers (Sara Deeping), Belle Bennett (Carla Light), Cyril Chadwick (Harry Avon), Ned Sparks (Adrian), Nick De Ruiz (Mueva), Anna May Wong (Harem Girl in play), Kalla Pasha (Pasha in play), Jane Winton.
The New York Times April 13, 1925: "Mr. Fitzmaurice has made shrewd use of color photography in sequences that are emphatically effective ... this film is a little too long and the story is rather ragged in places."
Variety April 22, 1925: "It is a well-done tale ... in the color shots there are some studies of remarkable beauty."

Synopsis: Mining engineer John Douglas falls in love with a popular Broadway star, Carla King. His former love, Sara Deeping, agrees to back Douglas in a new mining venture. He and Carla leave for South America, agreeing to live together platonically before making the commitment to marry. After just a year of rough living, Carla longs for the comforts of home, and Douglas begins to fear that his gold mine will fail.

Sara arrives hoping to win back Douglas' love. Added to his problems, the miners strike and a fire destroys Douglas' cabin and almost kills him. Saved by Carla, the pair returns to New York, followed by Sara. John takes up with Sara again, and Carla agrees to marry an aged millionaire in return for his backing Douglas' project. Hearing of this, Douglas leaves Sara and secures some independent capital. Carla rejoins Douglas and they sail for South America to begin their new life.

Print status: No known copies extant.
Anna May had but one scene in this production, but it is one of the two Technicolor sequences. At the beginning of the film, she is seen as a dancer in a Turkish harem scene, which is part of the play in which Blanche Sweet's character stars.

Ronald Colman (1891–1958) was just a year away from full stardom, a status which he would attain with the release of *Beau Geste* (1926). He would remain a star through the fifties, becoming an even greater one in sound films.

Blanche Sweet (1895–1986) had reached stardom under D. W. Griffith's direction in the teens. Her star faded at the end of the silent era and she made few sound pictures.

Fifth Avenue

Belasco Productions/Producers Distributing Corp.; Released January 24, 1926; 6 reels
Director: Robert G. Vignola; *Producer*: A. H. Sebastian; *Scenario*: Anthony Coldeway; *Photography*: James Van Trees; *Titles*: Fanny Hatton, Frederic Hatton; *Art Director*: Charles L. Cadwallader; *Assistant Art Directors*: Philip Carle, T.E. Dickson
Cast: Marguerite De La Motte (Barbara Pelham), Allan Forrest (Neil Heffner), Louise Dresser (Claudine Kemp), William V. Mong (Peter Heffner), Crawford Kent (Allan Trainor), Lucille Lee Stewart (Natalie Van Loon), Anna May Wong (Nan Lo), Lillian Langdon (Mrs. Van Loon), Josephine Norman, Sally Long (Greenwich Follies Girls), Flora Finch (Mrs. Pettygrew, of Indiana).
Motion Picture News February 6, 1926: "...from the artistic viewpoint leaves nothing to be desired ... has a good deal of heart appeal...."
Moving Picture World February 20, 1926: "...an exceptionally interesting human interest document ... smooth and skillful direction engrosses the interest and proves absorbing entertainment."

Synopsis: Neil Heffner, son of Peter Heffner, wealthy cotton broker of New York, is a social lion who devotes his spare time to sport. His fiancée, Natalie Van Loon, is interested in Neil because of the great fortune he is due to inherit. In the south lives Barbara Pelham, the last of her line, with her maiden aunt Sally. Barbara's sole source of income is her cotton crop, which is destroyed by fire, leaving her practically stranded, but determined as ever to go to New York and see Heffner with a view to obtaining an advance upon the coming season's cotton crop.

On the train Barbara meets Mrs. Claudine Kemp, who invites her to stay at her home during her visit to New York. She accepts, and on her arrival in the city, calls on the elder Heffner, who treats her overtures for money coldly until she mentions that she is staying at Mrs. Kemp's house. He then shows interest in her and promises to call upon her that evening. At Kemp's, Heffner makes advances which Barbara repulses. Opening one door, she interrupts a riotous crap game; opening another she witnesses a scene that forces her to run away in despair. One of the gamesters, caught cheating, fires two shots which bring the police, but they are cleverly outwitted by Mrs. Kemp.

Barbara finds new quarters in Washington Square, but Mrs. Kemp does not lose sight of her. Meanwhile, Neil realizes that Natalie's motives are purely mercenary and breaks off their engagement. He then asks his father for a job and is sent to inspect the elder Heffner's holdings in Washington Square. He finds Barbara in a ramshackle house. Believing him to be a burglar, she flees to the roof. There she is met by one Allan Trainor, who tries to embrace her. He is thrashed by Neil, who becomes friends with Barbara. Neil agrees to provide Barbara with lace to mend if she, still convinced that he is a crook, will "reform" him. She makes good and their friendship ripens. One day Neil takes her to his father's house to announce their engagement. The elder Heffner exposes Barbara as having been an inmate of Mrs. Kemp's house, but Neil still insists on marrying her. Heffner calls upon Mrs. Kemp to substantiate his charge.

When she arrives, Barbara appeals to her to tell the truth and kisses her. She exonerates the girl; Heffner apologizes and accepts her as his daughter-in-law.

Print status: No known copies extant.

Anna May's role was merely that of one of Mrs. Kemp's girls. Much was made of a fashion show (unmentioned in the synopsis) in press releases and reviews.

A Trip to Chinatown

Fox Films; Released June 6, 1926; 6 reels
Director: Robert P. Kerr; *Producer*: William Fox; *Supervisor*: George Marshall ; *Scenario*: Beatrice Van; *Photography*: Barney McGill
Cast: Margaret Livingston (Alicia Cuyer), Earle Fox (Welland Strong), J. Farrell MacDonald (Benjamin Strong), Anna May Wong (Ohati), Harry Woods (Norman Blood), Marie Astaire (Rose Blood), Gladys McConnell (Marion Haste), Charles Farrell (Gayne Wilder), Hazel Howell (Henrietta Lott), Wilson Benge (Slavin), George Kuwa (Tulung).
Harrison's Reports June 12, 1926: "A good farce-comedy. Robert P. Kerr's directorial work is very good."
The Film Daily June 20, 1926: "The comedy is of a helter-skelter sort and runs along in a disjointed fashion. The plot is secondary."
The Bioscope July 8, 1926: "...there is a Chinese butler and a very attractive Chinese maid ... the chief ladies' parts are charmingly taken by Margaret Livingston, Gladys McConnell and Anna May Wong. The settings ... are tasteful and elaborate and the photography is flawless."

Synopsis: Welland Strong is a hypochondriac who believes he has but six months to live. He decides to take a long trip, beginning on a train. He runs afoul of a jealous bridegroom. Though Strong is innocent of any hanky-panky, the husband feels otherwise. Strong spends the remainder of the ride dodging the irate husband. Finally arriving in San Francisco's Chinatown, Strong thinks he has shaken off the husband.

Print status: No known copies extant.

A Trip to Chinatown was based on the 1891 farce by Charles Hoyt, a very successful playwright of the period, who referred to it as "a musical trifle." It was revived many times in different venues and gave the world two song standards: "The Bowery" and "Chinatown, My Chinatown." The rights to nine other of Hoyt's plays were bought at the same time by Fox.

The Silk Bouquet (a.k.a. The Dragon Horse)

Fairmont Productions/Hi-Mark Productions; Released June 25, 1926; 8 reels
Director: Harry J. Revier
Cast: Anna May Wong, James B. Leong, Ernie Viebare, Fay Kam Chung, Marie Muggley, K. Namien.

Print status: No known copies extant.

This all–Chinese production was originally called *The Dragon Horse*, a title which was re-instated in January 1927. An item in *Variety* for February 10, 1926 announced that it was being produced by the China Educational Film Co., with financial backing from Chinese capital from San Francisco. Most all–Chinese films were not shown outside of San Francisco or Los Angeles, proving too difficult for white audiences to understand. *The Silk Bouquet*, however, had a life well beyond California. The Motion Picture Division of the State of New York Education Department granted Hi-Mark Productions a license to be exhibited in New York state in December 1927 after changes were made to two intertitles. It also somehow found its way to Argentina in 1928 under the title *El Caballo Fantasma* (*The Ghost Horse*).

Shanghai-born James B. Leong (1889–1967) had formed his own company in 1921 and produced one film, which he co-directed with Frank Grandon. Entitled *Lotus Blossom*, it starred the vaudeville singer Lady Tsen Mei, but also featured a pair of Caucasian character actors, Noah Beery and Tully Marshall, in yellowface.

The Desert's Toll (a.k.a. The Devil's Toll)

Metro-Goldwyn-Mayer; Released November 14, 1926; 6 reels
Director: Clifford Smith; *Camera*: Jack Roach, George Stevens; *Titles*: Gardner Bradford; *Editor*: Richard Currier
Cast: Francis McDonald (Frank Darwin), Kathleen Key (Muriel Cooper), Chief Big Tree (Red Eagle), Anna May Wong (Oneta), Tom Santschi (Jasper Martin), Lew Meehan, Gwynne Williams (Martin's Henchmen), Josef Swickard (Simon Cooper), Broderick O'Farrell (Henry Fenwick, lawyer), Charles Brinley (Sheriff).
Film Daily November 21, 1926: "It is fairly routine in substance but director Clifford Smith has been unusually successful in lifting considerable of the story's triteness through careful handling of the situations.... There is some first-rate suspense in the development...."
Variety December 1, 1926: "Compared to some of the westerns turned out recently, this one is a classic. Picture shows good direction."
The Bioscope January 27, 1927: "The story is a good one of its type, owing much to the magnificent natural settings ... very good performances are given by Big Tree, as the Indian servant, and the fascinating Anna May Wong as his daughter."

Synopsis: Frank Darwin seeks refuge from a woman's scorn in Death Valley. He becomes known in the area as The Pinnacle Man from Hidden Cave since he lives among some oddly shaped rock formations.

Out in the desert, an old miner named Simon Cooper strikes gold. He runs into Jasper Martin and his henchmen and is murdered by the former for his map. However, the killers are driven off by Frank before they get the map. At Frank's cabin, Cooper is tended to by Indian guide Chief Red Eagle and his sister, Oneta.

Meanwhile, in Chicago, Simon's wealthy brother John wishes to contact his sibling, from whom he has been estranged for many years. John's daughter Muriel overhears her father tell his lawyer, Fenwick, of his quest. She decides to go west before the lawyer is able to leave. Arriving in the town near Frank's abode, Muriel meets Martin and tells him of her search. Martin lies and tells her that Frank has murdered Simon. She believes him, even though she is wounded by one of Martin's men during the search. Frank takes her to his cabin, where she is cared for by Oneta. Muriel's contempt for Frank arouses the Indian girl's jealousy.

Frank is later captured by Martin, stripped to the waist, and tied to a stake in the blazing sun. Frank manages to start a smoke message and Red Eagle frees him. Muriel is taken to the cabin again and is almost attacked by Frank and stabbed by Oneta, who has dressed Frank's wounds.

In town, Frank convinces the sheriff of Martin's guilt. The latter's gang is rounded up, with Frank jumping Martin off his horse from a roof. When Muriel learns the truth, she forgives her uncle.

Print status: Copy at George Eastman House, Rochester, New York.

Driven from Home

Chadwick Pictures; Released January 15, 1927; 7 reels
Director: James Young; *Producer*: Jess J. Goldberg; *Scenario*: Enid Hibbard, Ethel Hill, from the play by Hal Reid; *Photography*: Ernest Miller
Cast: Ray Hallor (Henry Elliott), Virginia Lee Corbin (Mary Hillary), Pauline Garon, Sojin (Lo-Sing), Anna May Wong (Cho-Son), Melbourne McDowell (Jacob Hillary), Virginia Pearson (Madame Bubberly), Margaret Seddon, Sheldon Lewis, Eric Mayne, Alfred Fisher.
Film Daily February 6, 1927: "The story is the old hokum, handled in true hokum fashion but appropriately so considering the plot in hand."
Variety May 25, 1927: "An old-time melodrama, with lots of plot, has been made into a fairly good programmer. All in all, not so good, but a long way from being bad."

Synopsis: Mary Hillary is turned out of her home by her father when she chooses his poor secretary over a count whom her father had selected for her. A Chinese chop suey magnate attempts to kidnap Mary. A chase ensues; venues include a hop joint and an undersea tunnel cave. All ends well as Mary weds the secretary.

Print status: Copy at Cinematheque Royale, Brussels, Belgium.

Chadwick Pictures was an independent producer of feature films which was active only from 1924 to 1928. Their studio was located at Sunset and Gower, aka "Poverty Row." This film was advertised in *Moving Picture World* as a Chadwick "Special."

The Honorable Mr. Buggs

Pathé/Hal Roach; Released April 24, 1927; 2 reels
Director: Fred Jackman; *Producer*: Hal Roach; *Scenario*: Stan Laurel, A.B. Barringer, Ted Bersten, Frank Butler and Alf Goulding; *Photography*: George Stevens, Len Powers; *Supervisor*: Del Henderson; *Assistant Directors*: Lloyd French, Joe Barry; *Assistant Photographer*: Harry Wheeler
Cast: Matt Moore (Mr. Buggs), Anna May Wong (Baroness Stoloff), Oliver Hardy (butler), Sojin (other thief), Martha Sleeper (the fiancée), Laura La Varnie, Tyler Brooks, James Finlayson.
Motion Picture News April 22, 1927: "...will prove a highly amusing addition to any program ... Anna May Wong, the serio-comic adventuress...."
Moving Picture World, May 2, 1927: "...this Hal Roach comedy has the distinction of presenting two of the best known Chinese players, Anna May Wong and So-Jin [sic] in prominent roles. Comedy and melodrama are smoothly combined...."

Synopsis: Mr. Buggs, a bachelor and entomologist, becomes engaged to be married. The beautiful Baroness Stoloff, wanted by the police for the theft of a royal ruby, calls on Buggs with a rare specimen. While she is there, Buggs' fiancée and her aunt visit. Suspecting something is amiss, the aunt begins snooping about and finds her suspicions justified when another Asian crook appears in search of the baroness. When the police arrive on the scene, a mad scramble ensues and the baroness is arrested. Buggs forgives his fiancée for her jealous outburst and they make up.

Print status: Private collections only.

This was Anna May Wong's only two-reel comedy. She had been signed to a multiple picture deal by Roach, but apparently he could find no other appropriate roles for her, although she was mentioned in some press releases for other films, like the Laurel and Hardy vehicle *Why Girls Love Sailors* (1927). Having viewed this film, this writer noted the absence of Anna May or any other Asian performer; all the action takes place aboard a ship.

The critic for *Moving Picture World* erred in referring to Sojin as being Chinese; he was a native-born Japanese. Oliver Hardy (1892–1957) appeared here in blackface.

Mr. Wu

Metro-Goldwyn-Mayer; Released May 16, 1927; 8 reels

Director: William Nigh; *Producer*: Harry Rapf; *Scenario*: Lorna Moon, from the play by Maurice Vernon and Harold Owen; *Titles*: Lotta Wood; *Camera*: John Arnold; *Sets*: Cedric Gibbons and Richard Day; *Editor*: Ben Lewis; *Wardrobe*: Lucia Coulter; *Assistant Director*: M.K. Wilson; *Set Musicians*: Sam and Jack Feinberg

Cast: Lon Chaney(Mr. Wu/Wu's Grandfather), Renee Adorée (Nang Ping), Louise Dresser (Mrs. Gregory), Holmes Herbert (Mr. Gregory), Ralph Forbes (Basil Gregory), Gertrude Olmstead (Hilda Gregory), Mrs. Wong Wing (Ah Wong), Anna May Wong (Loo Song), Sonny Loy (Little Wu), Claude King (Mr. Muir), Toshioye Ichioka (Friend of Nang Ping), Komaie (Wu's Servant).

Previously filmed by Stoll in Great Britain in 1919.

Variety April 20, 1927: "…the first half is a draggy cumbersome series of sequences…. Anna May Wong as the companion of Nan Ping, played it in a loyal and sympathetic way."

The New York Times May 16, 1927: "On this picture [Mr. Wu's] vengeance is more limited than it was in the play. It is narrative that could have been told with infinitely greater depth…."

Synopsis: Mr. Wu wants his grandson to be taught western ways, so he hires Mr. Muir as a tutor for him. "Arm my grandson with the wisdom of your people. The West is coming to the East. Little Wu must be taught to hold his own."

Young Wu marries when he reaches adulthood and receives his grandfather's blessing. His wife dies one year later, having borne no son, only a daughter. Wu becomes wealthier and a mandarin. In time, his daughter Nan Ping is ready for marriage.

A carefree girl, she plays with her companions in one of the spacious gardens on Wu's estate. They throw coins over a wall to a blind flute player. They follow these with flowers, unaware that he has left. A young Englishman driving by is pelted with the petals. He stops, looks up, and climbs the wall, frightening Nan Ping's companions. They all turn and run, but Nan Ping hurts her ankle. The young man drops his hat inside as an excuse to drop in and retrieve it. Nan Ping loses her slipper and they grab for it simultaneously. They look into each other's eyes and the man kisses the girl on the lips. She does not know what to think and calls Loo Song. They converse in Chinese; the Briton says he wishes they spoke English and is amazed to hear Nan Ping respond in that language. Loo Song leaves them alone.

Over the next several months the two meet secretly in the garden. At one such meeting the Briton, Basil Gregory, tells

Mr. Wu (MGM, 1927): Renée Adoreé, Anna May Wong

Nan Ping that her father has invited his family for tea. They hide when they see Wu approaching, but one of his servants spots them. The man tells Wu what he saw and Wu takes the man's knife and kills him.

Gregory tells Nan Ping that his family is returning home and he must go with them. She becomes distressed, afraid that he will never return. Gregory is unable to console her; Nan Ping informs him that she is pregnant. She is suddenly summoned by her father; Gregory departs.

Wu tells his daughter that her bridal journey will begin at dawn; he then informs her of his invitation to the Gregorys and watches her reaction. She closes her eyes and bows in acquiescence. He adds that he has been called away and she will have to receive them in his place.

As the introductions are made, Wu watches from the bushes. Mr. Gregory throws his tea onto the ground and makes a face when offered a Chinese delicacy: "You Chinese eat the silliest food." His wife makes excuses for him. The family strolls about the property. Mrs. Gregory drops a locket containing a lock of her son's baby hair. She remarks how she loves babies: "Ours have such blue eyes and white skin." Nan Ping tries to speak, but cannot. Later she says to Loo Song: "The words of his mother are plain. There is no place for me in the West."

Nan Ping speaks to Basil through the garden door, agreeing to see him one more time. Loo Song lets him in, looking at the westerner with disapproval, then watches the pair. Nan Ping admits that she lied about being with child; she wanted to see if he was honorable. She reminds him of her forthcoming marriage. They embrace and kiss even as Loo Song begs them to cease. Wu sees them together just before Gregory departs. Outside the gate he is grabbed by Wu's servants; Nan Ping faints upon seeing this. Wu carries her inside and is secretly followed by Loo Song. Wu places his daughter on her bed; when he leaves, Loo Song enters the room. Nan Ping awakes and finds her father's beads next to her, and knows that he knows.

Wu summons Nan Ping; Loo Song watches her, knowing full well what will happen. Nan Ping kneels at her father's feet; she tells of her love and asks that Basil Gregory be spared. "Do you know why I called you?" "Yes, and I am not afraid." She walks to an altar in another part of the palace. Wu follows her and picks up a large sword off the altar. As he raises it, the curtain before the altar slowly closes.

Mrs. Gregory and her daughter visit Mr. Wu again. The mandarin apologizes for his absence on the previous day. He presents the daughter with a shawl and tells her to look at herself in Nan Ping's mirror. He tells Mrs. Gregory he has something of interest, then inquires after Basil. She replies that he did not come home last night, that he probably stayed with friends. "Perhaps an amorous adventure." suggests Wu.

"He's just a boy. One learns to forgive many things."

"That's your Western attitude. Let me show you ours."

Through a panel Mrs. Gregory sees her son tied to a pillar, guarded by a man with a sword. Shocked, she learns of her son's affair with Nan Ping from Wu and why he was forced to kill his own daughter. Wu swears he will avenge himself on Basil. Mrs. Gregory begs that her son be spared. Wu tells her there is one way. "Anything!" Through another wall panel she sees her daughter in a room with a Chinese man. Wu discloses to her that before the sun sets one or the other will die. If he strikes a gong, the son will die. "No!" He opens the panel to the room and nods at the man inside. The latter puts his hands on the daughter, who screams. Mrs. Gregory cries, "You dare not submit her to that! You dare not!" She pleads with Wu, who tries to calm her with tea. She notices a dagger on a nearby table and sits as Wu drinks his tea. He looks through the window at the sun about to set, apprising Mrs. Gregory of the fact. She glances at the dagger.

"Have you made your decision?" inquires Wu.

"My son would choose to die — to save his sister."

As Wu goes to have the daughter set free, Mrs. Gregory grabs the dagger and hides it behind her back. As Wu is about to strike the gong, she calls to him: "Mr. Wu ... there is another way." He walks over to her. "Take my life," she says. "That would be too easy. In China, it is the parent who must live — and suffer." The desperate mother drops to her knees before him. "Will nothing make you relent?" He shakes his head. She suddenly stabs him in the abdomen. Wu heads for the gong, but Mrs. Gregory pulls at his arm. Nan Ping's spirit suddenly appears to Wu, shaking her head. Wu drops the stick and follows the image. Mrs. Gregory's daughter appears. Wu, dying, picks up a large sword and leans on it. Mr. Muir enters and touches Wu on the shoulder; the mandarin falls over, dead.

Print status: Available on video.

The original ending of this film showed Wu and his daughter ascending heavenward on a light beam; no surviving print contains this shot. The picture's worldwide gross was over one million dollars.

This was the first film in which Anna May Wong acted in support of a Caucasian actress in yellowface. As Nan Ping's companion, she caters to that character's every whim. One can only speculate as to what she was thinking. French actress Renée Adoreé (1898–1933) was the daughter of circus performers. She attained stardom with her sensitive portrayal of John Gilbert's love interest in *The Big Parade* (1925). In *Mr. Wu* she played Nan Ping in stereotypical fashion, with mincing steps and insufferable shyness.

Mr. Wu was originally a stage play presented in London and New York in 1914. British actor Matheson Lang (1879–1948) nearly made a career playing the title role, also starring in the 1919 film version directed by Maurice Elvey.

Old San Francisco

Warner Bros.; Released June 21, 1927; 8 reels
Director: Alan Crosland; *Screenplay*: Anthony Coldeway; *Story*: Darryl F. Zanuck; *Photography*: Hal Mohr; *Titles by*: Jack Jarmuth; *Editor*: Harold McCord; *Set Direction*: Ben Carré; *Assistant Director*: Gordon Hollingshead; *Electrical Effects*: P.N. Murphy; *Costumes*: "Alpharetta"; *Art Titles*: Victor Vance; *Music Score*: Hugo Riesenfeld; Synchronized by The Vitaphone Symphony Orchestra, Josiah Zuro conducting
Cast: Dolores Costello (Dolores Vasquez), Warner Oland (Chris Buckwell), Charles Emmett Mack (Terrance O'Shaugnessy), Josef Swickard (Don Hernandez Vasquez), John Miljan (Don Luis), Anders Randolf (Michael Brandon), Anna May Wong (Chinese Girl), Angelo Rossito (Chang Loo), Sojin (Lu Fong), Rose Dione (Madame Rose), Lawson Butt (Capt. Enrique De Solano Y Vasquez), Otto Mattiesen, Walter McGrail (Vasquez' Grandsons), Martha Mattox (Mother), Tom Santschi (Capt. Stoner).
The New York Times June 22, 1927: "A roaring melodrama ... a very lurid piece of work.... The settings are quite interesting and the trap doors are ingenious.... Anna May Wong does very well with her part."
Harrison's Reports July 16, 1927: " ...lavishly produced and spectacular in the extreme ... directed by Alan Crosland with praiseworthy skill and good judgement."

Synopsis: The film opens with a prologue showing Capt. Enrique De Solano Y Vasquez claiming the area around San Francisco Bay for Spain in 1769. The Vasquez family prospers in the area until 1848, when gold is discovered at Sutter's Mill. Their workers gradually leave to join the rush. When Capt. Stoner attempts to steal some horses from his employer, he is ordered back to his ship. He defies Vasquez and shoots him when attacked. Vasquez' brother lassos him off his horse and kills Stoner with the family sword.

Another time lapse to 1906 — San Francisco is thriving, ruled by greedy businessmen, while the Vasquez' fortunes have declined. Don Hernandez Vasquez dreams of the old days; his granddaughter assures him their past will be restored. A lawyer named Brandon and his nephew Terrance O'Shaughnessy appear at the ranch with an offer to buy the estate. As Brandon deals with Don Hernandez, his nephew becomes smitten by Dolores, Don Hernandez' granddaughter. He tarries with her until his uncle leaves after being told the ranch is not for sale. Brandon threatens to take the place, for the man for whom he works can break a dozen Vasquezs.

The most powerful man in San Francisco is Chris Buckwell, a Chinese masquerading as a Caucasian. Known as the "Czar of the Tenderloin," he keeps his true heritage hidden while persecuting his own people. He has a Buddhist shrine in his basement, where he also keeps his dwarf brother locked in a cage. Angered when he learns that Vasquez will not sell, he says he will have the ranch condemned. Terrance objects to this tactic and Brandon explains to Buckwell about Vasquez' granddaughter. Buckwell orders Brandon to start condemnation proceedings. Downstairs in his shrine, he prays for forgiveness for the crimes he has committed against his own people. His brother, Chang Loo, taunts him and Buckwell reaches for his knife. Chang Loo urges his brother to kill him, for he will welcome the peace of death. This gives Buckwell pause and he does nothing.

A Chinese girl, Buckwell's eyes and

Old San Francisco (Warner Bros., 1927): Anna May Wong, Warner Oland, Dolores Costello

ears, warns him that Chinatown is outraged by his latest doings, forcing a group of Chinese businessmen to sell back some property outside Chinatown they had purchased.

Terrance goes to the Vasquez place to warn them of Buckwell's plan. Don Hernandez says he does not want his help; Dolores asks him to hear out the young man. He does, but says he does not fear Buckwell; he shows Terrance the family sword, adding that he will hold his land with it. Family friend Don Luis drops by and learns of the Vasquez' predicament. Asked for assistance, he states that he is unable to help. Seeing him, Terrance thinks he is Dolores' fiancé and goes to drown his disappointment at the Poodle Dog in San Francisco.

After hearing Don Luis, Dolores secretly goes to the Poodle Dog to seek Terrance's aid. Buckwell notices her as she arrives there. She finds Terry in a drunken state and departs, deeply hurt. Buckwell tells Brandon he will now handle the Vasquez matter.

At the Vasquez ranch, Buckwell pretends to pray at their outdoor shrine, knowing the Vasquezs are watching him. He asks if he may come often to pray and is told the place has been condemned. He feigns incredulity and offers to help. He tells Don Hernanadez to take his land grants to an address in San Francisco where an expert will examine them.

Terrance arrives later, begging Dolores' forgiveness for his actions on the previous night. He tells her that when he learned of her engagement he did not care what happened. She then informs him that she is not engaged.

When Vasquez brings his papers to the specified address, he finds Brandon is the expert. The lawyer tells Vasquez that he is retained by someone friendly to him and the most powerful man in town. Terry passes by then, and, seeing Vasquez in his uncle's office, enters. He warns the old gentleman of the plot to rob his land. Vasquez takes back his papers and departs. Brandon tells his nephew that their careers are ruined — all for a girl. Terrance says he loves Dolores and Brandon tells him he is out of luck. Not understanding, Terrance is asked why does he think Buckwell arranged for Dolores to be alone that night?

At the ranch, Buckwell makes advances upon Dolores, then grabs her; as they struggle, Vasquez appears, followed shortly by Terry, who gives Buckwell a good thrashing. The businessman tells them they will regret what has just happened.

The next day, surveyors appear on the Vasquez estate. Vasquez orders them off his property, rushing at them with his cane. They grab him and push him away. Dolores hands him the family sword; when he brandishes the weapon, the surveyors scatter.

Buckwell comes again that night; Vasquez points his sword at him and orders him out. Buckwell tells the old man he can have him jailed for interfering with official surveyors, then pushes him down. As he threatens Buckwell with his sword, Vasquez suffers a fatal heart attack.

Dolores grabs the sword and tells Buckwell that her father is now with his god, who is a god of vengeance. Buckwell looks worried, as the servant rings the chapel bells, the businessman becomes visibly frightened; "Stop — stop those accursed Christian bells!" he cries. Light appears on the shrine statue and on Dolores' face as she glares at Buckwell, who shields his face with his cape, Dracula-like. "In the awful light of an outraged, wrathful, Christian God, the heathen soul of the Mongol stood revealed." Buckwell lowers his cape, eyes narrowed, and flees, aware that Dolores knows his secret.

After her father's burial, Dolores tells Terry what she has learned about Buckwell. The young man informs her that his own people will avenge her. He advises her to see Lu Fong, who can submit Buckwell to the proper punishment from his own race. At Lu Fong's the news brings astonishment to all present. The Chinese girl is eavesdropping, however, and slips away to warn Buckwell, stopping on the way to order some thugs to waylay Terry and Dolores. She watches from a doorway as the thugs surround the pair and then continues on her way.

Later, when the Chinese group and the white bosses of the city converge at Buckwell's home, he appears unruffled. He asks for proof of the charge they bring against him; Lu Fong says they have the word of Dolores. Buckwell laughs and says she is presently his guest and has her brought into the room. Only she and Buckwell know that Terry is tied to a pillar in the basement. Buckwell drums his fingers on a hidden button, which causes a light to flash below. If he stops drumming his fingers and the light goes out, it is a sign for the Chinese girl to kill Terry. Aware of this, too, Dolores lies to the company. Buckwell moves away from the button and Dolores jumps in front of it, placing a rod on it to keep the light on and tells the truth, admitting she was forced to lie. She informs the men of Terry's situation, adding that she can prove what she says. Buckwell is grabbed and Dolores leads the men downstairs. Terry is freed while Dolores points out the shrine and Buckwell's caged brother. The Chinese girl throws a knife at the light fuses and the room is plunged into darkness. In the confusion, Buckwell grabs Dolores and he and the Chinese girl escape through a hidden passage. When the light is restored, Terry frees Chang Loo and they go after them.

Buckwell goes to the house of Chang Sue Lee, an opium dealer and white slaver. Buckwell orders a woman to dress up Dolores for an auction. The girl struggles, then faints. At Lee's she is displayed on a stage, but runs off it. Every where she turns she is blocked by a Chinese man and recoils in horror. Lee strikes a deal with Buckwell; as he goes for his money, an earthquake hits the city. Both the Chinese girl and Buckwell are buried under falling debris. Terry finds Dolores lying on a floor, unconscious but alive. Buckwell is found by his brother, who taunts him and laughs at him as he lays dying.

The city is rebuilt in time; Terry and Dolores look out over it as their daughter plays.

Print status: Shown on Turner Classic Movies.

A well-produced film, *Old San Francisco* is seriously marred by unabashed anti–Asian racism. There are several derogatory allusions to Asians and the terms "Chinaman" and "Mongolian" are used interchangeably and the subject of white slavery is included. That such a biased tale could be written by a man who would later head a major studio seems rather unjust, even given the temper of the times. Darryl F. Zanuck (1902–1979) began as a screenwriter at Warner Bros. in 1923 and five years later became studio manager. Following a policy dispute with the Warners in 1933, Zanuck left and formed Twentieth Century Pictures with Joseph Schenck. Merging his company with Fox in 1935, Zanuck produced a number of fine films until his resignation in 1971.

Anna May's character is introduced with the intertitle: "A flower of the Orient, stifled and poisoned in Chinatown's sunless cellars." She has no name (in the Photoplay edition of the story, she is called "San Toy" and is also described therein as a half-caste). Anna May wears but one costume throughout the picture, but her character is important.

Daedalus would have admired the intricate passageways and stairwells abounding beneath the buildings. The realistic earthquake scenes were tinted red, then orange once the fire begins. The photography is exceptional, with much artistic use of light.

The working title of this film was *A Million Bid*, and as such was promised to theater owners in December 1926. Over the next four months its progress was followed in *Moving Picture World* until *A Million Bid* emerged as another film with some of the same cast—Costello and Oland—but an entirely different story and a different director, Michael Curtiz. *Old San Francisco* was released in June, but with the director originally announced for the other film, Alan Crosland. Oddly, in the novelization of *Old San Francisco*, there is a sequence in which Dolores Costello's character is auctioned, and the last bid is one million dollars. In *Old San Francisco*, she is about to be auctioned when she tries to flee; as she is recaptured, the earthquake hits.

Dolores Costello (1905–1979) was the daughter of early film matinee idol Maurice Costello (1877–1950) and the sister of Helene (1902–1957). She was Warner Bros.' leading female star at the time of this picture. Her greatest achievement was being married to John Barrymore (1882–1942) for several years.

Warner Oland (1880–1938) had been in films since the mid-teens, usually portraying an Asian character. He was one of the few actors who did so without recourse to yellowface. This was the first of three films in which he appeared with Anna May Wong.

German-born Josef Swickard (1866–1940) had an enviable head of hair even in his sixties, and could act as well.

The Chinese Parrot

Universal; Released October 23, 1927; 7 reels
Director: Paul Leni; *Producer*: Carl Laemmle; *Adaptation-Scenario*: J. Grubb Alexander, from the novel by Earl Derr Biggers; *Story-Continuity*: John Francis Natteford; *Photography*: Ben Kline; *Titles*: Walter Anthony
Cast: Marion Nixon (Sally Phillmore), Florence

Turner (Sally Phillmore, older), Hobart Bosworth (Phillip Madden/Jerry Delaney), Edward Burns (Robert Eden), Albert Conti (Martin Thorn), Sojin (Charlie Chan), Fred Esmelton (Alexander Eden), Ed Kennedy (Maydorf), George Kuwa (Louie Wong), Slim Summerville, Dan Mason (Prospectors), Anna May Wong (Nautch Dancer), Etta Lee (Gambling Den Habitué), Jack Trent (Jordan).

The New York Times January 2, 1928: "...Mr. Leni once more proves that with individual treatment an only fair-to-middling story can be made into a film that is at once original and imaginative ... ingenious use of shadows, lights and special effects...."

Variety January 16, 1928: "Anna May Wong looked oke as a cooch dancer in the prolog, but she passed out on the knife route ... that meant one day's work and featuring. Leni's directorial work quite outstanding...."

Synopsis: Sally Randall, daughter of a rich Hawaiian planter, marries Phillmore, her father's choice for her husband. By doing so, she jilted P. J. Madden, the man to whom she had sworn her love. Madden rips the pearls, that are Sally's wedding gift from her father, from her throat, vowing that he will one day buy her for the price of the necklace.

Twenty years later Mrs. Phillmore is a widow and in financial straits. She returns to San Francisco and offers the pearls for sale through her jeweler, Robert Eden. He finds a buyer and Mrs. Phillmore and her daughter Sally go to Eden's office to meet him. He turns out to be Madden, now a millionaire.

Mrs. Phillmore is stunned and then humiliated as Madden looks lustfully upon her daughter. She is unable to deliver the pearls then, having entrusted them to a Chinese detective named Chan. Rather than wait for the detective, Madden instructs Mrs. Phillmore to bring the pearls to his desert hacienda on the next day, adding the stipulation that her daughter must accompany her.

When Madden arrives at his home, he is knocked out by thugs, who hold him prisoner in his home. One of them, Jerry Delaney, bears a striking resemblance to Madden and decides to impersonate the millionaire. He is abetted by Madden's secretary, a notorious crook. The Phillmores arrive with Alexander Eden, the jeweler's son. Sally and Alexander sense a tense atmosphere and are amazed to discover that Chan, still carrying the pearls, has arrived before them disguised as a prospector. He has been hired as a cook by Madden and orders the pair to keep silent while he investigates the situation.

At dinner, a strange voice shouts, "Help! I am being murdered!" Investigation reveals that the sound was made by a parrot belonging to a Chinese servant who has disappeared. The parrot speaks only Chinese; Chan removes it and tries to get it to reveal its secret. Another day passes and Alexander, who believes Sally loves Madden, is anxious to return to San Francisco. He demands the pearls from Chan and is about to turn them over to Delaney when another of the crooks, afraid he is being doublecrossed, knocks on the door, arousing Alexander's suspicions. He hides the pearls under a newspaper in the living room. The pearls are gone when he later returns. He accuses Delaney of taking them; Delaney in turn accuses members of the gang. Just then Mr. Phillmore and Robert Eden arrive. As Alexander tries to explain the situation, the real Madden appears, having been freed by Chan. Chan explains that the Chinese parrot had witnessed the kidnapping and told him about it. The crooks are arrested, Mrs. Phillmore falls into Madden's arms and Sally and Alexander realize their love for each other. Chan gives the pearls to Madden who hurls them into the desert, explaining that as they have caused nothing but trouble, everyone is better off without them.

Print status: No known copies extant.

Paul Leni (1885–1929) was one of the influx of German talent which was respon-

The Chinese Parrot (Universal, 1927): Anna May Wong

sible for some of the finest American films of the late silent era. A former set designer for Max Reinhardt and art director in his native country, he became a film director in 1916. He designed the sets for all his films as well. His first American effort was the hugely successful *The Cat and the Canary*, released earlier in 1927.

This was the second film to feature the character of Chinese detective Charlie Chan, and the final silent one. In neither is he the leading character; not until Warner Oland assumed the role in 1931 did he become the central figure.

The Devil Dancer

Samuel Goldwyn/United Artists; Released November 3, 1927; 8 reels
Director: Fred Niblo; *Scenario*: D. G. Miller; *Titles*: Edwin Justus Mayer; *Story*: Harry Hervey; *Camera*: George Barnes, Thomas Brannigan; *Editor*: Viola Lawrence; *Set Design*: Willy Pogany, Harold Grieve; *Assistant Director*: H.B. Humberstone
Cast: Gilda Gray (Takla, the Devil Dancer), Clive Brook (Stephen Athelstan), Anna May Wong (Sada, the Guilty One), Serge Temoff (Beppo, the tom-tom boy), Michael Vavitch (Hassim), Sojin (Sadik Lama), Ura Mita (Tana, servant woman), Albert Conti (Arnold Guthrie), Clarissa Selwyn (Isabel), Kalla Pasha (Toy), James B. Leong (The Grand Lama), William H. Tooker (Lathrop), Claire DuBrey (Audrey), Nora Cecil (Julia), Barbara Tennant (The White Woman).
Academy Award Nomination: Best Cinematography (1927–28)
The New York Times December 19, 1927: "This production is wonderfully convincing in its atmosphere and rich in scenery...."
Harrison's Reports December 24, 1927: "Mr. Niblo, who directed the picture, and Mr. Willy Pongany [sic], who designed the sets, have certainly done an artistic piece of work. As a result of it, one is made to think as if seeing the real thing ... there is nothing to

the story.... Clarissa Selwyn, Sojin, Anna May Wong and others are in the supporting cast."

Synopsis: In the mountains of Tibet, a weary white woman drags a yak cart bearing the body of her husband. An English missionary, he had been slain by bandits. The pregnant woman is taken in by the Black Lamas of the Monastery of Lakhang-gompa and dies after giving birth to a daughter.

To the Lamas this is a sign of the gods; accordingly, the newborn is taken into the great temple and the mark of the sect, a swastika, is tattooed on its arm. She is the consecrated vestal virgin who belongs to the devil-god and dances her wild dances before the idol in the temple. Here she is doomed to seclusion among the Lamas until the appointed time when she follows the previous dancer as Bride of the Gods.

Twenty-five years pass and Takla, the White One, is still a prisoner under the care of Tana, an aged Tibetan serving woman confined to her quarters and garden. The devil dancer now in the temple, Sada, is caught in a love affair with one of the monks, and the Great Lama sentences both to be buried alive. Sadik Lama, ruler of the devil dancers, notifies Takla that she is to be Sada's successor.

Stephen Athelstan, a British government explorer disguised as a Nepalese trader, is encamped in the valley below the monastery. Hearing a thunderous gong, he learns from his Chinese caravan man that it means an execution within the monastery. The two join the throngs at the temple, although discovery means death.

Haunted by the white hands he saw protruding from Takla's veil, Stephen attends the Festival of the Gods the next day. This is the rite celebrating her marriage to the devil deity. Stirred by the beauty of her dance and convinced she is an English girl, he gains entrance to her closely guarded chamber that night. At first his presence terrifies her, but his friendliness calms her. He appears again the following night and persuades Takla to escape with him. She agrees to do so the next night. She confides in Tana, who promises to keep watch. As Stephen arrives, Sadik Lama comes to take Takla to the evening service. Tana, disguised as Takla, intercepts him, giving the pair a chance to escape. Tana is soon found out and tortured into revealing the escape, but by then Stephen's caravan is far into the desert.

Arriving at Kalem, a small town in the Himalayas, Stephen introduces Takla to his brother-in-law, the British Commissioner, and his sister, Isabel. The latter is horror-stricken to learn that Takla has agreed to marry her brother. At a party for Stephen, Takla is introduced to all the British residents of the colony. She is hurt when her manners embarrass Stephen and by his sister's unpleasantness toward her.

A traveling nautch troupe, owned by a brutal, swaggering Moslem named Hassim, takes its post near the commissioner's home and entertains the party guests. The troupe consists of six nautch dancers, a snake charmer, a juggler and a frail white boy who beats the tuba drums for the dancers and slinks helplessly at Hassim's command.

Stephen's sister bribes Hassim to kidnap Takla. Fearing that the dancer has been spirited away by the Lamas, Stephen rushes off in pursuit. Meanwhile, Hassim convinces Takla that it was Stephen who bribed him to take her away because he was ashamed of her. She becomes contemptuous of Stephen and willingly joins the nautch troupe.

The next engagement of Hassim's troupe is at a nautch house in Delhi, where Takla becomes a sensation. Hassim schemes endlessly to win her, and in futile desperation, attacks her. Beppo, who has become Takla's friend, interferes, and the two plan an escape the following night.

The Devil Dancer (Goldwyn/United Artists, 1927): Anna May Wong, Serge Temoff (courtesy John Cocchi)

Stephen's search finally brings him and the commissioner to the Delhi nautch house. Hassim spots him and forbids Takla to dance that night. Takla, upon seeing the lover whom she believes has deceived her, assents.

Stephen corners Hassim, whom he had suspected in Takla's disappearance, and forces a confession from him. Meanwhile, Takla is met by Sadik Lama in her dressing room. Resigned to her fate, the dancer summons Stephen to her room by note — a trap for his death at the hands of the Lama. Beppo becomes the victim as he rushes to her aid, but fights back death to inform Takla of Hassim's lie about Stephen. Stephen then lunges into the room and hurls himself upon the Lama, toppling him over the balcony. The lovers sink to their knees over the body of Beppo and fall into each other's arms.

Print status: No known copies extant.

As Sada, the one caught with a monk, Anna May does not have much screen time in this melodrama. Her character is executed about two reels into the film.

A troubled production, *The Devil Dancer* had two directors, Alfred Reboch and Lynn Shores, before Fred Niblo finally completed it.

Streets of Shanghai

Tiffany-Stahl Productions; Released December 15, 1927; 6 reels
Director: Louis Gasnier; *Photography*: Max Dupont and Earle Walker; *Story-Continuity*: John Francis Natteford; *Editor*: Martin G.

Cohn; *Titles*: Viola Brothers Shore; *Set Designer*: George E. Sawley

Cast: Pauline Stark (Mary Sanger), Kenneth Harlan (Sgt. Lee), Eddie Gribbon (Swede), Margaret Livingston (Sadie), Jason Robards (Eugene Fong), Mathilde Comont (Buttercup, Mary's Companion), Sojin (Fong Kiang), Anna May Wong (Su Quan), Tetsu Komai (Chang Ho), Toshiye Ichioka (Girl Wife), Media Ichioka (F'aien Shi, the Chinese Girl).

The New York Times February 21, 1928: "It is a yellow melodrama, with yellow flames, yellow villains and even yellow gunfire. Just when this picture seems to be going along about rationally something pops up that makes one wonder when it is going to finish."

Variety February 29, 1928: "Cast principals play this one okay and Gasnier keeps it moving. The kick footage is the attack on the mission by the heavy's followers, with much gun play...."

Synopsis: Mary Sanger calls on the proprietor of the House of the Cage, asking him to relinquish F'aien Shi, the little Chinese girl he stole from her mission. The proprietor claims ignorance, igniting a heated argument. Some marines led by Lee and Swede happen along and swear they will find F'aine Shi if they have to tear down the entire place. While Swede and the other marines guard the stairs, Lee and Mary go upstairs in search of the girl. Lee knocks upon a door which is opened by Sadie, who is only too glad to welcome such a personable young American as a customer. Even when told of his quest she is nothing daunted and attaches herself to him. Meanwhile, Mary has located F'aien Shi behind a locked door and calls to Lee for aid. He breaks down the door, and while Mary calms the frightened child, Sadie continues her vamping tactics, stopping just long enough to thrust Lee aside as she sees a yellow hand in the barred window fling a knife at him. Lee rewards her by pinning his marine clasp on her waist, and Sadie thinks she has made a conquest. After finding out her name and address and telling her to expect him soon, Lee puts Mary and F'aien Shi in a rickshaw and they head for the mission. As the marines are about to leave, Sadie wants to know what's to become of her; Lee tells her to come along to the consulate where he'll see she gets protection. The marine installs her in a bungalow with a female missionary who is greatly shocked by Sadie's speech and manners.

Next morning Mary gets a visit from Lee in her classroom. He wants her to seek protection at the consulate, since she made enemies by her actions on the previous day. She refuses at first, but then agrees to go for a week. While gathering her things at the mission, Mary is visited by Eugene Fong, a young Americanized Chinese who is madly in love with her. He is saddened by the news of her departure and begs her not to go. Meanwhile, Eugene's father, Fong Kiang, learns of his son's whereabouts and becomes angry, for he is the owner of the House of the Cage and bitter towards Mary.

When Lee brings Mary to the consulate he installs her in the same bungalow with Sadie, who has taken a great dislike to her. Mary is puzzled by her attitude, for she has been cordial toward her. She questions Sadie and learns that Sadie considers Lee her man and that Mary better keep her distance, which is what Mary decides to do, despite her liking for Lee.

After several unsuccessful attempts, Lee gets Mary alone and finds out why she has been avoiding him. He swears to her that she is the only girl he has ever loved.

Later, Sadie goes to Lee's quarters and is told by the marine that he is grateful for her having saved his life, but he does not love her and wants to be left alone. Sadie agrees, but as they are about to go out, she deliberately tears her dress and explains that she cannot go out with a torn dress. Lee goes in search of a needle and thread. Mary shows up at Lee's quarters and looks

Streets of Shanghai (Tiffany-Stahl, 1927): Anna May Wong, Jason Robards (courtesy John Cocchi)

through a window; Sadie shows her the torn dress. Mary is deeply hurt and shocked and cannot help but think that Lee really belongs to Sadie. The situation is exacerbated when Lee returns and Sadie flings her arms about him and kisses him. Lee sees Mary at the window and, throwing Sadie from him, goes after her. He is stopped by an officer who gives him an order. Mary goes to her bungalow and packs her things.

In the home of Fong Kiang there is a party, but even this does not take Eugene's mind off Mary. He looks out a window and sees a light in the mission, so he rushes over to visit Mary. When his father finds out, he orders a henchman, Chang Ho, to rob the mission and kill the white woman.

Lee rushes to the mission as soon as he is able. Mary and her maid are putting things in order, preparatory to retiring. Little F'aien Shi is putting out the cat when Lee bursts in and demands to be heard. Mary will have none of him; in desperation Lee tells her he'll prove he's telling the truth by bringing Sadie and forcing the truth from her. He brings Sadie to the mission, but she refuses to clear him and Mary refuses to believe him. Suddenly a bullet misses Mary by an inch. Lee bustles about, barricading the place, then secures rifles with which the besieged repulse Chang Ho's first attack. As he prepares a second assault, Eugene appears at the door, begging to be admitted. Mary recognizes his voice, but as she opens the door, Eugene is shot. Now out of ammunition, Lee begs Mary to believe in his love for her, now that they face death. She does, and they embrace just as their assailants break into the mission. A small army of marines suddenly appears, brought by F'aien Shi, who had slipped away earlier to get help. Led by Swede, they rout Chang Ho's men.

Swede gravitates toward Sadie, who, seeing Mary and Lee resume their interrupted embrace, shrugs her shoulders and turns her attention to Swede.

Print status: No known copies extant.

Despite being a Poverty Row company, Tiffany managed to have this film tinted in one tone — yellow. Once again Anna May is unmentioned in the synopsis; she was probably either a denizen of the House of the Cage or a resident of the mission.

The Dove

United Artists; Released January 1, 1928; 9 reels
Produced and Directed by: Roland West; *Photography*: Olive Marsh; *Scenario*: Wallace Smith and Paul Bern, from the play by Willard Mack
Cast: Norma Talmadge (Dolores), Noah Beery (Don Jose Maria y Sandoval), Gilbert Roland (Johnny Powell), Eddie Borden (Billy), Harry Myers (Mike), Michael Vavitch (Gomez), Brindsley Shaw (The Patriot), Kalla Pasha (The Commandante), Charles Darvas (The Commandante's Captain), Michael Dark (Sandoval's Captain), Walter Daniels (The Drunk).
Remade as *The Girl of the Rio* by RKO in 1932 and as *The Girl and the Gambler* by RKO in 1939.
Academy Award: For Best Art Direction, to William Cameron Menzies, who was also cited for his work on another United Artists production, *The Tempest* (1927–28).
Anna May Wong's footage was completely excised from this film.
Harrison's Reports January 7, 1928: "…has been directed with skill by Roland West…. But on the whole the picture is nothing that any exhibitor can brag about it [sic] to his patrons."
Variety January 11, 1928: "…hasn't the dramatic intensity of the play. It's spasmodically slow. Marsh's camera work is a predominate feature throughout."

Synopsis: Johnny Powell is a young gambler employed at Charlie's gambling emporium in Costa Roja. Every night at dinner time he slips over to "The Yellow Pig Cafe" to hear Dolores, known as "The Dove," a fiery young woman who sings and plays guitar. One night the wealthy and egotistical Don Jose Maria Y Sandoval takes over the entertainment chores himself, toasting the ladies and declaring himself the best dancer in all Costa Roja. Smitten by Dolores, he makes advances, but is repulsed. The cafe proprietor, Mike Downey, scolds Dolores for her treatment of so wealthy a patron as Don Jose. She ignores his order to placate Don Jose. Johnny Powell watches in helpless anger. When Downey and Don Jose leave, Johnny offers his aid to the now frightened singer. The two quickly fall in love.

A murderous cousin of Don Jose's, Gomez, is ordered by Don Jose and Downey to make trouble for Johnny at the cafe. He substitutes phony dice for real ones; Johnny becomes suspicious at Gomez' winning streak and substitutes his own dice. Gomez calls foul and reaches for his gun, but is beaten to the draw by Johnny. Don Jose, expecting to find Johnny dead, sees his cousin dead instead. He accuses Johnny of murder; despite a plea of self-defense and Dolores' statement of a frame-up, Johnny is taken to jail.

With the help of Johnny's friend Billy, Dolores collects enough money to bribe the commandante at the jail into letting Johnny go. Don Jose meanwhile orders the commandante to let Johnny escape, so he can be shot as he climbs the last wall. Dolores meets with Johnny in the tower of an old fortress. She is surprised to find Downey and Don Jose there. She is shocked when she learns of the latter's plan for Johnny. In order to save him, Dolores agrees to go with Don Jose to his hacienda if Johnny is given his freedom. She meets with Johnny again and tells him their affair must end; as she does so, Powell sees a face peering around a corner at them and suspects the truth. He pretends to agree and heads for the coast.

At Don Jose's hacienda, a wedding breakfast is held. As Don Jose tests the champagne, Dolores puts poison into her glass. Don Jose sees this and knocks the glass from her hand before she can drink. As he embraces the singer, Powell leaps from the wall into the courtyard with gun drawn. Don Jose throws some wine into Johnny's face, temporarily blinding him, but finds himself facing Billy, who also has a gun. Dolores and Johnny escape, only to be caught again by Don Jose's guards; Johnny is sentenced to be shot.

Dolores pleads for her lover's life, but in vain. As the firing squad makes ready, she runs to Johnny's side and announces that she will die with him. This act, and Johnny's bravery, appeal to the watching crowd, and Don Jose becomes uneasy, but orders the execution to proceed. Dolores appeals to the crowd with a fiery speech directed against Don Jose. She ridicules his boast at being the best dancer in Costa Roja and calls him a coward for his fear of the American, naming Johnny the best caballero in the town.

In order to save face and assuage his vanity, Don Jose sets the couple free. As a final gesture, he lends the lovers his carriage, causing Dolores to acknowledge him as the best caballero in Costa Roja.

Print status: Reels 1, 3, 4, and 8 only at the Library of Congress, Washington, D.C.

Though set in Mexico, there is "A Chinaman" listed in the cast for the play; possibly Anna May could have played his wife or daughter. Since the role is not listed for the film, the producers apparently opted to delete the characters altogether.

The play which was adapted for this production ran on Broadway in 1925. *The New York Times* of February 12, 1925 said of it: "…makes no pretense of being a serious drama.."

The Crimson City

Warner Bros.; Released April 7, 1928; 6 reels
Director: Archie Mayo; *Story*: Anthony Coldeway; *Titles*: James A. Starr; *Cinematography*: Barney McGill; *Assistant Director*: Gordon Hollingshead; *Intertitle Writer*: James A. Starr
Cast: Myrna Loy (Onoto), John Miljan (Gregory Kent), Leila Hyams (Nadine Howells), Matthew Betz ("Dagger" Foo), Anders Randolf (Major Howells), Sojin (Sing Yoy), Anna May Wong (Su), Richard Tucker (Richard Brand).
Working title: *City of Sin*.
Variety April 18, 1928: "Story … is strained melodrama with leering Chinese menace and all the old tricks of Oriental melodrama.… Material is handled in directorial sense far better than the subject matter merits.…"
Harrison's Reports April 28, 1928: "A pretty good melodrama.… There are several thrilling situations. Anna May Wong … and others are in the cast."

Synopsis: Richard Brand, manager of the Anglo-Oriental oil fields, entertains Major Howells and his daughter Nadine, whom he hopes to marry. Nadine's former fiancé, a young English aristocrat named Gregory Kent, has fled Britain after being charged with embezzlement and gone to China. Aware that Nadine is there too, he has not the courage to seek her out.

Kent visits a notorious waterfront establishment called the House of a Thousand Daggers. Onoto, a slave girl, has been promised to Sing Yoy, a wealthy Chinese, by "Dagger" Foo, the owner of the House. She tries to escape, but is caught and subjected to torture. Kent intercedes, demanding that Onoto sit at his table while he orders food.

Tyler Jordan arrives from England with documents proving Kent's innocence. Brand bargains with Foo to secure the papers. Kent is dispatched to steal the papers that would mean his own freedom, with the stipulation that Onoto be freed as a reward. Onoto discovers the truth about the documents. After a terrific fight with Foo, Gregory recovers what he believes to be his pardon, and heads for Brand's home. The envelope which Kent presents to Nadine's father reveals only blank paper.

Onoto arrives, declaring that she loves Kent and pleading that he be allowed to go with her. As Kent is about to leave, Onoto realizes the futility of her love and hands the real proof of Kent's innocence, which she had stolen, to Nadine. Nadine and Kent embrace and Onoto returns to the House of a Thousand Daggers.

Print status: Trailer only at the Library of Congress, Washington, D.C.

This was the film which determined Anna May Wong to leave Hollywood for Europe. Playing second fiddle to Myrna Loy in yellowface was the last straw for the proud actress. Advertising blurbs like "Exotic Myrna Loy Perfectly Cast as the Alluring Temptress of the House of a Thousand Daggers!" and "The Crimson City Will Keep the Box Office Out of the Red!" undoubtedly aided her in this decision. Ironically, when Anna May returned to the film capital a few years later, Loy was still being cast as exotics. Both actresses would play the daughter of Fu Manchu — Wong in *Daughter of the Dragon* (1931) [q.v.] and Loy in *The Mask of Fu Manchu* (1932). Needless to say, it was not long before Anna May was back in Europe.

The original name of Anna May's character, as stated in her contract, was Cherry Blossom.

Chinatown Charlie

First National Pictures; Released April 15, 1928; 7 reels

Director: Charles Hines; *Producer*: C.C. Burr; *Scenario*: Roland Asher, John Grey; *Story*: Owen Davis; *Cinematography*: William J. Miller; *Titles*: Paul Perez; *Editor*: George Amy

Cast: Johnny Hines (Charlie), Louise Lorraine (Annie Gordon), Harry Gribbon (Red Mike), Fred Kohler (Monk), Sojin (The Mandarin), Scooter Lowry (Oswald), Anna May Wong (The Mandarin's Sweetheart), George Kuwa (Hip Sing Toy), John Burdette (Gyp).

Harrison's Reports March 31, 1928: "The comedy is the usual Hines sort, horse-play mostly ... thrills are caused by the abduction of the heroine in New York's Chinatown...."

Variety June 13, 1928: "No story unless a trip to Chinatown on a sight-seeing bus is a plot. Screen adaptation and comedy business extremely poor and direction at a low grade."

Synopsis: "Chinatown Charlie" is the genial orator on a Chinatown sightseeing bus. One night the bus includes a pretty girl named Annie Gordon, who is immediately attracted to Charlie. The other passengers include a bothersome child named Oswald and a number of out-of-towners and underworld characters.

Charlie notices Annie and the two quickly become acquainted. Annie asks Charlie about a Chinese ring she is wearing. He tells her that as soon as they reach the Port Shanghai Chop Suey Palace, he will ask the proprietor, Hip Sing Toy, about it.

The first stop is the Old Mission, where Charlie has an encounter with Gyp, a tough underworld character. From there they go to the Port Shanghai Chop Suey Palace, where an acrobatic troupe is providing entertainment. Charlie asks Hip Sing Toy about the ring. The man becomes excited when he recognizes it as the ring which once belonged to an emperor and has great powers. A Chinese man overhears them and slips out to tell Monk, a gang leader, of his discovery.

The next stop is a wax museum containing figures of historical personages. As they leave the museum, two Chinese men try to kidnap Annie, but are scared off by Red Mike. Charlie takes the ring for safekeeping, but Annie suddenly disappears.

Red Mike and Charlie look for her and encounter Monk at the back of the wax museum. Monk denies knowing of Annie's

Chinatown Charlie (First National, 1928): Anna May Wong, Johnny Hines, Louise Lorraine

whereabouts, but a tapping sound makes Charlie believe she is a prisoner somewhere inside.

He later discovers a note from the girl stating she has been taken to the Mandarin's Palace. He sends Red Mike to the police for help. He uses the ring to gain admission to the mandarin's place. Finding himself in the mandarin's bedroom, he disguises himself in Oriental robes as the mandarin.

He runs into Annie, who tries to fight him off, believing he is the mandarin. He then encounters the mandarin's girl, who wants to make love to him. The real mandarin enters and a meleé ensues.

Red Mike arrives then and sees the acrobatic troupe seated on windows near a fire escape across the street from the mandarin's place. He shouts instructions at them; they form a human chain from the fire escape to the mandarin's window on the second floor. Charlie and Annie eventually escape across this human bridge.

Print status: No known copies extant.

One of the few comedies in which Anna May appeared, *Chinatown Charlie* sounds rather lame from the synopsis. Existing stills tend to support this criticism.

Across to Singapore

Metro-Goldwyn-Mayer; Released April 28, 1928; 7 reels

Director: William Nigh; *Adaptation*: Ted Shane, from the book *All the Brothers Were Valiant* by Ben Ames Williams; *Photography*: John Seitz; *Continuity*: Richard Schayer; *Titles*: Joe Farnham; *Settings*: Cedric Gibbons; *Wardrobe*: Donald Cox; *Editor*: Ben Lewis

62 • Across to Singapore (1928)

Cast: Ramon Novarro (Joel Shore), Ernest Torrence (Capt. Mark Shore), Joan Crawford (Priscilla Crowninshield), Frank Currier (Jeremiah Shore), Don Wollheim (Noah Shore), James Mason (Finch), Edward Connelly (Joshua Crowninshield), Duke Martin (Matthew Shore), Anna May Wong (Bailarina).

Working title: *China Bound*

Previously filmed by Metro in 1923 as *All the Brothers Were Valiant*.

Remade by MGM in 1953 as *All the Brothers Were Valiant*.

The New York Times April 28, 1928: "It is an out-and-out tale, with good points mixed with poor ones in many of its episodes. William Nigh does not always give his characters credit for sufficient intelligence...."

Variety May 2, 1928: "...the film is a marvel of artistic excellence. Not one incident or character really lives."

Synopsis: Joel Shore, youngest son in a seafaring family, wants to go on his first voyage. His oldest brother Mark says only a man who can prove he can fight can sail with him. Joel and Mark are rivals for the affections of Priscilla Crowninshield, to whom the latter is engaged by their respective parents.

All the brothers go drinking to celebrate Mark's engagement and get into a fight with another ship's crew at the tavern. Joel fakes beating up a tough sailor and wins the admiration of his brothers and the chance to sail with them.

Mark's engagement to Priscilla is announced in church. Neither Joel nor Priscilla are happy; Mark notices this but says nothing.

The next day the Shores set sail for the Far East. Priscilla sees Joel off and tells him that she does not love Mark. Joel returns her embrace, but she refuses Mark's kiss. Mark tries to forget Priscilla, but has visions of her.

A storm hits the ship off Cape Horn. Mark is drunk in his cabin; Joel tells him that Priscilla only has eyes for him, but Mark says she loves someone else. Joel persists, and Mark finally goes on deck to help the crew. Noah Shore is swept overboard and Joel is made first mate.

A sailor named Finch becomes disgruntled for being overlooked for promotion and vows to put Capt. Mark out of the way in Singapore.

When the ship docks at Singapore, Joel remains on board because of his age. In a bar, a local girl plays up to Mark: "Kinda recognize beauty when you lay eyes on it, don't you?" Finch plots against Mark with an Indian who likes the girl. Joel appears and finds Mark with the girl on his lap. He pulls her off and tells Mark he must remember Priscilla. "Why should I remember Priscilla? She'll be happier if I forget her! She doesn't love *me*!" cries Mark. He continues drinking, blaming Priscilla for his state and tells Joel he will throttle him if he ever mentions her name again. He orders two of the crew to take his younger brother back to the ship. Joel struggles with them, but is knocked out. The girl takes the drunken Mark outside, where he is attacked by the Indian and his gang and left for dead. The girl and an older woman help Mark up to the girl's room. The older woman later tells Finch that Mark was killed and his body dumped into the bay.

The ship returns and Mr. Shore is informed of the deaths of two of his sons. Joel is in irons, because Finch says he deserted Mark in the fight in which Mark was killed. Mr. Shore asks Joel for his side of the story, but the young man says nothing. Finch says that his silence is a sign of his guilt. His father calls Joel a coward and slaps him. When Finch opens Joel's handcuffs, Joel attacks him, telling his father that the sailor lied. Priscilla arrives and is later told by Joel that he believes Mark is still alive. He further tells her that she is the only one who can bring him back; she repeats that she does not love Mark. Joel informs her that he is returning to Singapore that night and she is going with him. He takes command of the ship after knocking down Finch.

In Singapore, Mark has moved in with the girl from the bar, but is continually drunk, repeating the same song over and over again. The girl is going out of her mind: "Stop! Stop! For six months all I hear is the same crazy song!" Mark goes outside and spots his ship entering the port.

Priscilla admits to Joel that if Mark is found, she must put everyone else from her mind. Joel reminds her that she is pledged to Mark, but the girl insists she loves him. "No! You belong to Mark!" he says nobly. Meanwhile, Finch informs his cronies that if Mark is found, they will all go to jail. Joel has Finch take him to the spot where he last saw Mark. As Joel hugs Priscilla, Mark appears suddenly. Joel goes to him but Mark asks Priscilla what kind of girl is she, being pledged to him but loving his brother instead. He struggles with Joel and threatens to kill the pair with a belaying pin. Joel knocks him down and has him placed in irons and tells him the ship will be his when he returns to his senses. Mark threatens to feed Joel to the sharks when he is freed. Joel informs him that Priscilla came only to find him and tells Finch to speak the truth. Finch lies again, telling Mark that Joel quit him in Singapore so he would be killed and the younger brother could have Priscilla. Joel and Finch fight; as the sailor gains the upper hand, Mark threatens him and gets

Across to Singapore (MGM, 1928): Anna May Wong

loose. Finch flees, locking the cell door behind him. "You're both where I want you at last! Now this ship's mine ... and the woman too!" Finch cries in the best tradition of movie villains. Mark asks Joel for forgiveness as the factions fight on deck. The two brothers escape and join the fray. Their side wins, but Finch kills Mark from behind. Joel chases him up into the rigging and knocks him off into the sea. With his last breath, the dying Mark tells his younger brother to be good to Priscilla.

Print status: Shown on Turner Classic Movies.

Anna May does not appear until well into this picture, looking almost gaunt, and dressed in an outfit apparently borrowed from Gypsy Central. She is the object of Mark's affections until the attack upon him. She then becomes his nurse until Joel returns for his brother.

Ramon Novarro (1899–1968) was at the peak of his stardom and about to make a smooth transition into sound pictures. Ernest Torrence, usually a heavy, turns in a good performance as the older brother who loses in love. Future major star Joan Crawford (1904–1977) had been in films only a few years and was still playing ingenues.

II

European Silent Films

Anna May Wong's first stop was the German capital city of Berlin, then experiencing an explosion of expression in every artistic area. Gone were the nightmares of inflation, starvation and defeat; life was for living and Berlin was the place to live. Among the dominant names in the cultural pantheon there were Bertold Brecht, Kurt Weill, Max Reinhardt and Richard Strauss, in those exciting but uneasy days before the National Socialist takeover.

The experienced actress was signed by director Richard Eichberg (1888–1952). In 1914, Eichberg became one of the first directors to head his own company, Eichberg Film. In February 1928 he took advantage of the reciprocity existing between British and German filmmakers to close a four-picture deal with British International Pictures. That company had gone public the year before and had absorbed W & F Film Service and Wardour, becoming the largest and best equipped studio in Britain. Located at Elstree, it attracted filmmakers from all over the globe, including a local young man who had made a splash at Gainsborough in 1926, Alfred Hitchcock (1899–1980), destined to direct the first British talkie for BIP, and later make the move to Hollywood where he became very highly regarded as a director of superior suspense films. Acquiring the German distributor Sudfilm at the same time as Eichberg's services, BIP announced that the director's films would be made in Germany and distributed there by Sudfilm, while Wardour would handle the British distribution.

Song
(U.K.: Show Life;
U.S.: Wasted Love)

Richard Eichberg Film/British International/Wardour; Released July 30, 1928; 94 minutes.

Director: Richard Eichberg; *Camera*: Heinrich Gartner, Bruno Mondi; *Scenario*: Helen Gosewish, Adolf Lantz, from the book *Schmutziges Geld* (*Dirty Money*) by Karl Vollmoller; *Art Director*: W.A. Hermann; *Editor*: Alfred Booth

Cast: Anna May Wong (Song), Mary Kid (Gloria), Heinrich George (John), Hans Adalbert von Schlettow (James Prager), Paul Horbiger (Carletto), Julius E. Herrmann.

The New York Times August 22, 1928: "...is a hapless piece of work that is years behind the times. Anna May Wong is a competent little actress, but it would take far more than good acting, coupled with pleasing photography, to make this production half-way diverting."

The Bioscope September 19, 1928: "...Anna May Wong scores a veritable triumph ... the star's personality and acting, which from start to finish enchains the attention.... Anna May Wong's acting [is] a masterpiece of subtlety.

Variety January 1, 1930: "Miss Wong is the only one with the slightest knowledge of what to do before a camera. Promiscuous use of shears has robbed theme of any continuity and makes it unravel like a cumbersome trailer. Story is patchwork."

Synopsis: A young woman is attacked by two thugs on a beach outside a

66 • Song (1928)

Anna May Wong in Berlin, 1928

Malaysian city. A down-and-out performer who has been living there comes to her aid. The men turn on him, but the woman grabs the performer's knife and holds them while the man beats them. As the man leaves, the woman calls after him, but he fails to respond.

That night, in pouring rain, the woman finds the man's shack and enters, with the intention of returning his knife and introducing herself. He is less than polite, preferring to show his skill as a knife-thrower. He uses the woman, Song, to demonstrate his proficiency with knives by having her stand against a door while he outlines her with the weapons. Song loses her initial fear of John and they form a knife-throwing act. With the help of a one-man band named Carletto, the pair is given an engagement at the Blue Moon, a working man's club.

Song acquires a sandwich board to use as a table top. The image of the ballerina Gloria Lee dissolves into the real woman as Song looks at it. Miss Lee has just arrived in the city from England with her troupe. She is taken to dinner by James Prager, a local promoter. He gives her an expensive bracelet; she suddenly decides she would rather dine at a more interesting restaurant.

Meanwhile, Song shows the board to John, who recognizes her as his former partner. In a flashback, Gloria flirts with another man aboard a ship. John sees them and knocks the man overboard. He dives in to rescue the man; a newspaper article reports that both men were lost at sea.

James and Gloria go to the Blue Moon, where Song is performing Malay dances to the accompaniment of a piano and Carletto. John and Song perform their knife-throwing act; when it is over, John notices Gloria. They stare at each other in disbelief, then Gloria offers John money, but he only wants her love. She invites him to join her and Prager while Song sells pinup photos of herself. Prager buys them all and makes advances toward Song, but she ignores him.

Back at his shack, John fails to appreciate Song's attentions, so she pours soup over Gloria's image on the table top. Still smitten with Gloria, John takes Carletto to see her perform. After the show, John slips into Gloria's dressing room with a small sprig of flowers. He is embarrassed by all the large bouquets he finds there and hides behind a screen. Gloria spots his feet beneath it and she tells him that all is over between them. As he leaves, Prager enters.

Aware that he could not match Prager's gift, John agrees to join Carletto and his gang, who are planning a mail train robbery. Knowing John's reason for doing this, Song alerts the police.

The gang subdues the signalman; John puts on his uniform and stops the train. The police arrive then and arrest everyone except Carletto, who gets away. As John realizes what has happened, he hides under the locomotive until it departs. Carletto saves him and takes him home. The next night when Song's finger is grazed by John's knife, it is clear that his vision has been impaired by the steam from the locomotive.

At John's shack, he and Carletto figure it was Song who told the police about the caper, since she was the only one who knew of it. John chases her about the shack with knives, but stumbles over the furniture. Though terrified, Song nurses John when he collapses, noticing that he is unable to see the light of a candle.

In desperation, Song goes to Gloria's dressing room, but the dancer refuses to visit her former partner. She gives Song a bouquet and some money for a doctor. The doctor tells him an operation is necessary to restore his sight.

John sends Song to Gloria to ask for money for the operation. She is readying her troupe for a return to Europe. She orders her maid to give Song a valuable coat she no longer wants. Before Song can ask for the money, Prager interrupts her. Song uses the opportunity to reluctantly steal some hotel money from Gloria's dressing table. When the hotelier calls for his money, Prager pays him out of pocket after figuring what Song had done.

When Song returns to John's place, her mistakes he for Gloria when he feels the fancy coat. Song says nothing, though she is hurt. She leaves and then comes back as herself with the money. John gets ready to go to the hospital.

Prager sees Gloria off at the dock and then goes to the Blue Moon. He tells Song he could have her arrested for stealing his money, but prefers that she appear in one of his shows. Soon thereafter she is wearing the finery intended for Gloria as she dances at the Palace Hotel cabaret. Meanwhile, John's operation is a success, but he must keep his eyes covered for three days. At home, John complains about not receiving a visit from Gloria, so Song puts on the fine coat and pretends to be the dancer. John tells her he can see, and Song inadvertently speaks. Realizing the girl's deception, John rips off his bandages and throws her out. He runs to the theater to see Gloria, only to be told that she had left a month earlier.

Heartbroken, Song goes to the Palace Hotel. Prager makes advances, which she rejects. The promoter tells her she must choose between him and John.

John finally realizes Song's devotion and goes to the Blue Moon. Carletto informs him that she is with Prager, so John rushes over to the Palace Hotel. Song is doing a dangerous dance involving knives pointed upwards from a small revolving section of the floor. When John bursts in, she fears he has come to harass her; she loses her concentration and falls and is impaled on one of the knives. Prager rushes to her, but John holds him back. He takes the wounded girl to his shack and makes her comfortable, but her wounds are mortal and she dies.

Print status: Copy at National Film Archive, England.

Anna May Wong finally achieved true stardom with the release of this production. She appeared at the trade showing of the film and "...received an ovation from a large and enthusiastic audience." according to *The Bioscope* review.

Heinrich George (1893–1946) was a stage actor and director at the famed Schiller Theatre in Berlin who entered films in 1910. His work in both media was very highly regarded.

Hans Adalbert von Schlettow (1888–1945) was also a stage actor until entering films in 1919. He appeared in many silent and sound features, including D.W. Griffith's *Isn't Life Wonderful?* (1924).

Variety's 1930 review listed the running time as only 65 minutes, indicating that serious cuts had been made since the film's original release. This undoubtedly accounted for their negative review.

Grosstadt-Schmetterling (U. K.: The Pavement Butterfly; U. S.: The City Butterfly)

Richard Eichberg Film/British International/Wardour; Released April 10, 1929 (Germany); April 30, 1930 (U.K.); May 1929 (U.S.); 90 minutes

Director: Richard Eichberg; *Photography*: Heinrich Gartner, Otto Baecker; *Screenplay*: Hans Kyser, from the novel by Adolf Lantz; *Art Directors*: W. A. Herrmann, Werner Schlichting, Fritz Maurischat

Cast: Anna May Wong (Mah), Louis Lerch (Kusmin, the artist), Alexander Granach (Koko), E.F. Bostwick (Working, the art dealer), Tilla Garden (Ellis, Working's daughter), Gaston Jacquet (Baron de Neuwe), Szoke Szakall (Paul Bennett), Nien Son Ling (Mr. Wu), John Hoxter.

Variety May 8, 1929: "This time he has not caught her [Anna May Wong] personality and her exotic charm half as completely. There is something to be made of Anna May Wong in the silent film..."

The Bioscope December 18, 1929: "...a charming story of no great dramatic strength, but interesting as a vehicle for the varied talent of the charming star. The direction is efficient.... Her [Wong's] delicate art makes the little Chinese girl a figure of pathetic charm."

Synopsis: Mah, a Chinese circus artist, has an act with a Chinese man. He performs "The Flying Hara-Kiri" act—jumping through a wooden frame lined with sharp knives. Koko, another performer, lusts after Mah. He murders her partner and she is blamed. She runs through the streets, finally taking refuge in the apartment of an artist. Mah models for him, and her portrait is sold to a wealthy art patron. On her way to the bank to deposit the money, Mah is robbed by Koko. Again she is blamed for the crime and thrown out by Kusmin. She moves in with the buyer of her portrait, a baron, who takes her to the Riviera. There she encounters the artist again, as well as Koko, who is using the stolen money to gamble. He wins big; Mah somehow gets his winnings, with which she repays Kusmin, restoring her reputation. The artist loves another, however, so Mah goes out of his life.

Print status: Copy at National Film Archive, England.

Apparently another triumph for Anna May, judging by the review in *The Bioscope*. It is a great pity that the films she made for Eichberg are not readily available; they would undoubtedly add a new dimension to the general opinion of her talent. Another actress who had departed Hollywood (though for different reasons than Miss Wong), Louise Brooks (1906–1985), arrived in Berlin some months later and starred in a film which immortalized her and became a silent classic. She was fortunate in having a highly regarded director, G. W. Pabst (1885–1967) and a property whose filmization was eagerly awaited. Though not a success upon its release at the end of the silent era in late

Grosstadt-Schmetterling (Eichberg/BIP, 1929): Poster

January 1929, the rediscovery of *Pandora's Box* decades later and its availability gave both the film and the actress exposure that Anna May Wong has yet to receive.

Piccadilly

British International/Wardour; Released February 1929 (U.K.), 105 min.; June 1, 1929 (U.S.), 92 minutes; Toned

Director: E.A. Dupont; *Script*: Arnold Bennett; *Set Decoration*: Alfred Junge; *Cinematography*: Werner Brandes; *Editor*: J. N. McConaughty; *Assistant Director*: Rona D. Goetz; *Music*: Eugene Contie; Sound prologue, music and effects by RCA Photophone (3% dialogue)

Cast: Gilda Gray (Mabel Greenfield), Jameson Thomas (Valentine Wilmot), Anna May Wong (Sho-Sho), King Ho Chang (Jim), Cyril Ritchard (Victor Smiles), Hannah Jones (Bessie), Charles Laughton (Dissatisfied Customer), Ellen Pollock (Vamp), Harry Terry (Publican), Gordon Begg (Coroner), Charles Paton (Doorman), Debroy Somers and His Band.

The Bioscope February 6, 1929: "...this is the most striking film issued recently from a British studio and reflects every possible credit on all concerned in its making. Anna May Wong is perfectly fitted as the little scullery maid whose head is easily turned by sudden success."

The New York Times July 15, 1929: "Of the players besides Miss Gray and Miss Wong, King Ho Chang gives a good performance.... The director has managed to get the most from his situations without overdoing them."

Variety July 24, 1929: "From the moment Miss Wong dances in the kitchen's rear, she steals 'Piccadilly' from Miss Gray; in fact Miss Wong also steals Gilda's cooch ... this is one British-made that can go around the world."

Synopsis: Vic and Mabel, a dance team, are the star attraction at Valentine Wilmot's Piccadilly Club. Both men are in love with Mabel.

One evening a customer complains of a dirty plate. This is brought to Wilmot's attention. He goes to the kitchen and then the scullery to discover the reason. There he finds a Chinese girl dancing on a table top for her co-workers. When his presence is discovered, everyone returns to work. He berates the woman in charge for the dirty plate and informs her there is to be no more "skylarking" in the scullery. If there is any, he will fire the lot.

He then fires Victor, who says Mabel is in love with him, which she denies. Victor's angry reaction causes Wilmot to knock him down.

After Victor's departure, business becomes slow. One evening Wilmot runs into the Chinese scullery maid. She had been looking for her mascot, a Chinese figurine, which she shows to the club owner. He remembers her and asks her up to his office to dance for him.

Next evening at dinner, she tells her boyfriend that she lost the mascot he gave her. "Well, that means you lost your luck," he informs her. A co-worker appears to take her to Wilmot, who offers her a chance to dance at the club. She tells him that she danced in public once, in Limehouse, where she lives, and that there was trouble with knives and police. Wilmot is sketching her image on a napkin as they speak. Mabel arrives and Wilmot crumples up the napkin and tosses it into a wastepaper basket. Mabel thinks there is trouble in the scullery when she sees Sho-Sho. After she leaves, Sho-Sho and Wilmot discuss their deal. The girl says she will pick out her costume from a Chinese shop in Limehouse. Wilmot agrees to meet her there. The girl selects an expensive costume and insists that her boyfriend, Jim, play her music. Wilmot grudgingly consents to her terms.

At the club, Mabel shows Wilmot a new dance step; he informs her of Sho-Sho's debut that night. Upset, Mabel insists that the Chinese girl cannot dance and will be laughed at. The girl's debut is a resounding success; Mabel faints upon hearing the thunderous applause.

Now ready to sign a contract, Sho-

Piccadilly (Warner/Sono-Art World Wide, 1929): Jameson Thomas, Anna May Wong (Courtesy BFI Stills, Posters and Designs)

Sho is told by Wilmot that the papers are in his office; she asks Jim to fetch them. In the owner's office, Jim sees Sho-Sho's mascot on Wilmot's desk. Realizing the truth, he is angered, but does not let on when he hands the papers to Sho-Sho in the doorway. Wilmot looks at the girl and she slowly closes the door on Jim with her back. Wilmot drives her home, but she insists on getting out at the corner of her block.

He then visits Mabel, who tells him that she knows Sho-Sho danced for him at night privately. Admitting jealousy, she quits her job at the club.

Soon after, Sho-Sho takes Wilmot on a tour of her neighborhood haunts in the East End. Afterwards, they go to her flat. "You are the first visitor to my new rooms," Sho-Sho informs Wilmot. She changes into a shimmering gown and lace shawl, then leans back on a sofa, smiling. Wilmot attempts to kiss her hand, but she pulls it away. She touches her mouth with her fingers; as Wilmot leans forward to kiss her, the scene jumps to the alley outside, where a shadow appears on a wall. The club owner leaves; Jim receives a tip for showing him out. The shadow appears again and Jim is convinced to let Mabel inside; it is her shadow. In Sho-Sho's flat Mabel asks the girl to leave Wilmot alone. Mabel admits her love for Wilmot and says that Sho-Sho does not, and Wilmot does not love her. "I want him and I shall keep him!" cries the Chinese girl. Mabel opens her purse, revealing a gun. Fearful, Sho-

Sho pulls a knife from a wall. Mabel points the gun, then faints.

The next day, newspaper headlines tell of Sho-Sho's murder. At the inquest, Jim says he saw Wilmot at Sho-Sho's before he went home. He tells about the triangle, that he warned Sho-Sho that Wilmot would soon tire of her. The club owner admits the murder weapon is his, but will not talk about what transpired at Sho-Sho's flat. The judge orders the jury to convene when Mabel suddenly comes forward to testify. She says she took the gun from Wilmot's desk and followed him and the girl to the girl's flat. There she asked Sho-Sho to stop seeing Wilmot and the girl refused. She relates that she threatened Sho-Sho with the gun, but passed out before firing it. The judge recalls Jim, stating that either he or Wilmot is committing perjury. The bailiff returns, informing the judge, "The Chinese boy has shot himself. He's lying in a room just down the hall." The judge goes out to the hall and Jim says weakly, "We belonged to each other. I'll tell you everything." He relates how he confronted Sho-Sho after Wilmot's departure. They argued and struggled; Jim was knocked to the floor, where he saw Mabel's gun. In a rage he grabbed it and shot Sho-Sho. This is shown in flashback; Jim dies after completing his confession.

The final shot is of some men bearing sandwich boards with the ad: "Life Goes On — new show at the Scala."

Print status: Available on video.

Anna May Wong's final silent film is one of her best. Her seduction of the club owner is especially memorable, as she accomplishes it with just her eyes and a slight gesture of her hand, slowly lowering a lace shawl before her face. In the scene where her boyfriend, Jim, goes to Wilmot's office for the contract, she indicates that Wilmot is her new man by closing the door on Jim with her back, not even glancing at him.

The story was written by one of England's leading novelists, Arnold Bennett (1867–1931), who was also a journalist and playwright.

For the film's American release, a sound prologue and sound effects were added. In the prologue, Valentine Wilmot explains to a fellow Briton just returned from China (John Longden) his reasons for quitting Piccadilly. The film tells his story.

German director E. A. Dupont (1891–1956), who had helmed the memorable *Variety* is his homeland four years earlier, showed he had not lost his touch. The opening credits are displayed on boards atop double decker buses. He keeps his camera moving, whether to showcase the vastness of the Club Piccadilly with its numerous patrons, or in dingy Limehouse bars where a cosmopolitan clientele gathers. The one jarring note is the jump cut utilized when Wilmot and Sho-Sho are about to kiss; here the director was overruled by the censors.

In only his third film appearance, Charles Laughton (sporting a moustache) has only one scene, but sets the plot in motion when he complains about a dirty plate, which leads the club owner to the scullery where he discovers Sho-Sho.

Future Hollywood star Ray Milland (1907–1986) appeared as an extra.

An excerpt from *Piccadilly* was utilized in the 1952 Associated British film *Elstree Story*.

III

European Sound Films

Film technology in Europe was a bit behind that of the United States at the start of the talkie era. In Germany, sound had been successfully allied with film as early as 1903 when Oskar Messter (1866–1943) demonstrated his *Biophon Tonbilder der Specht*. The sound came from a small disc with a running time of up to four minutes. Up until 1914, Messter produced hundreds of short films, many featuring established stars of stage and opera. By then the public began showing its preference for longer productions, even though they lacked the feature of sound. A system called Tri-Ergon was developed by three young scientists in 1921. Various factors kept it from replacing silent films until 1929, when it merged with Klangfilm, an outfit which had made great strides with electrical sound recording. It was March 1929 when the first feature length sound pictures were released in Germany. Another six years passed before all German theatres were converted to sound. In England, British International Pictures bought the RCA sound on disk system and began sound production in 1929. The French initially used B.I.P.'s studio to make sound films, but soon thereafter had two studios wired for sound and released their first home-made talking picture in November 1929.

European directors embraced the new feature and quickly proved their adaptability. The one technique that was yet a few years away was dubbing, so that a film had to be made more than once, usually with different casts, for each language desired. Having mastered French and German for her stage act, Anna May Wong starred in three versions of her first sound feature.

Hai-Tang (Der Weg Zur Schande)

Eichberg Film/British International Pictures/Süd-Film; Released February 26, 1930 (Germany); January 25, 1930 (U.K.); 81 minutes

Director: Richard Eichberg; *Scenario*: Dr. Ludwig Wolff and Monckton Hoffe, from an idea by W. Goldschmidt; *Cinematography*: Heinrich Gartner and Bruno Mondi; *Art Direction*: Willi A. Hermann and Clarence Elder; *Music*: Hans May; *Sound*: Cecil V. Thornton; *Choreography*: Alexander Oumansky; *Costumes*: Leopold Verch; *Songs*: "Without a Woman or Love, a Russian Cannot Survive," "If You Believe I Love You," "One Day the Wonder of Love Comes" Fritz Rotter; British International Symphony Orchestra conducted by John Reynders

Cast: Anna May Wong (Hai-Tang), Franz Lederer (Lt. Boris Borriskoff), Hugo Werner-Kahle (Oberst Moravjev), Georg Schnell (General Governor Pawel), Edith d'Amara (Yvette), Ley On (Wang-Hu, Hai-Tang's brother), Hai Yung (Dschung Dschow), Hermann Blass (Birnbaum), Charles Lincoln.

Print status: Copy at National Film Archive, England.

Variety, March 26, 1930: "Expectations were high for the girl's [Anna May Wong] first talker ... her voice is guttural and uncultivated in comparison to the lightness and delicacy of her bodily make-up.... Anna in the

74 • Hai-Tang (1930)

talkers is not the Anna of the silent screen. Of the cast only Herman Blass stood out."

Daily Film Renter [date unknown]: "Anna May Wong gives a beautiful performance."

News of the World [date unknown]: "Provides Miss Wong with every opportunity of the exercise of her very real talents as an actress of the exotic kind. Her voice surpasses all expectations."

Daily Telegraph [date unknown]: "Anna May Wong has deservedly won high renown as a film actress."

Synopsis: A Chinese dance troupe led by the beautiful Hai-Tang is touring pre-revolutionary Russia. One Lt. Borriskoff falls in love with Hai-Tang, making Yvette, a French dancer who has eyes for him, jealous. At a gala performance, the Grand Duke sees Hai-Tang and orders a colonel to tell Lt. Borriskoff to bring her to him at the infamous Orpheum Cafe. Hai-Tang refuses the invitation and prepares to depart. Borriskoff informs the colonel that the performer has already arranged to leave by the night express. Furious, the colonel orders Boris personally to see that the girl goes to the Orpheum, then returns to the Grand Duke with the word that she has accepted. Boris rushes to Hai-Tang and tells her that his duty compels him to ask her to be present. She gradually realizes the terrible predicament in which this places her lover and so gives her acceptance. Boris conducts her to the cafe.

At the cafe, a group of Cossacks clears

Hai Tang (Eichberg/BIP, 1930): Production shot. Director Eichberg in center, Franz Lederer seated on ground, Anna May Wong (Courtesy BFI Stills, Posters and Designs)

the place for the Grand Duke. A private room is prepared for him and dinner for two is served. A pianist named Birnbaum is ordered to entertain the Grand Duke and his guest. He is placed behind a screen so as to be heard, but not seen. Hai-Tang arrives and is shown into the Grand Duke's room, while Boris waits outside.

Downstairs, Yvette and the colonel enjoy a wild party. Yvette later goes upstairs and flirts with Boris, but his polite coldness brings a threat from the singer. Wang-Hu, Hai-Tang's brother, has managed to get a temporary job at the cafe as a waiter so as to watch his sister. He is about to enter the Duke's room with a loaded tray when he and Boris hear Hai-Tang call for help. Wang Hu quietly enters and shoots the Duke in the arm with a revolver. The Duke orders Wang Hu to be taken away by the Guard. He follows them, ignoring Hai-Tang's plea that the culprit is her brother.

Birnbaum promises to help Hai-Tang if he can. The next day, the Grand Duke signs an order for Wang Hu's execution on the following morning.

Boris tries to intercede with the Duke for the boy's life and inadvertently admits his love for Hai-Tang. Receiving a refusal, Boris turns to his friend, the officer in charge of the firing party, and they arrange a plan to save Wang Hu's life. Meanwhile, Hai-Tang's friends urge her to plead with the Grand Duke for her brother's life. She decides to make the sacrifice.

Unknown to Boris, his officer friend is ordered to St. Petersburg, and another officer, unaware of the plot, replaces him.

Hai-Tang (Eichberg/BIP, 1930): George Schnell, Anna May Wong, Ley On

The Grand Duke signs a reprieve with the condition that Hai-Tang yield herself to him. He phones the colonel, who is drunk at the Cafe, and he sends the paper to the Duke by an orderly. Yvette has seen the colonel send the paper and gets him so drunk he falls asleep before the orderly can return with the signed document. When the orderly returns, Yvette refuses to awaken the colonel. Birnbaum begs her to do so, but she refuses. The two struggle; the pianist is determined to take the document to the officer in charge of the firing party himself. Yvette locks him out of the room, so Birnbaum rushes to the prison and tries to get the officer to believe that a reprieve has been granted to Wang Hu. He is kicked out. The colonel awakens twenty minutes before the execution is due to occur. He learns of the reprieve and curses Yvette for not waking him earlier.

Just as Wang Hu is being led from his cell, the colonel arrives and announces that a reprieve has been granted. In her room, Hai-Tang prays to her gods. The lieutenant hurries to Hai-Tang with the good news, but is too late; she has taken poison and dies in his arms.

Hai-Tang was banned in Budapest due to alleged "anti-monarchist tendencies." These "tendencies" were the Russian grand duke's desire for a Chinese woman. Apparently not all of Europe was as tolerant as some places on the continent. The German title translates to "The Path of Shame."

Elstree Calling

Elstree Productions/British International Pictures; Released February 1930; 94 minutes
Director: Adrian Brunel; *Sketches and other interpolated items by*: Alfred Hitchcock ; *Ensemble Numbers Staged by*: Adrian Charlot, Jack Hulbert, Paul Murray; *Lyrics by*: Douglas Furber, Rowland Leigh, and Donovan Parsons; *Music by*: Reg Casson, Vivian Ellis, Chick Endor, Ivor Novello, Jack Strachey; *Musical Conductors*: Teddy Brown, Sydney Baynes, John Reynders; *Photography*: Claude Friese-Greene; *Scenario*: Val Valentine; *Production Manager*: J. Sloan; *Sound recordist*: Alec Murray; *Edited by*: A. P. Hammond; *Supervising Editor*: Emile De Ruelle
Cast: Will Fyffe, Jack Hulbert, Cicely Courtneidge, Lily Morris, Anna May Wong, Tommy Handley, Helen Burnell, The Berkoffs, Bobby Comber, Lawrence Green, Ivor McLaren, Jameson Thomas, John Longden, Donald Calthrop, Gordon Harker, Hannah Jones, Teddy Brown, The Three Eddies, The Balalaika Choral Orchestra, supported by The Adelphi Girls and The Charlot Girls.

The Bioscope February 12, 1930: "...Mr. Calthrop scores heavily with his burlesque of "Taming of the Shrew" with Anna May Wong ... the whole revue is a very successful attempt to present together so many varied and brilliant a collection of popular artists."

Variety, March 5, 1930: "...the material is old where it's not amateurish. All you see of Anna May Wong is in trunks throwing custard pies in a burlesque on 'Taming of the Shrew' which starts well ... and then falls to bits."

The New York Times—London Film Notes—March 1930: "...is distinctly disappointing. It is a variety show ... but it is second-rate variety.... Elstree will have to call much louder to catch the ear of an American or any other foreign public."

Synopsis: This film is presented in revue format linked together by emcee Tommy Handley purveying some very weak humor and a group of people watching the show on primitive television sets.

Print status: Shown on British television.

The Bioscope reviewed the film again in its May 14, 1930 issue, noting that certain segments had been tinted.

Anna May, the only American in the cast, appears in the penultimate number with Donald Calthrop in a spoof of the Fairbanks-Pickford *The Taming of the Shrew* (1929). Wearing a revealing two-piece silver lamé outfit, she throws automobile tires, furniture and shoes down a long staircase and adroitly hurls cream pies at her Petruchio, all the while shouting in Cantonese. When William Shakespeare himself appears, he also receives a pie in the face. Not exactly high-brow stuff, but the actress seemed to enjoy herself.

Most of the performers appeared in more than one segment, and three sequences were tinted amber — two with Helen Burnell (who surely was to dance what Charles Bronson was to comedy) and the final one with Cicely Courtneidge. The direction is only fair; Busby Berkeley could have done much more with the dance numbers; so could Tod Browning for that matter.

The Flame of Love (a.k.a. The Road to Dishonour)

Richard Eichberg Film/British International Pictures; Released October 7, 1930 (U.K.), November 1930 (U.S.); 81 minutes

Directors: Richard Eichberg, Walter Summers; *Script*: Monckton Hoffe, Ludwig Wolff; *Photography*: Heinrich Gartner and Bruno Mondi; *Editor*: Emile de Ruelle; *Art Directors*: Willi Hermann, Werner Schlichting; *Musical Direction*: John Reynders;

Cast: Anna May Wong (Hai-Tang), John Longden (Lt. Boris Boriskoff), George H. Schnell (Grand Duke), Percy Standing (Col. Moravjev), Mona Goya (Yvette), J. Ley-On (Wang Hu), Fred Schwartz (Birnbaum).

Print status: Copy at National Film Archive, England.

The Flame of Love (Eichberg/BIP, 1930): Anna May Wong

The Bioscope March 12, 1930: "It is on the whole well-played and most effectively mounted. Anna May Wong ... gives a very effective performance, in which her grace and skill as a dancer are supplemented by her skill as a vocalist. Her speaking voice has hardly the same appeal, and the tragic ending is rather lacking in emotional power."

The New York Times, March 23, 1930: "Miss Wong is not allowed to do much talking, but the audience is allowed to see a good deal of her in various varieties of inextensive attire ... altogether the story holds the spectator's interest throughout."

The New York Times November 3, 1930: "...the stilted dialogue of this version makes the entire production seem unreal and obscures the haunting Oriental beauty of the star, Anna May Wong. Miss Wong is one of the few cinema luminaries able to convey poignant emotion with restraint. The principal theme ... requires a more sophisticated treatment than it receives."

Variety, November 5, 1930: "...a couple of excellent and lively cabaret scenes.... Miss Wong talks flat American.... Miss Wong as an actress probably did as well as she could...."

Harrison's Reports, November 15, 1930: "Well acted, but the story is unpleasant, for it deals with a love affair between a white man and an oriental woman."

Synopsis: This is the English version of Hai-Tang.

This last review is a sterling example of the anti–Asian bias typical of the time. That love could be "unpleasant" is something of an oxymoron, while the author of the review is just a moron.

Much was made of Anna May Wong's first English sound film (made prior to, but released after *Elstree Calling*) in the advertising copy—"The Triumph of a Great Star"; "See and Hear the Alluring Anna May Wong in Her First Talkie."

Hai-Tang
(a.k.a. L'Amour Maitre Des Choses)

Richard Eichberg Film/British International Pictures/Etablissements Jacques Haik, Paris; Released September 19, 1930 (France), April 1931 (U.S.); approx. 81 minutes

Directors: Jean Kemm, Richard Eichberg; *Screenplay*: Pierre Maudru from the story by Monckton Hoffe and Ludwig Wolff; *Photography*: Heinrich Gartner and Bruno Mondi; *Music*: Hans May; *Musical Direction*: John Reynders; *Songs*: Marguerite Chanal and Albert Chantrier

Cast: Anna May Wong (Hai Tang), Marcel Vibert (Grand Duke), Robert Ancelin (Lt. Boris Ivanoff), Armand Lurville (Col. Mouraview), Francois Vigulier (Wang Hu), Helene Darly (Yvette), Gaston Dupray (Pierre Baron), Claire Roman, Mona Goya.

Print status: No known copies extant.

Variety, October 8, 1930: "Acting fair, with a tendency to overact ... Sound good and photography okay."

The New York Times, April 2, 1931: "...is a production with some interesting interludes, but in quite a number of sequences the vocal recording is faulty. Here and there one hears poorly synchronized songs from Miss Wong and M. Ancelin."

Synopsis: This is the French version of Hai-Tang.

This version was shot at Elstree Studios in London, as were the others. The French premiere occurred on September 19, 1930 at the re-opening of the famed Colisée.

Tiger Bay

Wyndham/Associated British; Released March 19, 1934 (U.K.); Not released in the U.S.; 68 minutes

Director: J. Elder Wills; *Producer*: Bray Wyndham; *Screenplay*: Jon Quin, based on a story by J. Elder Wills and Eric Ansell; *Editors*: David Lean, Ian Thomson; *Photography*: Robert G. Martin and Alan Lawson; *Art Director*: J. Elder Wills; *Music*: Eric Ansell; *Sound*: A.D. Valentine

Cast: Anna May Wong (Lui Chang), Henry Victor (Olaf), Rene Ray (Letty), Lawrence Grossmith ("Whistling" Rufus), Victor Garland (Michael Brooke), Ben Soutten ("Stumpy"), Margaret Yarde (Fay), Wally Patch (Wally), Ernest Jay (Alf), Brian Buchel (Tony), Ley On (Ho Tang), Judy Kelly, Ruth Ambler.

Picturegoer March 17, 1934: "Anna May Wong certainly looks the part of the calm, fatalistic Chinese woman ... the production is very conventional, artificial and strained in construction. Dialogue is commonplace and the Eastern atmosphere distinctly synthetic."

Synopsis: A young British gent is enthralled by the tale of Tiger Bay told by some older associates at a men's club. Told it is "not friendly to foreigners," he goes there anyhow.

At a night spot featuring a Chinese dancer, he gets into a fight with a sailor named Olaf who is manhandling a young girl named Letty. When the dancer intervenes, she is thrown aside. The young man is stabbed in the arm by the sailor, who finally leaves.

The dancer and young woman tend to the wounded man. It turns out that the dancer is Lui Chang, the proprietress of the club, and the girl is her ward. Lui had told the girl not to come to the club at night, for that sailor has been around before looking for trouble. Lui knows she is to be his next extortion victim. When he returns offering her security against damage, she puts him off. The sailor's gang frightens most of the help at the club into leaving.

While the young man is recovering, Lui tells him her history. In a flashback she is shown as a child caring for an infant when a revolution breaks out in China. With their city under attack, she flees with her father and the babe, eventually making her way to Tiger Bay, which is shown on the map to be in Brazil. The Briton confesses that he loves Letty, who overhears him as she returns from shopping. Lui tells the Briton that when Letty returns his love, he can speak with her about arrangements.

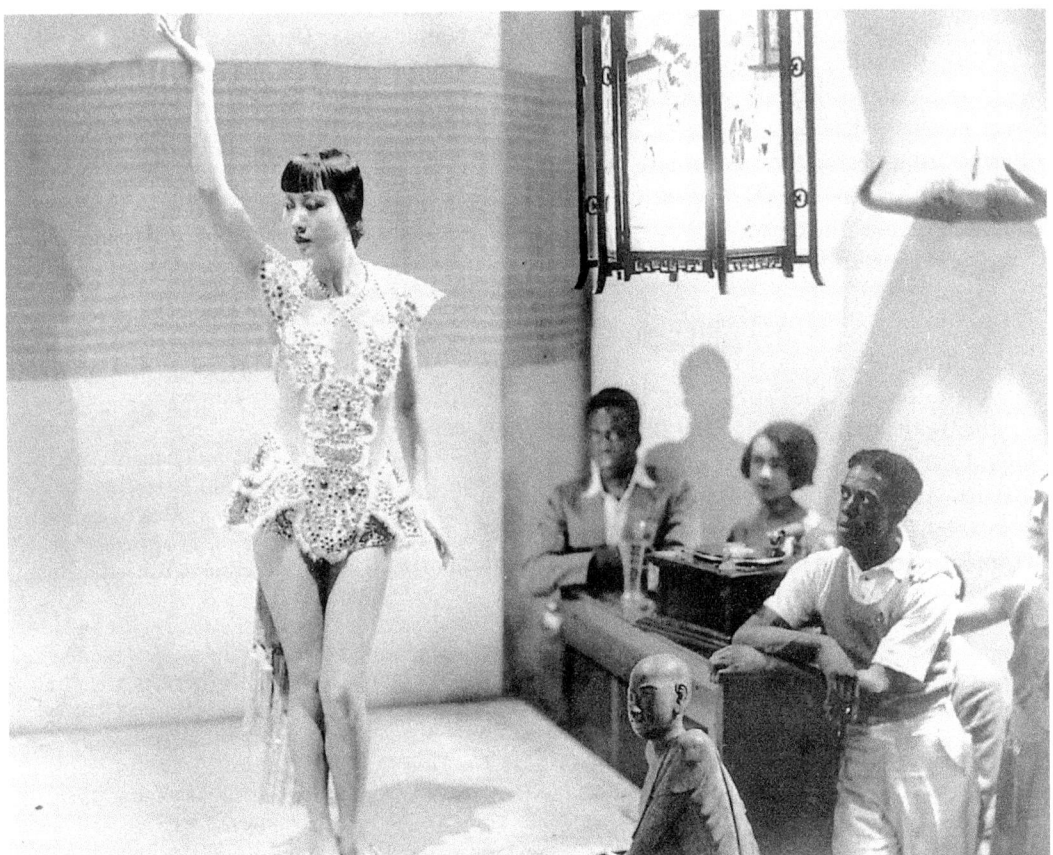

Tiger Bay (Wyndham/Associated British, 1933): Anna May Wong (Courtesy BFI Stills, Posters and Designs)

When Olaf murders one of Lui's regular patrons, she goes to the police. Though she has no proof of Olaf's guilt, the police agree to watch the sailor.

After having a meal at Lui's, the gang is told by her that she has been doing the cooking since her help fled. They leave, believing they have been poisoned. Olaf decides to get to Lui through Letty.

He kidnaps the girl while she is secretly seeing the young Briton, against Lui's orders. He is beaten and later taken to the police station. Olaf goes to Lui with the girl's necklace as proof that he has her. Meanwhile, the police raid the gang's hideout and the girl is freed by the Briton. Olaf gets his money from Lui but as he leaves, she cries, "You forgot something!" As he turns she throws his knife into his chest: "Your knife!" Inquiring about Olaf's death, the police inspector tells Lui she has committed murder. She refuses to go to jail after all she has done for Letty. Taking a ring from her finger, she jabs it into her wrist, poisoning herself. She recites a Chinese poem as she dies.

Print status: Copy at National Film Archive, England.

Produced at ATP Studios, Ealing, London, *Tiger Bay* was one of the notorious "quota quickies" produced in Britain during the early thirties. The British film industry was in a sad state in the twenties, with American pictures dominating the market. The government finally stepped in and passed the Quota Act in December 1927, which stipulated that a certain percentage of films shown in Britain also had to be made there. Hoping this would improve the quality as well as the quantity of British-made pictures, they were sadly disappointed. The result was a deluge of films poorly made on all levels, which did nothing to improve the reputation of British motion pictures.

Anna May is first seen in a tight closeup, her hair tied back. Acting as if unaware of the lack of production values, she gives her usual spirited performance and grabs the viewer's eye throughout the picture.

Censors forced the setting to be changed from London to South America due to the fact that Anna May's restaurant was frequented by "all the riff-raff of the seven seas."

Chu Chin Chow

Gaumont-British; Released July 1934 (U.K.), September 1934 (U.S.); 96 minutes
Producer: Michael Balcon; *Director*: Walter Forde; *Screenplay*: Sidney Gilliat, L. DuGarde Peach, Edward Knoblock; Based on the musical by Oscar Asche and Frederic Norton; *Photography*: Mutz Greenbaum; *Music*: Frederick Norton; *Costumes*: Cathleen Mann; *Editor*: Derek N. Twist; *Choreography*: Anton Dolin; *Musical Director*: Louis Levy; *Musical Conductor*: Hubert Bath; *Art Direction*: Ernest Metzner; *Sound Recordist*: A. O'Donoghue; *Unit Production Manager*: Victor Peers
Cast: Anna May Wong (Zahrat), George Robey (Ali Baba), Fritz Kortner (Abu Hassan), John Garrick (Nur-al-Din), Pearl Argyle (Marjanah), Dennis Hoey (Rakham), Sydney Fairbrother (Mahbubah), Lawrence Hannay (Kasim Baba), Frank Cochrane (Mustafa), Thelma Tuson (Alcolom), Kyoshi Takase (Entertainer), Francis Sullivan (Caliph), Jetsam (Abdullah).
Previously filmed in 1923 by Graham-Wilcox in Berlin, with American Betty Blythe as Zahrat, directed by Herbert Wilcox.
A spoof entitled *Two-Chinned Chow* was made in 1923 under the direction of Adrian Brunel for Atlas-Biocraft.
Re-released in 1953 as *Ali Baba Nights* by Lippert Productions minus the musical numbers.
The New York Times, September 22, 1934: "...a tuneful, spectacular and robust adaptation ... Anna May Wong as the slave..."
The Film Daily September 22, 1934: "...Anna May Wong is very alluring as Zahrat...."
Motion Picture Exhibitor, October 1, 1934: "...the picture ... is of international appeal. There are a few names familiar to American audiences, but the vastness of the picture and its scope are dominant."

Synopsis: Ali Baba is the poor brother of wealthy merchant Kasim Baba. When out fetching wood in the Dark Forest for Kasim's upcoming banquet, Ali Baba is nearby when Hassan's band rides out and hears the secret password, "Open, O Sesame!", which he uses to gain entry to the robber's lair. He takes enough gold coins to set himself up as a wealthy merchant.

His son Nur-Al-Din is in love with a slave girl named Marjanah, who is owned by his uncle. Another of his slaves is Zahrat, who is a spy for the robber chief Abu Hassan. Kasim is throwing a feast for the great merchant Chu Chin Chow. Zahrat overhears Kasim telling his wife where Chow is camped and sends word to Abu Hassan via pigeon. Hassan and his band ride to Chow's camp and kill all the men except Chow. Hassan takes a medallion from the merchant which is his means of identification, then pushes Chow into a pit and has him covered with sand.

Assuming Chu Chin Chow's identity, Abu Hassan is welcomed in Baghdad. At the banquet, Kasim is surprised when his brother Ali and his family arrive dressed in finery. He tells Kasim he has made a fortune but refuses to tell how. Later, Kasim gets Ali drunk and learns the secret of the bandits' cave.

That same night, Marjanah spies on Zahrat's meeting with Chow and learns the truth about the real Chow's fate. Hassan and Zahrat make plans for the slave auction to be held the following morning. Zahrat is to be sold; she tells Hassan not to attack until she is put up for sale; "The merchants of Baghdad will bid high for me," she says confidently. She says the word "sold" will be the signal for the thieves to attack. "By Satan! Even a woman can have an idea!" cries Hassan in his best sexist manner. Zahrat then sings for Hassan as Marjanah slips away.

Kasim heads for the cave as the auction begins. A bearded basso sings of the "properties" to be auctioned as the bidders gather. Meanwhile, Marjanah tells Nur-al-Din of Hassan's plot and urges him to bid for Zahrat as long as he can: "Go on bidding till I return." He bids as high as possible, but Hassan gets the high bid. Just as the auctioneer is about to shout "Sold!" Marjanah arrives with a group of guards and denounces Hassan and Zahrat. She says she had heard Zahrat tell of the real Chu Chin Chow's death at Hassan's hand. The robber chief calls to his men and a meleé ensues. Hassan has one of his men grab Zahrat as the band flees back to their lair. Kasim is still there; hearing the robbers' song, he hides with two large bags of loot. As the thieves celebrate, Hassan calls for Zahrat and has her bound to the wheel which operates the mechanism for opening and closing the entrance. The other slaves are all dumb and blind; Zahrat is horrified that she will meet the same fate. The entrance is opened and Kasim tries to escape, then goes back for one bag of treasure. He is caught and killed by the bandits.

Ali and his son go to bring back Kasim, and find his remains hanging just inside the entrance. They also find Chu Chin Chow's headpiece and realize the truth about the merchant. Taking Kasim's corpse and some ruby jewelry from a casket, they return home.

When the bandits return and Hassan discovers the missing body and rubies he moans, "My drops of blood! Of all my treasures, the dearest! Is there no honesty left that even a robber must be robbed?" One of his men discovers a shoe on the cave floor. Abu Hassan disguises himself as a peddler and returns to Baghdad where he finds the cobbler who had stitched a shroud for Kasim. Hassan pays him to take him to Ali Baba's house. When the cobbler asks for more money, Hassan twists his arm, causing him to cry out. Ali Baba and

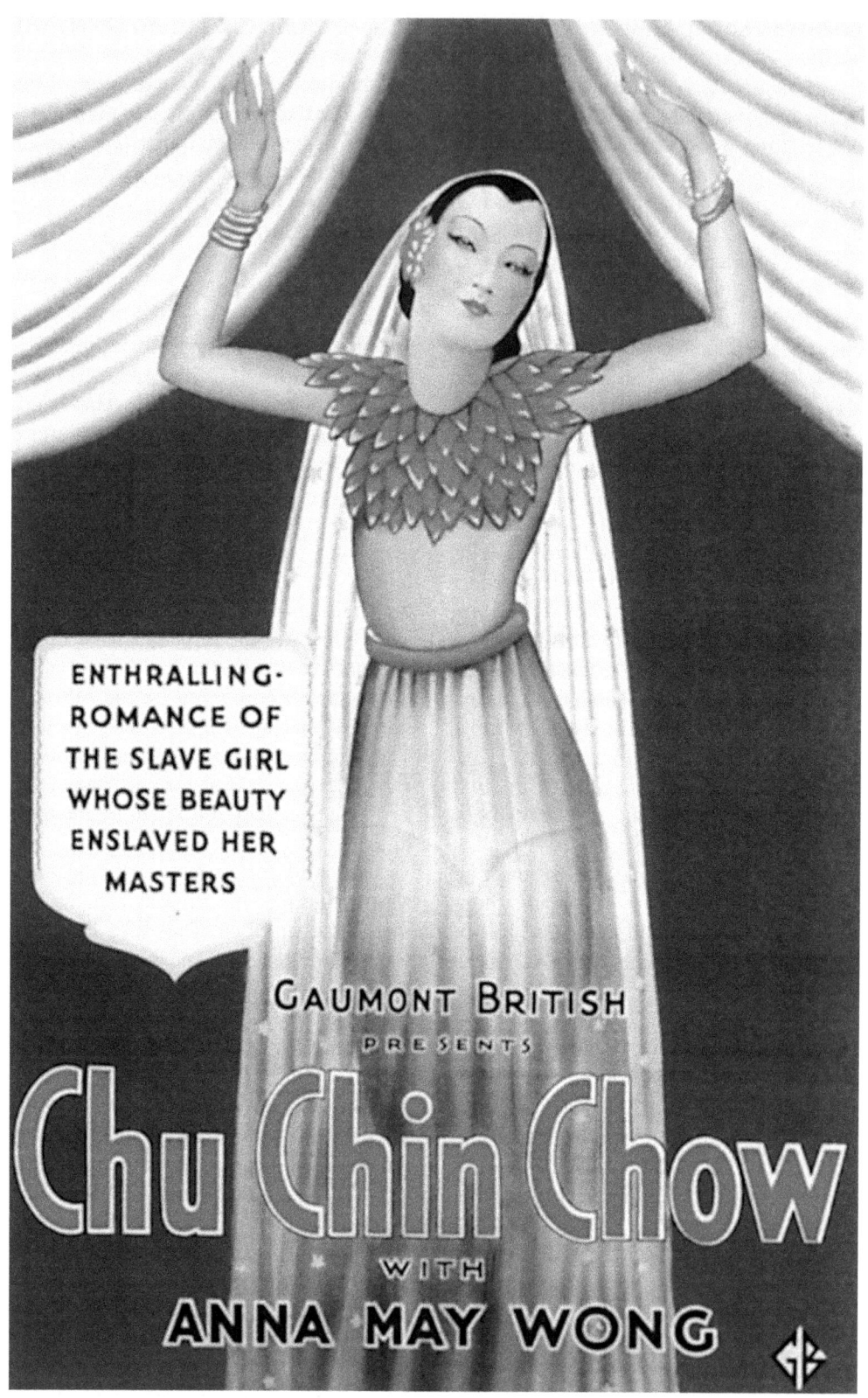

Chu Chin Chow (Gaumont-British, 1934): Poster

his sister-in-law come to the balcony and Hassan notices his ruby necklace on the woman. Now he knows that Ali Baba has the password to his lair. Knowing the caliph is dining with Ali Baba the next evening, Hassan plans his revenge. Since a gift is needed by every guest, he hides his band of forty in large oil jars and tells them that three strokes on a gong will be their signal to attack. He refuses to tell what his disguise will be so that none may betray him. Meanwhile, one of his men takes water to the slaves of the wheel and is strangled with a chain by Zahrat, who takes his knife and cuts her bonds. She overhears Hassan's plan and hides in one of the jars.

At the palace, Nur-al-Din and Marjanah meet outside the palace. The girl must dance for the caliph and be given to him if she pleases the ruler. Just then Zahrat emerges from her jar and tells them of Hassan's scheme. She says she will take Marjanah's place as she feels she can penetrate any disguise that Hassan may assume and will keep him from giving the signal. Afraid she may fail, Nur-al-Din has the jars rolled into a deep pit and boiling oil poured over them.

Zahrat dances for the caliph wearing a veil over the lower half of her face. Dancing past all the guests seeking Hassan, she spots him made up as a black servant. "Hassan!" she cries. The bandit chief looks at her in shock: "Zahrat!" and reaches for a knife. Zahrat draws one first and hurls it into his chest. She gloats over him as he falls to his knees, grabbing his hair and commanding, "Lift up your head so that I may see your face and taste my vengeance to the full!" Hassan rises and tries to stab the slave girl, but Nur-al-Din shoots an arrow into his chest. Hassan staggers up a staircase and attempts to strike the gong, but falls; he and the gong roll down the steps together and he expires.

As a reward for providing such wonderful entertainment for the caliph, Marjanah is granted her freedom so that she and Nur-al-Din may marry.

Print status: Copy at National Film Archive, England.

Anna May does not have a lot of screen time in this film, even though she gets top billing, but is the commanding presence in the climactic scene. She again proves herself a more than capable actress, speaking her lines with the required feeling, be it anger, sympathy, or flattery. Still only twenty-nine years old when she made this picture, the much-traveled performer brought a wealth of experience to her role, though her singing was dubbed.

Fritz Kortner (1892–1970) was a Viennese who achieved renown on the Berlin stage in the years following World War I, both as actor and director. He served the same functions in a number of German silent films before fleeing the Nazi regime. After a stint in Europe, he settled in the United States in 1938. In 1947 he returned to Germany, where he recaptured his earlier stature. In *Chu Chin Chow* he takes the role of the chief heavy and runs with it, ordering murders and other mayhem with unrestrained glee. He also served as Anna May's escort to the premiere of the film.

George Robey (1869–1954) was a fixture in British music halls for many years and was a model for both Charlie Chaplin and Stan Laurel. Known as "The Prime Minister of Mirth," he appeared in every British music hall at least once during his long career. He drew on his lengthy experience to create a humorous and human Ali Baba. He was given a knighthood in early 1954.

The actor billed as "Jetsam" was in reality Malcolm McEachem of the popular vaudeville team of Flotsam and Jetsam.

Shot at Islington Studio, *Chu Chin Chow* benefited from superior production values, rivaling those of any film produced by Britain's leading studio, London Films. The sets and photography are equally

Java Head

Java Head (Associated Talking Pictures/Associated British Film Distributors, 1934): Anna May Wong

Associated Talking Pictures/Associated British Film Distributors; Released October 15, 1934 (U.K.), 85 minutes; September 1, 1935 (U.S.), 70 minutes
Director: J. Walter Ruben; *Producer*: Basil Dean; *Screenplay*: Martin Brown, Gordon Wellesley, based on the novel by Joseph Hergesheimer; *Photography*: Robert G. Martin; *Editor*: Thorold Dickinson; *Art Director*: Edward Carrick; *Music*: Ernest Irving
Cast: Anna May Wong (Taou Yen), Elizabeth Allan (Nettie Vollar), John Loder (Gerrit Ammidon), Edmund Gwenn (Jeremy Ammidon), Ralph Richardson (William Ammidon), Herbert Lomas (Barzil Dunsack), George Curzon (Edward Dunsack), Roy Emerton (Broadrick), John Marriner (John Stone), Gray Blake (Roger Brevard), Amy Brandon Thomas (Rhoda Ammidon), Frances Carson (Kate Vollar), Mavis Claire (Laurel Ammidon).
Previously filmed in 1923 by Paramount in the U.S. with Leatrice Joy as Taou Yen.
The London Times, August 20, 1934: "The story, though well constructed, is slight and chiefly serves to introduce the most fascinating object ... the daughter of a Chinese mandarin (Miss Anna May Wong) married to an English sailor.... The actors play their parts very well in the story...."
Motion Picture Exhibitor, July 1, 1935: "...sometimes brilliantly cast ... it is a surprise to find a picture of such lavish beauty, evident high production cost under the independent banner ... bit players push Loder, Wong, Allan to their greatest efforts."

Synopsis: In nineteenth century Bristol, a distinguished shipping family, the Ammidons, try to cope with various issues. The oldest son, Gerrit, is friendly with Nettie Vollar, the granddaughter of a former shipmate of his father's. The two older gentlemen have not spoken for years. Ammidon's younger son, William, argues over buying clipper ships for their company; Jeremy is adamantly opposed. When Jeremy Ammidon learns of Barzil Dunsack's being ill, he goes to see Barzil to bury the hatchet. At first, all goes well, but Jeremy brings up an old memory which

impressive, the former suggesting spacious palaces and deserts, the latter abounding in lights and shadows. One shot of Anna May is especially lovely. As she releases the pigeon carrying a note to Hassan from a balcony, the camera zooms into a tight closeup of her, followed by a dissolve into the bird in flight.

The direction is also exceptional. The camera moves freely and multiple angles are employed throughout. It is a real pity that this production was made before Technicolor was perfected, for it would have been even more memorable. As it stands, *Chu Chin Chow* deserves far more attention than it has received.

The source play, by Oscar Asche, had been a huge success in London, where it opened on August 31, 1916 and ran for 2,000 performances at His Majesty's Theatre. The first U.S. production was at the Metropolitan Opera House in New York in 1917.

angers the very religious Barzil and Ammidon leaves in a huff.

News arrives that Gerrit is late returning from the Orient and Jeremy has a mild seizure. When Gerrit does return, it is with a Chinese wife named Taou Yen. She kneels before Jeremy to show her respect. The family is stunned. William cries, "It's incredible, Gerrit, horrifying! I can't pretend anything else," after she is shown to her room. Gerrit apologizes for not having sent advance notice of his marriage. He informs William that her father is a Manchu prince. Word spreads quickly throughout the town that Gerrit Ammidon has married "a heathen Chinese." Only Nettie Vollar refuses to believe it.

Gerrit's niece Laurel watches Taou Yen apply her makeup as she prepares to attend church services with the family. All the churchgoers gape at Taou Yen, dressed in her Chinese finery. Nettie's uncle, Edward Dunsack, is a Sinophile and an opium addict. He is quite taken by Taou Yen. The vicar welcomes the new Mrs. Ammidon; when he learns she is a follower of Confucius, he asks if he may visit to discuss Confucian philosophy. They do so that afternoon. Edward Dunsack drops by uninvited, along with Nettie. Taou Yen is entertaining the group with music. When Dunsack is introduced to Taou Yen, he flatters her, but she sees right through him. Seeing her disturbed look, Gerrit thanks Dunsack for calling. "I shall dream of this afternoon," he says. After he is gone, Taou Yen tells Gerrit, "I saw at once that his mind was ill. China is bad for men like him."

At the celebration for the queen's birthday, Nettie goes out to view the festivities and meets the Ammidons. Gerrit notices that she seems unhappy and walks her home. He learns that her uncle is in bad shape. "Now I know why he lost his position in Shanghai," she says, without mentioning his addiction by name. Gerrit asks her if Edward is going back to China. She replies that his only chance is here, for his business is failing. Gerrit offers to help, but Nettie must not tell her grandfather. "You've got to be safe, secure—no other consideration matters." he adds.

Alone with Taou Yen, Gerrit admits to being foolish. She replies, "To be sad without reason shows presence of evil spirits." In anger he responds, "You will have your evil spirits, won't you?" As she changes her clothes, Gerrit looks askance at the Chinese decorations in the room. He tells his wife he will be leaving on another voyage soon. She says she is content in Bristol, for it is her home now. He remarks that she is so different and she agreeably replies that she came willingly.

William argues again with his father about progress and confesses to having already ordered four clipper ships and two steam packets. Jeremy respects his courage and agrees to look at his plans. Accidentally spotting a certain manifest, the old man suffers another seizure; William admits to having been in the opium trade for two years. Jeremy dies and Gerrit blames William, saying he can never forget nor forgive what he has done. He quits the company, taking his ship, the *Nautilus*, and his share in cash.

Gerrit loses his temper with Taou Yen as she mourns for his father her way. Ceasing to pray when he leaves, she looks very unhappy. Nettie and her grandfather come to pay their respects and Gerrit tells her that all is arranged regarding her uncle's business. She need only finish the details in town the following day.

In town the next day, Taou Yen and Gerrit's niece wait in the carriage while Rhoda goes shopping. A barrel falls off a passing wagon and hits one of their horses in the legs. The frightened animal bolts, but the women are unable to control them. Nettie steps into the street and is struck by them as they pass. Gerrit's niece becomes hysterical, but Taou Yen remains calm and tries to comfort her. The horses finally slow down when they come up on a hay wagon and sample its contents. Edward Dunsack calls on Gerrit, saying that Nettie has been asking for him. When he leaves, Dunsack remains and makes a pass at Taou Yen. "Your compliments do not interest me," she informs him. "But it's the truth! I worship you! No one, not even Gerrit, has my power to realize your perfection!" he assures her. He adds that Gerrit loves Nettie, but Taou Yen tells him that it is over between them. "Perhaps it's only begun," says Dunsack, smugly. Taou Yen tells him to leave and he replies they are destined for each other. She threatens to call the servants. Just then Laurel enters dressed up like Taou Yen, asking if she looks like her, and Dunsack departs.

At Nettie's home, Gerrit learns she has been given opium for her pain and warns her about the drug. She promises to take no more. He tells her that he would have come without her message and discovers that she sent none. Gerrit reveals his plan to make his headquarters in the east. The two say they will miss each other and wish mutual good luck. Gerrit then kneels beside Nettie's bed and kisses her, admitting his love. She asks why must he go and he replies that he is responsible for Taou Yen's life; Nettie cries after he leaves.

Back at Java Head, the Ammidon residence, Gerrit apologizes to his wife for having left her alone with Dunsack. She reports what happened and says an apology is unnecessary. Gerrit orders her to pack, for they leave in a week. Alone in their room later, Taou Yen reads a Chinese story about a man who had two wives, comparing her culture to that of Britain. She asks Gerrit if an Englishman could love two women equally. He replies that one could, but only for a moment. She adds, "Then one love would die — and the other grow stronger." "We English are very single-minded," says Gerrit. Taou Yen says nothing, but wears an understanding look.

Taou Yen visits Nettie, wearing an elaborate Manchu outfit. She tells the Englishwoman that she is aware of Gerrit's love for her. Nettie assures the Chinese woman that Gerrit will never leave her. Taou Yen smells the opium Nettie had been taking and suggests that she take an overdose as a solution; Nettie orders her out. Taou Yen is about to strangle Nettie with a silk kerchief when she screams and Edward Dunsack appears, looking much the worse for wear. Seeing him, Taou Yen quickly swallows all the opium in the bowl, takes a few faltering steps and dies in Dunsack's arms. The final shot shows Gerrit and Nettie sailing away together.

Print status: Copy at National Film Archive, England. Also available on video.

Anna May Wong's final British vehicle was made at Ealing Studios and tradeshown on July 20, 1934. Fifteen minutes were cut for its U.S. release.

Joseph Hergesheimer's 1918 novel was set in Salem, Massachusetts; apparently the producers wanted their audience to be better able to identify with the characters, so they moved the setting to Bristol.

Anna May looks stunning throughout in her elaborate Chinese costumes. For the first time she was kissed by a Caucasian, though only lightly on the lips. This was allowed because it was already established that the man was her husband. She again uses her eyes to convincingly express a range of emotions and carries herself in a manner befitting royalty. Her performance is one of her best, as she underplays superbly. She carries herself regally and her measured speech befits that of someone for whom English is a second language.

Ralph Richardson (1902–1983) was a noted stage actor who appeared in many British and Hollywood films. He received a knighthood in 1947.

Both Elizabeth Allan (1908–1990) and

John Loder (1898–1988) achieved popularity in British and Hollywood productions in the 1930s and 1940s.

Edmund Gwenn (1875–1959) was also a veteran stage actor in both London and New York, but is best remembered as a character actor in Hollywood films of the 1940s. He won an Academy Award as Best Supporting Actor for his work in *Miracle on 34th Street* (1947).

IV

American Sound Films

Before beginning her run in *On the Spot* in Los Angeles, Anna May Wong signed a contract with Paramount which must have contained a clause allowing her to appear on stage and visit Europe whenever she wished. In the next four years the busy actress spent more time across the pond than in the U.S. She traveled back and forth constantly, really racking up the "frequent sailor" miles. (See "European Sound Films.")

On November 10, 1930, her mother was struck by a motorist in Los Angeles and died from her injuries on the following day. Appearing on Broadway at the time, Miss Wong remained in New York, further estranging herself from her family.

In 1931, a tale of a Chinese peasant couple's daily struggles called *The Good Earth* was published. Written by Pearl S. Buck (1892–1973), it won a Pulitzer prize for its author the following year. The daughter of Presbyterian missionaries, she received her early education in Shanghai, and wrote a number of novels with Chinese settings. The film rights were snapped up by MGM, and Anna May saw her chance at a meaningful role, one which would show the Chinese in a sympathetic light. Lobbying hard to secure the role of O-Lan, the peasant wife, she was initially assured of the coveted part by director W. S. Van Dyke (1889–1943). The now seasoned actress was once more passed over when Van Dyke was replaced, however. Offered the role of the second wife instead, Anna May flatly refused to portray a concubine, an unattractive character. With her background in silent film acting, Anna May would have undoubtedly done herself proud, for the character of O-Lan has but fourteen lines of dialogue throughout the lengthy picture. We shall never know, however. At around the same time Anna May was announced for the role of Mah Li in *The Bitter Tea of General Yen*, to be directed by Herbert Brenon and starring Constance Cummings. Again she was denied a role in a major film; both star and director were also replaced, by Barbara Stanwyck and Frank Capra respectively. The part of Mah Li was given to Toshia Mori, a Japanese actress. Though the first film to play New York's magnificent new Radio City Music Hall in January 1933, it was a financial failure.

These upsetting experiences caused Miss Wong to once more flee America for Europe. In 1933 and 1934, she appeared in three more British pictures, which turned out to be her final foreign films. (See "European Sound Films.") The experienced entertainer also took her stage act to a number of venues throughout the British Isles, later touring the continent from Spain to Scandinavia. (See "Stage Work.")

In 1936 the veteran actress made her only visit to her ancestral homeland of China. She spent almost nine months there, during which time she visited Star Studios in Shanghai and met Butterfly Wu, China's leading film actress.

The history of film in that timeworn land was lethargic at first. While the first moving picture was shown in Shanghai in 1896, none was produced there until 1905, and the first feature film did not appear until 1921, the year Anna May Wong received her first screen credit. It was another decade before the first sound film was produced there. In China, as in most of the world, Hollywood productions reaped the lion's share of box office receipts. The domestic film situation did not reach appreciable figures until the late 1920s. Shanghai became home to scores of film companies in that period, and was known as "The Hollywood of the East," even though by the early 1930s the number had dwindled to a handful of large studios. Female film personalities garnered most of the attention, with Butterfly Wu, neé Hu Die (1908–1989) and Lily Yuen, neé Ruan Lingyu (1909?–1935) being the most famous.

Daughter of the Dragon (Paramount, 1931): publicity photo featuring Anna May Wong

When Anna May arrived in Shanghai, she discovered that her knowledge of Cantonese was useless, as Mandarin was the dialect spoken in that colorful cosmopolis. She was criticized for her portrayals of Chinese as evil people, and had to explain she had to take what roles she was offered in order to continue her career.

In March 1937 Anna May had her worst experience with the dark side of celebrity life. She received a note threatening her father with bodily harm and herself with disfigurement if she did not forward $20,000 toward the financing of a film. A similar note was received by the wife of producer David O. Selznick with the threat aimed at their two young sons. Famed evangelist Aimee Semple McPherson was also contacted by a local doctor, but for the purpose of her being in the proposed film. Another note, signed "The Gang," was received by the same physician and demanded that he act as intermediary; he was to receive the money. Anna gave the letter to her agent, who alerted the authorities. They took the note seriously and put everyone concerned under protection, including the doctor.

The gist of the letters was that the author resembled Christ and wanted to portray him in a movie. He needed financing and a connection with the film industry, hence the threats to film celebrities. The FBI was called in and the plot thickened; Miss Wong received a second threatening note within a week after the first one. That one made the same demands and was signed "She." Handwriting experts and a psychiatrist were employed and a plethora of names began appearing in the newspaper columns covering the case. Soon thereafter, Aimee Semple McPherson received another note demanding money; that one was traced to a woman from Minnesota. She was cleared of having had anything to do with the notes written to the film people, however, and the search continued. After much footwork and questioning of a number of suspects and matching similar extortion notes, the FBI determined that it was the local doctor who was the author of all the threatening letters. That was 1940, however, and the Los Angeles authorities had already closed the case due to lack of sufficient investigative evidence. Fortunately, the good doctor did not follow up on his threats and no one concerned in the case was ever harmed. He was characterized as a dangerous individual regarding extortion by the FBI and a watchful eye was kept on him in the future.

Even though she began getting sympathetic roles in the late 1930s, Anna May was still being passed over in favor of white actresses. Her own studio, Paramount, utilized her as technical advisor on *Disputed Passage* in 1939, in which Dorothy Lamour appeared in yellowface. She served the same function on *Panama Patrol* (Grand National, 1939), although she also tested for the role of Lia Maing, which eventually went to Caucasian actress Adrienne Ames.

It seems odd that Paramount never promoted Anna May Wong as the silver screen's "only Asian-American star" until one realizes that such a slogan would not have added much drawing power, in the opinion of studio executives. As long as there were popular white players who could be made up to portray Asians, why promote a true Asian performer? Add to this biased view the fact that after *Shanghai Express*, Anna May was given only "B" features and shorts, one can understand the disillusionment felt by the actress. Her fine work in all her European pictures seemed to have gone for naught. With Sessue Hayakawa now working in Europe, she was the only truly recognizable Asian name in American films, yet she was treated like some washed-up, aging silent film performer instead of one who had made the transition to sound smoothly and who was still in her early thirties.

In 1942, Anna May Wong signed a three-picture deal with Producers Releasing Corporation, a Poverty Row outfit which had been founded by Ben Judell in 1939 as Producers Distributing Corporation. Their early films were released under the Producers Pictures logo. Seven films and one year later, the company was almost bankrupt. Sigmund Neufield, brother of studio director Sam Newfield, started a production company called Producers Releasing Corporation, which took over PDC. In December 1940 the Pathé Corporation took full control, although the name was retained.

Only two of the films were made, *Bombs Over Burma* and *Lady from Chungking*, both released in 1942. The third, with the intriguing title of *The Devil's Sister*, was announced for release on May 29, 1942 in the April 4 issue of *Harrison's Reports*. The same trade paper announced in its May 16 issue that the picture's release date had been postponed; it never was made.

Following this association, Anna May Wong retired from films to concentrate on her work for Chinese War Relief and the USO. During the final two years of the war, she entertained U.S. troops in Canada and Alaska. She was also made an air raid warden in December 1942. With the cessation of hostilities in August 1945, the veteran entertainer took some time off from performing, living quietly in her Moongate Apartments in Santa Monica. She had purchased the property in 1939 and converted it into four apartments shortly after the war.

Having just entered middle age, Anna May slowed down considerably. One film appearance in 1949 and another in 1960 sandwiched around a score of television performances was all she added to her body of work.

In October 1955 the actress was hospitalized for two days for a gastrointestinal disturbance. She returned to television work in 1956, appearing in several dramatic series over the next four years. In 1960 she returned to Hollywood with a supporting role in a Lana Turner vehicle. The producer, Ross Hunter, then signed her for the role of "Auntie" in his upcoming production of *Flower Drum Song*. Fate stepped in and ended her long career when she passed away suddenly on February 3, 1961, at her brother Richard's home. The immediate cause of death was listed as a myocardial infarction, but Laennec's cirrhosis was included as a contributing factor. One final indignity which the proud Asian-American was fortunately unaware of was being called "Caucasian" in the "color or race" box on her death certificate. This obvious error remains inexplicable. She was cremated on February 9 and her ashes interred in Rosedale Cemetery. Her $85,000 estate was bequeathed to her sister Lulu and brother Richard only; Anna May felt she had given enough to her other three brothers over the years. (Her sister Mary died in 1940.)

Daughter of the Dragon

Paramount; Released August 1931; 70 minutes
Director: Lloyd Corrigan; *Adaptation-Script*: Lloyd Corrigan, Monte M. Katterjohn from the novel *The Daughter of Fu Manchu*, by Sax Rohmer; *Dialogue*: Sidney Buchman; *Photography*: Victor Milner; *Continuity*: Jane Storm; *Technical Advisor*: Tom Gubbins

Cast: Anna May Wong (Princess Ling Moy), Warner Oland (Fu Manchu), Sessue Hayakawa (Ah Kee), Bramwell Fletcher (Ronald Petrie), Frances Dade (Joan Marshall), Holmes Herbert (Sir John Petrie), Nella Walker (Lady Petrie), Nicholas Soussasin (Morloff), Lawrence Grant (Sir Basil), Harold Minjir (Rogers), E. Alyn Warren (Lu Chung), Harrington Reynolds (Hobbs), Tetsu Komai (Lao), Ole Chan (The Amah), Olaf Hytten (Butler).

The New York Times, August 22, 1931: "Miss Wong does quite well in some of her scenes. The production is lavishly staged, with dragons on the walls, secret panels..."

Variety, August 25, 1931: "...the dialog is mostly amateurish and inept. Anna May Wong and other Orientals will find the going tough in talkers.... The story ... is tangled."

Motion Picture Exhibitor, August 15, 1931: "Anna May Wong is splendid. It is a thriller that is certain to satisfy...."

Synopsis: Entertainer Ling Moy eagerly looks forward to meeting her father after many years, not knowing that he is the infamous Dr. Fu Manchu. When they meet, Fu Manchu reveals his identity and tells Ling Moy of his hatred of the Petries and his desire for revenge upon them as they were responsible for the deaths of his wife and son. He is shot trying to escape after murdering Sir John Petrie. Realizing he is dying, Fu Manchu will not allow his follower, Lu Chung, to seek revenge: "Only one of the house of Fu can redeem our honor." Ling Moy says, "The blood is mine. The hate is mine. The vengeance shall be mine!" "My flower daughter — the knife would wither in your petal fingers. Gods of my ancestors — if only thou had granted me another son!" "Father! Father! I will be your son! I will be your son!" cries Ling Moy. "Swear, man-daughter, to deliver the soul of Ronald Petrie to me, to our ancestors!" She raises her left hand and

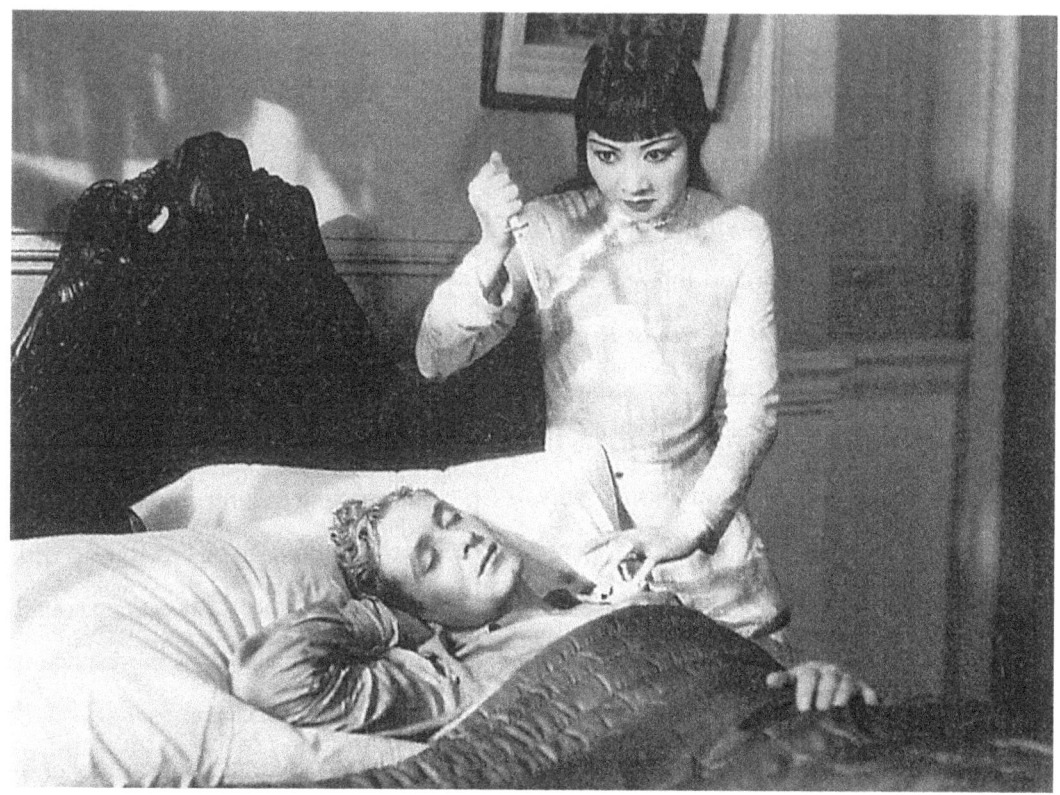

Daughter of the Dragon (Paramount, 1931): Bramwell Fletcher, Anna May Wong

swears. Fu Manchu continues, "Sovereign spirits, you have answered my deepest prayer—I have a son!" The arch villain devises a ruse to get young Petrie to sympathize with Ling Moy in order to facilitate her revenge. He pretends to threaten her life and is fatally shot by Ah Kee, a Chinese detective. She comes to care for Ronald, though, and delays her revenge. Lu Chung berates her for her weakness. She determines to do the deed and tells Lu Chung to tell her people that it will be done that very night. Ah Kee gets a secret message to be at the Petrie house that night from a Chinese merchant. Taking a secret passage leading from her house to Petrie's she enters his bedroom as Ah Kee enters below. As she exits the room, Lu Chung knocks out Ah Kee from behind. As the two leave through the secret passage, Chung knocks over a vase, awakening Rogers, who barely sees them leave, as he is not wearing his glasses. He finds Ah Kee, who asks after Petrie, who suddenly appears, unharmed.

Petrie and Ah Kee go to check on Ling Moy, since they believe she had been attacked by Fu Manchu. Morloff, another minion of Fu Manchu's, is surprised to see Petrie, believing Ling Moy had been successful. When Lu Chung learns of it, he is very upset. She says it was a moment of weakness. She goes to pray, admitting her love for Petrie and that she would rather kill herself than him. As she is about to stab herself, Lu Chung enters and grabs the knife from her hand: "A heartsick maiden would pour her blood on love's altar! Death would be her release! Her petty torment would then be ended and for the peace of this one miserable soul the souls of her ancestors will forever burn in dishonor!" She continues her prayer after he leaves and hears her father's voice saying that he will not rest until she has killed Petrie. She vows to do so.

The next morning she tells Lu Chung of her determination. He says it will be more difficult now as Ah Kee is guarding young Petrie. She phones Ah Kee and tells him she is leaving the country the next morning. Ah Kee, who has become attracted to her, begs to see her one more time. He has Rogers watch Petrie while he goes next door to see Ling Moy. While he is visiting her, Morloff goes to Petrie and tells him that Ling Moy has been kidnapped by Lu Chung. He says that Ah Kee has followed them and that he should call Scotland Yard and have them raid Lu Chung's place. The raid turns out to be a trap for Petrie and he is kidnapped.

Meanwhile, Ling Moy entertains Ah Kee; they pledge their love for each other. The detective asks Ling Moy to come to China with him. Just then she gets a signal from Lu Chung through a secret wall panel that all has gone according to plan. She does not answer Ah Kee's question, but goes into the next room, ostensibly to pray. There she finds an unconscious Petrie and makes plans with Chung, who says that Ah Kee must also die. Ling Moy replies that there is no need for further killing. Ah Kee notices something on the wall and discovers the hidden panel; peering in, he overhears the foregoing conversation. When Ling Moy appears again with some wine,

Daughter of the Dragon (Paramount, 1931): Sessue Hayakawa, Anna May Wong

Ah Kee at first pretends that nothing is amiss, then throws down the cup: "Why have you poisoned the wine — and our love?" Also inquiring about the presence of Lu Chung and the unconscious Petrie, he learns Ling Moy's true identity. He begs her not to kill Petrie; she tells him of her oath to her father and tells him to forget his hatred of the Manchu name, that she is a woman and can make him happy in China. Ah Kee says that is not possible. Ling Moy replies that he has thus chosen death. The detective tries to escape, but is caught by Ling Moy's minions and tied up.

Petrie's former flame, Joan, is kidnapped by Morloff and taken to the cellar of Ling Moy's house. Petrie awakes and is told by Ling Moy that she rescued him for herself. Hearing Joan's screams, Petrie asks about her. "Can you think of her now?" asks Ling Moy. "Why is she screaming like that?" Ling Moy agrees to take him to Joan. He finds her bound and gagged in a chair; he lowers the gag and she cries "It's Morloff!" Petrie leaps at Morloff but is restrained by Chinese guards. He tells Ling Moy that he cannot believe she could be so jealous. "No love now. No jealousy — just merciless vengeance! You will understand when I tell you, Ronald Petrie, I am the daughter of Fu Manchu!" Petrie says she can do what she likes with him, only leave Joan alone. Ling Moy refuses, saying he will have a thousand bitter tastes of death before dying. Lu Chung demonstrates the corrosiveness of the acid Ling Moy intends to use to eat away Joan's looks. The young woman faints.

Failing to find Petrie at home, the men from Scotland Yard decide to check with Morloff. Upstairs, Ah Kee has managed to stand and open a window. The police are met at the door by the *amah*, who says she is alone. As they leave to work from the Petrie house, Ah Kee tumbles down the roof onto the pathway. He tells the officers that Petrie is being killed, then passes out.

Joan comes to and the acid is prepared. Petrie begs Ling Moy not to harm her; Ling Moy says she is merciful. She has Petrie untied and hands him a knife, ordering him to kill Joan himself. He hesitates; the acid is brought closer; Joan cries to Petrie that she would rather die by his hand. As he moves toward her, the men from Scotland Yard burst in, shooting one man on the stairs and then the one holding the acid. Lu Chung turns out the light and grabs Ling Moy, taking her through the secret passage to the Petrie house. With the lights on again, one detective remarks it seems that the walls have swallowed Ling Moy and Lu Chung. That comment causes Rogers to remember what he saw the night of the first attempt on Petrie's life. He tells Ronald he knows where the pair has gone. At Petrie's, Rogers tells Ronald to turn off the light until he calls out. A moment later, Ling Moy and Lu Chung emerge from the passageway. Rogers calls out; as the lights come on, Lu Chung tries to flee back into the passage but is shot by Rogers. Ling Moy halts; Petrie says he will deal with her while Rogers goes for the police. She asks Ronald to let her surrender in the spirit of her family. Joan appears and calls to Petrie, who turns. As he does so, Ling Moy pulls a knife from her sleeve, but is shot by Ah Kee before she can strike, dying without a word. The detective, mortally wounded himself, falls and crawls over to Ling Moy's body: "Forever, Ling Moy? A flower need not love, but only be loved, as Ah Kee loved you." He grasps her hand and dies.

Print status: Available on video.

Should this film ever achieve wide exposure, it will undoubtedly become a cult classic. Played to the melodramatic hilt by all concerned, every line of dialogue ends with an exclamation point. The most laughable bit is Sessue Hayakawa as a *Chinese* detective; anyone with Asian friends would know him for a Japanese right away with his accent, if not for his looks. It is interesting to note that his character has to die also; even good Asians were not given a break in those intolerant days.

Anna May went with the flow, flailing her arms and widening her eyes at every opportunity. *Daughter of the Dragon* was Miss Wong's biggest hit and has become the quintessential Anna May Wong film, containing all the elements for which she was noted — dancing, villainy and the infamous dagger-in-the-sleeve. It is very likely that Fu Manchu creator Sax Rohmer (né Arthur Sarsfield Ward, 1886–1959) was pleased with this effort, as he was hardly known as a master of subtlety. He was also undoubtedly delighted with the $20,000 he received for the film rights on March 23, 1931.

Cinematographer Victor Milner (1893–1972) had been in film since he was fifteen and would later receive eight Academy Award nominations, winning one for his work on *Cleopatra* (Paramount, 1934).

Clips from *Daughter of the Dragon* appear in *The House That Shadows Built* (1931), Paramount's five-reel celebratory feature marking its twentieth anniversary in the industry.

Shanghai Express

Paramount; Released February 17, 1932; 80 minutes
Producer: Adolph Zukor; *Director*: Josef von Sternberg; *Screenplay*: Jules Furthman, based on a story by Harry Hervey; *Cinematography*: Lee Garmes; *Art Direction*: Hans Dreier; *Musical Score*: W. Franke Harling; *Costumes*: Travis Banton
Cast: Marlene Dietrich (Shanghai Lily), Clive Brook (Capt. Donald Harvey), Anna May Wong (Hue Fei), Warner Oland (Henry Chang), Eugene Pallette (Sam Salt), Louise Closser Hale (Mrs. Haggerty), Lawrence Grant (Mr. Carmichael), Emile Chautard (Major Lenard), Gustav von Seyffertitz (Eric Braun), Claude King, Willie Fung (train engineer).
Academy Award Nomination for Best Production (1931–32).
Academy Award Nomination for Best Director (1931–32).
Academy Award for Best Cinematography (1931–32).
Academy Award for Best Sound to the Paramount Sound Dept.
Remade by Paramount in 1943 as *Night Plane from Chunking*, and again in 1951 as *Peking Express*.
Motion Picture Exhibitor, February 10, 1932: "...splendid photography and excellent casting have triumphed over a familiar type of story."
The New York Times, February 18, 1932: "...by all odds the best picture that Josef von Sternberg has directed.... Anna May Wong makes the most of the role of the brave Chinese girl."
Variety, February 23, 1932: "Von Sternberg ... has made this effort interesting through a definite command of the lens. It climaxes ... after a Chinese woman (Anna May Wong) has revengefully daggered Oland to death. Cast performances are uniformly good outside the main pair...."

Synopsis: An eclectic group of travelers boards the title train in Peking bound for Shanghai. Among them is "Shanghai Lily," a notorious "coaster," a sort of wanton on wheels. Another is actually a Chinese warlord traveling incognito. The others are a reformed prostitute named Hue Fei on her way to a respectable marriage, a British medical officer going to Shanghai to operate on a government official, an American businessman, a retired French army officer, a missionary, a German coal mine owner and a boarding house proprietor.

Not long after leaving Peiping, the train stops while a cow is coaxed off the tracks. The British officer, Capt. Harvey, meets his old flame, who is now none other than the infamous "Shanghai Lily." "So you're Shanghai Lily," he responds, with all the interest a book collector would evince toward a pocket book edition. They renew their acquaintance and continue with a lot of silly banter.

When the missionary learns of Lily's

presence aboard the train, as well as that of Hue Fei, he warns Harvey about them. "One of them is yellow, the other is white, but both their souls are rotten!" he declares vehemently. The doctor is amazed how he can locate a soul and diagnose its condition.

At meal time, Lily and Hue Fei stop at Harvey's compartment; Lily asks if he will escort them to the diner. When she introduces Hue Fei, the latter extends her hand; Harvey says it is a great pleasure to meet her, but does not take her hand. She goes on to the dining car alone.

"You're very cruel, doc," comments Lily.

"I reserve the privilege of choosing my friends."

"She's no friend of mine; I was only trying to be — decent." replies Lily.

"Oh, professional courtesy?"

"Call it what you like…"

The train is stopped by government troops at night. Everyone goes outside with his or her passport. All are cleared except one Chinese man, who is taken away. Chang, the disguised warlord, tells Harvey he is probably a spy trying to return to his lines. He then wires ahead to his forces, informing them of the capture and ordering them to stop the Shanghai Express at midnight at any cost. Chang then goes to Hue Fei's compartment and begins to paw her, but she forces him out.

Later, the American businessman Sam Salt queries Chang about his ethnicity. "I can't make head or tail out of you, Mr. Chang — are you Chinese or white or what are you? "

"My mother is Chinese, my father is white."

"You look like a white man to me."

"I'm not proud of my white blood."

"What future is there in being a Chinaman? You're born, you eat your way through a handful of rice and you die. What a country! Let's have a drink!" (This is one of the stronger anti–Asian views expressed by the character; he makes several other disrespectful comments throughout the film.)

When the train stops for water at a small station, rebel troops attack, killing all the government soldiers aboard. The train having been seized, the passengers are ordered to dress and get off the train, leaving their baggage behind. Chang reveals his true identity and begins questioning the foreign passengers one by one inside the station in order to find a suitable hostage to exchange for his man.

The first one interviewed is the boarding house owner; when she returns downstairs, she tells the others it is Chang all dressed up in a military uniform who is the cause of the trouble. Hue Fei then remembers him and informs the others of the reward for him dead or alive. "It will be a great day for China when that price is paid."

When the French officer is called, Shanghai Lily goes with him to act as interpreter, as he does not speak English. It is revealed that he had been dishonorably discharged from the army, but wears a uniform so that his sister will not know of his disgrace. He is let go, but Lily is shown into the next room.

Capt. Harvey is next and learns that Chang's reason for holding up the train is to find a suitable hostage to exchange for his right-hand man. The warlord already knows of Harvey's reason for the journey — to operate on the governor-general of Shanghai immediately upon his arrival. He therefore chooses the doctor as his hostage and orders the others back to the train.

Chang makes a play for Lily, inviting her to his country palace. When he puts his hand on her, though, she cries, "Don't touch me!" Harvey, who had been listening from the next room, kicks in the door and strides over to Chang. Told by Chang

Shanghai Express (Paramount, 1932): Anna May Wong, Warner Oland

to mind his own business, the doctor knocks down the warlord with one punch. Chang backs off and says to Lily, "You are very fortunate in having Captain Harvey for a protector, as I promised to return him alive."

As Lily leaves the station, Hue Fei is dragged off the train by soldiers and taken to Chang.

Outside, Lily asks the missionary if he can do anything. He advises her to pray. She goes inside the train and does so; only her clasped hands are visible among the shadows. The missionary goes to a window and sees what he must have thought was a miracle.

At daybreak another train arrives, carrying Chang's man. A British official is informed that Harvey is still inside, but is made to wait before seeing him. Hue Fei appears, her hair disheveled and looking dazed. It is clear that Chang had his way with her. She goes straight to her compartment and takes a dagger from a satchel. Lily advises not to do anything foolish and she drops the weapon. Told to wait for Harvey, Hue Fei replies, "If he's up there, he may never come down." Lily runs out and bursts into Chang's room, asking why the doctor has not been released. Chang says he lives by his own code and that he is going to punish the officer for striking him. He tells Lily she can wait and lead him back to the train — blind. Lily says he is bluffing and offers money in exchange for Harvey's safety. "All the money in the world cannot wipe out his insult to me," replies the proud warlord.

Lily suddenly grabs a soldier's gun, but is immediately overpowered. Defeated, Lily offers to go with Chang. He makes her give her word of honor; this done, he accepts her offer. He frees the officer, who learns from the British official that the Chinese girl and Lily are still inside. Telling the man to have the train ready to leave, he takes the man's gun and returns into the station. He confronts Chang and is told that Lily has agreed to go with the warlord after all. Chang has Lily brought in and she tells Harvey that he speaks the truth. The doctor storms out. Chang dismisses everyone and says he will soon follow.

In his room, Hue Fei awaits in the shadows. As Chang sorts some papers, she stabs him twice in the back and flees.

When she appears downstairs, Harvey is ready to depart. "You'd better get her out of there; I've just killed Chang." Hue Fei advises the doctor. Harvey asks the official for a gun and goes inside, where he rescues Lily, knocking out a Chinese servant and a Chinese soldier in the process. They board the train and the journey is resumed.

Lily thanks her former lover, who replies, "I'd have done it for anybody," still disgusted with her. He later learns from the missionary that Lily prayed all night for him. The missionary goes to her and inquires why she decided to run off with Chang. She makes him promise secrecy if she tells. Learning the truth, the missionary begins to see Shanghai Lily in a differ-

Shanghai Express (Paramount, 1932): Louise Closser Hale, Gustav von Seyffertitz, Marlene Dietrich, Clive Brook, Lawrence Grant, Anna May Wong, Eugene Pallette, Emil Chautard

ent light. He calls Harvey a fool. When the doctor asks Lily why she prayed for him, she gives him tit for tat: "I would've done it for anybody."

As the train pulls into Shanghai four hours late, newspapers carry headlines of Chang's assassination. Hue Fei is surrounded by reporters, but quickly tires of them, saying something in Chinese and walking away.

Inside, Harvey asks for Lily's forgiveness, for he still loves her. She admits feeling the same; they kiss. Fadeout.

Print status: Available on video and DVD.

Shanghai Express is the only sound film in which Anna May Wong appeared to receive any recognition from the Academy of Motion Picture Arts and Sciences, being nominated for Best Production, Best Director and Best Cinematography, winning in the latter category. It is also the fourth and last film cinematographer Lee Garmes (1898–1978) lensed for von Sternberg. One of its most memorable features is the editing; every scene dissolves slowly into the next, creating a visual flow suggestive of the train's motion. Von Sternberg (1894–1969) obviously had a hand in this; he was the only Hollywood director to also be a member of the American Society of Cinematographers.

Had the Best Supporting Actress Award existed then (it began in 1936), many feel that Anna May would certainly have had a nomination. She says as much with her eyes as with her mouth, not having a lot of dialogue. When the snobbish boarding house owner gives her a business card, stating, "I'm sure you're quite respectable," Anna May replies "I must confess I don't know the standard of respectability you expect in your boarding house," in BBC English as she hands back the card to the shocked woman. Calmly playing solitaire and smoking cigarettes in her compartment for most of the trip, her detachment is broken only when Chang forgets his manners and when she exacts retribution for being raped. Even then she resists overacting. Marlene Dietrich's (1901–1992) constant eye-rolling is so flagrant it is almost comical.

Warner Oland, appearing for the last time with Anna May, shows his versatility by portraying Chang as a ruthless, proud and unbending individual. No trace of Charlie Chan's politeness is evident here.

Clive Brook's (1887–1974) stilted acting style is an acquired taste; his features are particularly devoid of animation. He has been quoted as stating that von Sternberg ordered his actors to "speak like a train."

Emile Chautard (1865?–1934), who played the bogus French officer, was the first director to offer a young von Sternberg work as his assistant. Prior to that, he had been a stage actor in his native France, where he also directed some films before his departure to the U.S. in 1914.

For this production, von Sternberg had a spur of the Santa Fe Railroad closed off and two stations transformed into Chinese terminals. One thousand Asian extras were hired and the train utilized was painted to specifications by the director. Filming began in late September 1931; location sites included San Bernardino and Chatsworth.

It is a wonder that the art direction did not also receive an Academy nomination, for it is exceptional. It takes several viewings to absorb all the detail that fills each frame, from the crowds at Peiping and Shanghai to the ramshackle station where Chang holds his interviews and is later killed.

Harry Hervey's story was very likely influenced by reports of the many train kidnappings by Chinese bandits during the 1920s. One 1923 incident included over a score of foreign passengers held for ransom.

Although banned in China, the film earned a worldwide gross of over $1,500,000, and garnered a modest profit for the studio. When Paramount sought to reissue *Shanghai Express* in 1935, it met with some resistance from the Production Code Administration, which had begun using its power in earnest in late 1934. Some of the violence and lines of dialogue were ordered trimmed.

Hollywood on Parade

Paramount/Criterion; Released 1932; 20 minutes
Producer: Louis Lewyn; *Host:* Eddie Kane
Cast: Roscoe Ates, Wheeler and Woolsey, Anna May Wong, Bob Bromley's Olivera Puppeteers, Helen Kane, Jackie Cooper, Douglas Fairbanks, Jr., Billie Dove, Jimmy Durante, Ben Lyon, Bebe Daniels, Tom Mix, Dorothy Ates.

All Anna May does in this revue-style short is graciously agree to recite a Chinese poem as a favor to host Kane after singer Helen Kane hurts her ankle and Kane nearly pulls Jackie Cooper's arm from its socket. The host asks to hear it first; when Miss Wong asks him if he liked the poem, Kane makes flippant remarks.

In another entry in the series, her name is spoken by a Chinese card girl, one of a group of girls of different nationalities promoting stars who shared the same birthplace.

Print status: Available on video.

A Study in Scarlet

KBS Productions/World Wide; Released May 14, 1933; 73 minutes
Producers: Burt Kelly, Samuel Bischoff, William Saul; *Director:* Edwin L. Marin; *Screenplay:* Robert Florey; *Continuity and Dialogue:* Reginald Owen; Suggested by the novella by Sir Arthur Conan Doyle; *Cinematography:* Arthur Edeson; *Settings:* Ralph DeLacy; *Music:* Val Burton; *Editor:* Rose Loewinger; *Supervising Editor:* Martin G. Cohn

Cast: Reginald Owen (Sherlock Holmes), Anna May Wong (Mrs. Pyke), June Clyde (Eileen Forrester), Allan Dinehart (Thaddeus Merrydew), John Warburton (John Stanford), Warburton Gamble (Dr. John H. Watson), J.M. Kerrigan (Jabez Wilson), Alan Mowbray (Inspector Lestrade), Doris Lloyd (Mrs. Murphy), Billy Bevan (Will Swallow), Leila Bennett (Daft Dolly), Cecil Reynolds (Baker), Wyndham Standing (Capt. Pyke), Halliwell Hobbes (Malcolm Dearing), Tetsu Komai (Ah Yet), Tempe Pigott (Mrs. Hudson), Hobart Cavanaugh (Publican), Olaf Hytten (Butler).
Working title: *The Scarlet Ring*.
The New York Times, June 1, 1933: "…this murder mystery is almost as exciting on the audible screen as it was in type in the days of yore. Anna May Wong does well in her part."
Variety, June 6, 1933: "Perhaps not the best done of any of the Sherlock Holmes adventures, this one has enough menace and murders, plus other factors, to land it moderate appreciation…. Warburton Gamble … Allan Dinehart and Anna May Wong are particularly up to their assignments."
Motion Picture Exhibitor, June 10, 1933: "Well produced Sherlock Holmes tale … feature players guarantee good going."

Synopsis: At Victoria Station, a cleaning woman is unable to open a compartment door. She gets the help of a conductor, who has a colleague break the window. Inside is the body of a murdered man.

Cut to an ad in a newspaper which reads:
692 3 7 13 7
 Scarlet 23 4 76
 Limehouse M

A young couple responds to it and go to a run-down building. The girl goes in alone; the pair is watched by a man with a briefcase who then enters the same building through another door. Inside, the man, a lawyer named Thaddeus Merrydew, heads a meeting which he called due to the death of one of the members of the group, James Murphy. He tells the others that the official verdict was suicide, therefore Murphy's estate is to be divided equally among those present. Included is the young girl, Miss Forrester, whose father had been a member until his recent death. Merrydew adds that the man's wife drove him to take his life.

Meanwhile, Sherlock Holmes is showing the same ad to Watson and asking what he deduces from it. "Obviously, an attempt to convey secret information," responds the good doctor. Holmes smiles and asks Watson if he could decipher the code. Watson says no and bets Holmes a shilling that he cannot, either. The latter says the answer will be found in a large book, because the numbers are large, and suggests the Bible. Just then Murphy's widow calls on Holmes. She tells the detective that her husband came to London after receiving a cryptic message, which she gives him. "Six Little Black Boys, Playing With A Hive, A Bumble-Bee Stung One And Then There Were Five." She adds that she received nothing from her husband, the money instead going to a fund run by Thaddeus Merrydew. Hearing that name, Holmes agrees to take the case, even though Mrs. Murphy cannot pay him. After she leaves, Holmes tells Watson that Merrydew is the "king of blackmailers" who has managed to escape the law until now, but will not this time.

Back at Limehouse, the meeting is breaking up; Merrydew tells Miss Forrester that she must not speak of what transpired that night to anyone. He learns that the young man awaiting her outside is her fiancé. He cautions her to consult him before marrying, because the organization will soon cease to exist and until its affairs are settled it would be unwise for her to wed. Suddenly Capt. Pyke, one of the members, comes rushing in, crying: "He's after me!" and falls down dead in the next room from a shot through a window. Merrydew tells the girl to wait while he checks outside. A menacing shadow appears inside; the girl screams. Merrydew is just outside the door; he checks his watch before going back inside. There he sees the girl is alright, but she notices that Pyke's body is gone. "What does it mean?" she cries. "The murderer must have had an accomplice and removed the body," replies the lawyer, adding that she is not to speak of this event, either.

At the city morgue Holmes looks at a body found drifting in the Thames. The face is unrecognizable, but a ring and the clothes identify the body as that of Capt. Pyke. Among the papers found on the body is a similar message to that received by Murphy, with some words altered to fit the diminishing numbers. Holmes talks to Pyke's widow in the next room and learns that she had dined with him the night before, that he left after 9 P.M. She identified the body from the ring, which was a gift from her when they married six years before in China. She tells Holmes she can be reached through her lawyer, Thaddeus Merrydew. After she leaves, Holmes tells Inspector Lestrade that it was murder and the lady is a liar.

A close-up of a list of names shows that of Capt. Pyke having a line drawn through it. The next name is that of Malcolm Dearing; at home he gets the cryptic message and tosses it away. A shadow appears on the wall behind him — "You! It's not possible! What do you want with me?" He runs but is shot dead.

Holmes and Lestrade investigate the crime; the latter calls it suicide. Holmes snoops about and from clues gets a description of the murderer. He informs Lestrade that the killer was in the house before the victim, who was shot twice, the second time to obliterate the wound of the first, making it appear a suicide.

Holmes visits Merrydew at his office and notes that the lawyer smokes the same brand of cigar as the wrapper found at Dearing's. The detective confronts the lawyer with Mrs. Murphy's charge and the murder of Dearing, another of his clients. Holmes writes something on a slip of paper after sneaking a look at a large book on the lawyer's desk. He hands the paper to Merrydew, who is taken aback to see the newspaper ad — so Holmes knows! Outside the office, Holmes tells Watson the answer to the code is in Whitaker's Almanac, the book he saw on Merrydew's desk. As they enter the elevator, Mrs. Pyke steps out and enters Merrydew's office.

Merrydew visits Miss Forrester to tell her that there will be another meeting at the same place and time the following night. Her fiancé, John, arrives as Merrydew leaves; she tells him of her father's will, the reason for her attending the meetings. John sees someone in the garden and goes to investigate, but the intruder gets away. John goes to Holmes, who orders him to watch her closely without being seen, for she is in terrible danger.

Holmes decodes the ad — "Meeting Scarlet Ring — Tuesday — Limehouse" — then places his own ad in the paper. Donning a disguise, he takes a trip to the Grange, the country estate owned by Pyke. At the local pub he finds a former employee of Pyke's to take him to the estate by cart. "You can't make English gentry out of the 'eathen Chinee, no how — not in these parts," philosophizes the driver. Holmes sees an auction sign as they near the place. He tells the driver to stop — "I'll walk the rest of the way; I'm in a hurry" — and asks the man to wait.

At the Grange he tells the maid he saw the sign and wishes to buy the estate. He pokes around a bit, and in Mrs. Pyke's bedroom pretends to have a seizure. While the maid is off getting him water, Holmes looks around. When the maid returns, he tells her it's a serious heart problem, he must have a doctor. Told there is no phone, he says she must run for a doctor, which she does, giving him ample time to look over things. He finds a hidden passage behind an armoire. Downstairs are some rooms; a box of Merrydew's brand of cigars is found in one. After walking through several more rooms, he finds a door leading to a landing to which a boat is tied.

Back in London, Jabez Wilson, one of the club members, meets with Mrs. Pyke in her hotel room. She tells him that she has always held him in high regard. "Oh, 'ave ya?" "Can you doubt it? You are the only one who knows of my husband's affairs." She goes on to say that they are in great disorder and wonders if he could come to the Grange as her guest and sort out the papers. He agrees to go the following night, as he has a meeting to attend that night.

Closeup of a newspaper ad: "Anyone supplying information concerning the 'Scarlet Ring' will be rewarded. Apply Sherlock Holmes, 221A Baker St."

Wilson is shown this by another member at the meeting: "Someone has given away the code! It's one of us, that's certain!" Merrydew is eavesdropping in the next room. When the two men become edgy, he enters and admits he overheard them. They say they do not want to end up dead. Merrydew reminds them that it was crime that brought them together, and crime will keep them together. He divulges the fact that he will have the money for which they have been waiting next week, and the Scarlet Ring will cease to be. The two still fear that they may not live to collect their shares. Merrydew informs them that if they write letters relinquishing any right to benefits from the Ring, it might guarantee that they will live. "What, and give up £200,000?" Miss Forrester arrives then, and Merrydew changes the topic.

Holmes gets a phone call from John, who followed the girl. He goes to Limehouse and waits outside the meeting place. All the members except the girl leave; he and John go in, smell gas and get the girl outside just in time. Holmes tells John to take the girl home and watch over her. Out in the street, Jabez Wilson is almost run over; he goes to Holmes' apartment where Watson tends him.

Merrydew welcomes someone unseen by the viewer to his office: "Any luck? Too bad. I have the securities." He continues that Ah Yet, the sole Asian member of the group, can be handled with money, and that speed is necessary due to the presence of Holmes. The lawyer goes on to say that all must end the next night at the Grange; he will make arrangements.

When Holmes returns to his rooms, Wilson tells of his narrow escape and about the Scarlet Ring. The detective tells him to hide at home and leave town tomorrow. Holmes and Watson grab guns and accompany Wilson to the door. The latter talks of his plan to meet Mrs. Pyke at the Grange and Holmes changes his plan. He says Wilson will be given the room next to Mrs. Pyke's, and there will be an adjoining door. Wilson should lock himself in overnight. As they open the street door, the body of Baker, another Ring member, falls in. A note on the body reads: "To Sherlock Holmes, with compliments," and another cryptic message.

Holmes and some police arrive at the pub near the Grange. As they leave, John arrives with news that Miss Forrester is gone and that he did not understand Holmes' telegram telling him to be at Dover. Realizing something was amiss when Holmes did not show, he raced back home and was told that Miss Forrester had left with a Chinese woman.

At the Grange, Mrs. Pyke remarks that Holmes is late. She tells Miss Forrester that she had handwritten instructions to bring her there. She figures if he does not arrive that night, he is certain to show up the next morning. When a knock is heard at the door, Ah Yet goes to answer, but is confronted by Wilson, who threatens him bodily harm if he does. Mrs. Pyke answers instead and is given a telegram for Miss Forrester. The girl opens it and finds a blank page; she shows it to Mrs. Pyke, who says nothing. Wilson retires and tells Miss Forrester to lock her door when she goes to bed.

Outside, the telegram courier reports to Holmes that the note was delivered. A policeman comes to Holmes and informs the detective that "he" arrived by boat fifteen minutes before. Holmes is upset at not being told sooner; the policeman says he was lost in the fog. Holmes and his men head for the Grange, where a mysterious figure is seen entering the cellar.

In her room, Mrs. Pyke turns as a figure (seen only as a shadow) enters: "I thought you would never come." The figure asks about Miss Forrester and Wilson and told the girl is in bed and Wilson is locked in his room. He tells Mrs. Pyke to offer any inducement to the latter to get him out. The figure appears in Miss Forrester's room; she screams and is heard by everyone. Mrs. Pyke knocks on Wilson's door, saying something terrible is happening to Miss Forrester; Ah Yet awaits beside her with a knife. The figure carries Miss Forrester downstairs just as Holmes arrives. He jumps the figure. Back upstairs, Wilson is attacked by Ah Yet and cries out; Holmes appears and shoots the Asian. The police arrive and handcuff Mrs. Pyke. The mystery man is revealed as Capt. Pyke; Holmes charges him with the murders and his wife as an accomplice. He tells how Pyke faked his death by breaking the window, making Miss Forrester think a bullet had passed through it, and then just running out when she fainted. A detective announces the arrival of someone by car. The person is Merrydew; when asked why he is there, he explains that he owns the mortgage to the house and had invited some friends for the weekend. Holmes charges him as an accomplice in the murders, but the lawyer is unruffled as he is taken away, confident to the end.

104 • A Study in Scarlet (1933)

The detective further clarifies the situation, relating how several years before some valuable gems had been stolen in China, a crime probably instigated by Pyke. He says he got a description of the killer from the clues at Dearing's home and that they fit Capt. Pyke. Holmes adds that Mrs. Pyke is really the captain's mistress, not his wife, but gives no reason.

Print status: Shown on American television.

In 1932 the former Tiffany Productions (Tiffany-Stahl from 1927–1929), renamed KBS for its owners Burt Kelly, Sam Bischoff and William Saal, bought the rights to the title only of the initial Sherlock Holmes adventure. Faced with the need for an original story, they utilized the services of the recently hired Robert Florey (1900–1979), a Frenchman who had been working at Universal. Finding the regime there too restrictive, he signed on with KBS, who allowed him more freedom. Initially he was supposed to direct as well as write the screenplay, but left for a more lucrative deal at Warner Bros. imme-

A Study in Scarlet (KBS/World Wide, 1933): Anna May Wong, Tetsu Komai

diately after collaborating on the story with star Reginald Owen (1887–1972). Edwin L. Marin (1899–1951), who had been Florey's assistant on his previous two films, was brought in as his replacement. Owen became the only actor to portray both Dr. Watson and Sherlock Holmes on film, having played the former character in *Sherlock Holmes* (Fox, 1932).

One stipulation for the writers was to create a part for Miss Wong. Oddly enough, she was made the wife of a British sea captain, though no romance was shown between the two. Again she uses her eyes to great effect, daring the viewer to guess what is going on in her mind. One aspect of Anna May's presence that is very apparent in this film is her height. At 5'7", she was taller than many of the males in her pictures, yet no attempt seems to have been made to create any equity. Perhaps her producers thought this added an extra element to her foreign appearance, or more likely, that it precluded any possibility of romance. The inexplicable addition of her being called Pyke's "mistress" rather than wife at the end of this film would appear to be yet another instance of anti–Asian bias.

Also inexplicable is the address of 22 "1A" Baker Street; even people who have never read the stories know that Holmes resided at 22 "1B" Baker Street.

Allan Dinehart (1889–1944) is appropriately slimy and confident as the crooked lawyer, Thaddeus Merrydew. Another Asian performer, Japanese actor Tetsu Komai (1894–1970) had nary a line of dialogue in this picture, which was normal for him. Like African-American actor Noble Johnson (1881–1978), Komai was utilized as an all-purpose exotic in minor roles, usually without dialogue.

By the time the picture opened, both KBS and World-Wide had gone under. The distribution was handled by Fox, which had a deal with World-Wide. *A Study in Scarlet* received fine reviews and is considered one of the studio's best productions.

Limehouse Blues (U.K.: East End Chant)

Paramount; Released November 9, 1934 (U.S.), April 8, 1935 (U.K.); 63 minutes
Director: Alexander Hall; *Producer*: Arthur Hornblow, Jr.; *Screenplay*: Arthur Phillips, Cyril Hume and Grover Jones, based on a story by Arthur Phillips; *Cinematography*: Harry Fishbeck, A.S.C.; *Music and Lyrics*: Sam Coslow; *Art Direction*: Hans Dreier and Robert Usher
Cast: George Raft (Harry Young), Jean Parker (Toni), Anna May Wong (Tu Tuan), Kent Taylor (Eric Benton), Montagu Love (Pug Talbot), John Rogers (Smokey), Robert Loraine (Inspector Sheridan), Billy Bevan (Herb), E. Alyn Warren (Ching Lee), Wyndham Standing (Asst. Commissioner Kenyon), Louis Vincenot (Rhama), Eily Malyon (Woman Who Finds Pug), Forrester Harvey (McDonald), Joe May (Taxi Driver), Colin Kenny (Davis), Eric Blore (Man Slummer), Desmond Roberts (Constable), Colin Tapley (Man Fighting with Wife), Rita Carlyle (Wife), Tempe Pigott (Maggie), Otto Yamaoka (Chinese Waiter on Boat), Dora Mayfield (Flower Woman), Clara Lou Sheridan (Girl with Couples), Elsie Prescott (Woman Employment Agent), Keith Kenneth (Policeman), Robert Adair (Alfred).
Motion Picture Exhibitor, November 15, 1934: "Familiar yarn of Chinese intrigue ... nothing to write home about."
The New York Times, December 12, 1934: "...owns the most child-like scenario that the grown-up Broadway area has seen in many weeks ... its chief virtue is to remind some of us novagenarians of the Yellow Peril literature of an earlier day...."
Variety, December 18, 1934: " ...Anna May Wong offers an authentic piece of work, capturing what minor sympathy the picture affords."
Kinematograph, January 3, 1935: "Jean Parker and Anna May Wong afford good dramatic contrast.... the efficiency of the presentation and direction permit it to provide good mass entertainment ... good thrills, spectacular staging and powerful cast."

106 • Limehouse Blues (1934)

Synopsis: Eurasian Harry Young operates a bar as a cover for his smuggling operations; the authorities are on to him, but cannot seem to catch him redhanded. Inspector Sheridan drops in at the Lily Gardens, Young's establishment, after a smuggling operation on the Thames. Young's Chinese mistress, Tu Tuan, is dancing on stage and spots the official. She signals Herb the piano player, who plays certain notes, alerting Young's bodyguard of trouble. He hurries into Young's office, where he helps his boss change into proper attire. The inspector notices that Young's tie is askew; Harry blames his pet cat for that and asks the officer to do it for him, as he is not good at it. Sheridan notices the long pinky nail on Young's hand. "Among the Chinese it's a sign of class. It shows a man who works with his head instead of his hands." "I have got an idea you work very well with both — too well." replies Sheridan. Asking how the river is tonight, Young learns that it will be unhealthy from now on.

A young woman pickpocket is chased through the streets by her victim and enters Young's office through the back door. When the victim arrives with a bobby, she denies the charge and allows the cop to search her; he finds nothing. Harry tells the cop the girl was with him all evening. The man and bobby leave; Young recognizes the girl as Pug Talbot's. "He's me stepfather." Young says the girl should be working for him. "Not me, mister; I know your New York Chinatown ways." He asks about the watch and she denies having it. "That's for the police; you can't fool me," says Harry. "No?" and she

Limehouse Blues (Paramount, 1934): John Rogers, Anna May Wong

removes the watch from his jacket pocket. Outside the girl runs into Talbot's minion Smokey. She asks him not to tell Pug she was in Young's place. He says he won't if she's nice to him; she walks off, clearly offended.

Pug is manhandling someone who had told him Harry Young would have given him a better deal. Talbot says he will kill Young for ruining his business. Smokey informs on the girl, Toni, and Pug confronts her. She relates what happened. Pug and Smokey go to Harry; the former tells him he's angry at losing business and wants a cut of the *Nanking* job Young has planned for the next night. Ching Lee, an associate of Young's, warns Talbot that "Only a fool makes powerful enemies." "You ain't 'eard the end of me!" cries Talbot and storms out. "One day, all Limehouse will hear the end of Pug Talbot," remarks Harry.

Limehouse Blues (Paramount, 1934): Anna May Wong

Young goes to a hidden room where he dons a Chinese robe and prays before an image of Buddha: "In thee, master, may I find greater wisdom, greater strength and greater courage." "And greater love," adds Tu Tuan, who has been assisting him. Harry repeats the phrase.

On his way to the river with Herb the next night, Young is warned by Toni not to go there. He goes anyhow and completes the transaction from his motor boat. The police are watching and give chase, but lose him in the fog. Smokey informs Talbot of Young's escape, saying he must have been tipped off. Pug knows it had to be Toni; he beats her with his belt. Shortly thereafter, Harry and Herb see a cop warning Talbot against further beatings. They figure he has beaten Toni for having warned them. "Looks like we'll have to settle with Pug Talbot right away," comments Harry as he hands a key to Herb. "You know what to say."

At Pug's, Herb tells Young's rival that Harry feels the two should work together after the close call he had that night. He invites Pug to Young's private flat the next night for a cut of the *Nanking* job, and gives him the key, telling him to let himself in. Smokey tells Pug he's balmy if he goes alone, after Herb has gone. Pug shows him a pistol.

The following night Harry is dancing with Tu Tuan on stage when Pug is due to visit. Upstairs in the flat, Talbot is knifed by Rhama, Young's bodyguard. He props up the body against an outside wall. When a woman asks the time of what she thinks is a live man, she touches his arm and the body falls over. A bobby appears and Young comes out of his place and identifies the body. The police commander holds a meeting of all concerned before the formal inquest. No one lets on to knowing anything, except Toni, who tells the police of the quarrel between Harry and Pug the day before the murder. Asked if she would testify to their rivalry, she replies that she could not, for the two made up the same day, adding that Pug had told her so. Everyone is dismissed. Feeling helpless, Sheridan asks for faster boats, or better yet, a gun. The commander replies that if he finds the occasion, he shall have his gun.

Young offers Toni a job at his place, noting that she would look beautiful in nice clothes: "I need a clever girl who remembers much, and can use all she knows." He gives her the room next to Tu Tuan's, who takes her there. The room is full of Chinese artifacts. Toni clearly is uncomfortable; Tu Tuan tells her she does not belong there, especially since she cannot appreciate Chinese culture, adding, "We're both in the same house now; you're good at remembering— remember to leave him alone."

Working at the Lily Gardens, Toni gets some information from a ship captain, who passes her a note. She is accosted by a drunk and Harry comes to her aid by tossing out the fellow. Herb says to Tu Tuan, who had been watching, that Harry is sweet on Toni and that she'd better watch out. "Perhaps the white girl had better be looking out!" hisses Tu Tuan with eyes ablaze. In Harry's office, Toni gives him some news when Tu Tuan comes in and orders Toni out: "Your place is at the bar with the white sailors!" Turning to Harry, she reminds him, "You had a white father, Harry, but you are of the east. The white girl is not for you." Harry says Toni means nothing to him and Tu Tuan, unconvinced, tells him that one day he will understand the difference between east and west.

Outside, the drunk, who is really an undercover cop, tells Sheridan he saw the sailor pass a note to Toni, but he was unable to get it. The inspector says he still wants the girl watched closely.

Young's friend Ching Lee also warns Harry about an affair with a white woman, asking if the girl loves him. Harry says, "No, but she will." The next time he sees Toni, Harry informs her that she need not work anymore and gives her money to treat herself. When Tu Tuan learns of this, she has Smokey follow Toni, offering him money if he discovers anything.

In another part of London, Toni meets a young man who runs a pet shop. Smokey spots them; Toni begins spending all her spare time with Eric, the young man.

The next time she sees Harry, he happens to grab her arm, and she complains that his long fingernail hurt. After she leaves, he cuts it off, just as Tu Tuan walks into the room. Asking what she wants, Harry is told that he could not understand.

Harry begins to wonder where Toni is spending her time. Tu Tuan says she knows someone who can tell him. Harry refurnishes Toni's room. When she does not respond, he asks what is wrong. She feels she cannot go on accepting things from him and wants to get a job. Harry allows her to keep the room until she finds employment. As he talks, he begins swinging the key to his private flat. Toni recognizes it as the one Pug had the night before he was killed. "You're good at remembering things, aren't you, Toni?" He then tells Herb to spread the word that no one in Limehouse is to give Toni a job.

Tu Tuan taunts Young: "Harry Young in love with a white girl." "Suppose I am?" "While she spends her days with a man of her own color." "I'm half white." "He's *all* white!" retorts Tu Tuan. He reminds her it is time for her dance. She informs him that she will dance there no more, that she is leaving for good.

Meanwhile Eric and Toni profess their love for each other. Toni reveals her past and tells Eric about Harry, but he is persistent, not caring about those things. She returns to Limehouse; Smokey goes up to Eric and offers to tell him where Toni lives.

Young orders Rhama to let him know whenever Toni goes out. Eric goes to Harry and asks for Toni, that he knows all about her situation, but still loves her and is convinced that she loves him. Harry invites Eric to visit him at his private flat that night and gives him the key. From her window Toni sees Eric departing and tries to warn him, but Harry intercepts her: "Did you have a visitor just now?" "Yes, Ching Lee," answers Harry, then asks Toni if she meant someone else. She says she heard voices and wondered. Acting very nervous, she returns to her room.

Inspector Sheridan meets secretly in a booth somewhere with Tu Tuan, who tells him of Harry's latest plan. He thanks her and asks if she wants protection, then figures she does not need it. While he phones headquarters, Tu Tuan turns off the light in the booth, pulls a dagger from her purse and stabs herself.

Harry and Toni go to a New Year's celebration on Ching Lee's boat. Toni is wearing Harry's mother's betrothal robe. Harry orders Herb to handle the smuggling operation. Herb says he can smell cops, but is assured by Harry that they have not been caught yet. Inside, Toni questions Harry about Eric, for she admits she knows it was he who came to see Harry, but Harry says he did not listen to what Eric said. She tries to cut him off by saying that Eric is just a kid who should not be out without a nurse maid. "No, he shouldn't," agrees Young.

Herb spots a police boat and tries to warn Harry, but Ching Lee's men will not let him inside. Meanwhile, Eric is on his way to Harry's flat.

At dinner, Toni is distracted; Harry asks her if she's thinking about Eric. She says she never wants to hear his name again. "You won't," Harry promises her. While Harry leans over to talk to someone, Toni notices the missing key, jumps up and runs out. Young follows; she pleads with him not to harm Eric and promises never to see him again. "You could never love me, could you?" asks Harry, finally resigned to the situation. He takes the robe from her and tears it up, vowing that no one will ever wear it. Harry heads for his motorboat; Herb says it's too late, the cops are all around. Young takes the wheel and Toni jumps on the back of the boat. The cops pursue; this time the inspector has a tommy gun. He fires at Young.

In Limehouse, Eric enters the building and takes the elevator up to Harry's flat. Young and Toni arrive just seconds later and see the open door. They race upstairs; Harry calls out to Rhama to hold as he is about to kill Eric. He tells the young couple to go out the back way and goes inside, where he dons his Chinese robe. Sheridan appears and tells Young he won't get away this time. "Yes I will, you shoot too straight," and falls to the floor. Toni notices blood drops on her arm and runs back to the flat, knowing Harry is hurt. As she kneels beside Young, he exonerates her with his dying breath.

Print status: Available on video.

Limehouse Blues, despite its brevity, gave Anna May Wong one of her better

roles. She gets to wear some interesting outfits, including a curve hugging, shimmering black full-length dress with a dragon pattern up the front and has two dance numbers, one of which is interrupted by the discovery of Pug's body. She also gets to speak some very catty dialogue, which she delivers with gusto and a dash of relish on the side. Her hair was done with a widow's peak rather than her trademark bangs.

George Raft (1895–1980) is his usual stoic self, save for a few scenes in which he speaks as if there really is blood running through his veins. His makeup is too exaggerated for a Eurasian; with his natural black hair, he would not look out of place among the extras.

The part of Toni would have been better served by Ida Lupino; Jean Parker (b. 1912) makes virtually no attempt at a cockney accent and her Montana twang jars on the nerves.

Hollywood Party

M-G-M; Released April 9, 1937; 2 reels; Technicolor
Director: Roy Rowland; *Producer*: Louis Lewyn; *Cinematography*: Aldo Ermini; *Dance Director*: Carlos Romero; *Dialogue*: John Krafft; *Technicolor Director*: Natalie Kalmus; *Hosts*: Charlie Chase and Elissa Landi
Cast: Clark Gable, Joan Bennett, Joe E. Brown, Freddie Bartholomew, Joe Morrison, Sonny O'Dea, Anna May Wong, Leon Errol, Leon Janney, Ahern Sisters, Betty Jane Rhodes, Jack Good, Jones Boys, Marcus Show Girls, Al Lyons and His Cocoanut Grove Orchestra.
Motion Picture Exhibitor, May 15, 1937: "This is quite interesting and novel."

Synopsis: Elissa Landi arrives in a ricksha. She welcomes the crowd and then says, "We're here to greet the celebrated magician who's come from the Orient to entertain you." Charlie "Chan" Chase arrives in a "China Clipper" automobile. They sit at a table where Charlie performs a simple trick and Landi introduces a number of stars who put their faces through a frame in a hedge. More patter, with Chase speaking pidgin English. Landi strikes a gong on the table to introduce Anna May Wong as "China lady of fashion." Two Chinese girls standing beside closed blinds open them to reveal Anna May after one strikes a gong. She speaks: "I've just returned to Hollywood, after a most marvelous year in China. My first visit to the ancestral country." She then proceeds to model three Chinese outfits as she describes them. Anna May returns through the blinds. Music utilized in this first reel included *Chinese Wedding Procession*, *In a Tea Garden*, *Chinatown My Chinatown*, *The Glory of Love* and *Shanghai Merriment* No. 611.

Anna May did not appear in the second reel, which featured Leon Errol trying vainly to be humorous with a Chinese waiter who speaks no English.

Print status: Shown on Turner Classic Movies.

The studio made a 68-minute feature with the same title in 1934 which was not well received, despite the presence of Laurel and Hardy and an animated sequence created by the Disney studio. Their reason for re-using the title is most likely for its appropriateness. *Hollywood Party* was filmed at the beautiful Berkheimer Estate in Los Angeles.

In this short, we see a rare glimpse of Anna in color, in stark contrast to all of her black and white movies, and for a change we get to see her simply talk to us.

Miss Wong no doubt gritted her teeth throughout her appearance in this short, not only because of its condescending nature, but for the fact that it was made by the studio which rejected her for a leading role in their super production released the

Opposite: Hollywood Party (MGM, 1937): Poster

same year, *The Good Earth*. It also marked her return to Hollywood after more than two years spent abroad.

Daughter of Shanghai (U.K.: Daughter of the Orient)

Paramount; Released January 21, 1938; 61 minutes

Producer: Edward T. Lowe; *Director*: Robert Florey; *Screenplay*: Gladys Unger and Garnett Weston, based on a story by Weston; *Cinematography*: Charles Schoenbaum; *Art Directors*: Hans Dreier and Robert Odell; *Editor*: Ellsworth Hoagland; *Music Direction*: Boris Morros; *Assistant Director*: Stanley Goldsmith

Cast: Anna May Wong (Lan Ying Lin), Philip Ahn (Kim Lee), Charles Bickford (Otto Hartman), Larry Crabbe (Andrew Sleete), Cecil Cunningham (Mrs. Mary Hunt), J. Carrol Naish (Frank Barden), Ching Wah Lee (Quan Lin), Evelyn Brent (Olga Derey), Anthony Quinn (Harry Morgan), Gino Corrado (Interpreter), John Patterson (James Lang), Fred Kohler (Capt. Gulner), Frank Sully (Jake Kelly), Maurice Liu (Ah Fong), Guy Bates Post (Lloyd Burkett), Virginia Dabney (Rita), Pierre Watkin (Mr. Yorkland), Archie Twitchell (Secretary), Mrs. Wong Wing (Amah), Ernest Whitman (Sam Blike), Mae Busch (Lil), Paul Fix (Miles), Charles Wilson (Schwartz), John Hart (Sailor), Lee Shumway (Ship's Officer), Carmen Bailey, Paulita Arvizu, Carmen LaRue, Tina Menard (Dancers), Bruce Wong (Chinese), Gwen Kenyon (Phone Girl), Marie Burton, Paula DiCordo, Alma Ross, Blanca Vischer (Girls).

Daughter of Shanghai (Paramount, 1938): Guy Bates Post, Anna May Wong, Philip Ahn, Cecil Cunningham

Pre-release title: *Across the River.*

The New York Times, December 25, 1937: "A tense, melodramatic atmosphere is successfully maintained.... Miss Anna May Wong, the attractive Oriental, as the daughter..."

Motion Picture Exhibitor, January 1, 1938: "It is well made, holding enough punch for action houses ... well paced, with the necessary melodramatic angles."

Synopsis: Newspaper headlines proclaim alien smuggling as a major problem. A plane with illegal aliens is chased by a government plane; unable to outrace it, the smugglers open the hatch and the aliens drop into the ocean where they drown. "There goes $6,000," remarks one of the smugglers.

The smugglers learn that a Chinese federal agent, Kim Lee, is being assigned to the case in San Francisco. They figure "the boss" will handle him, but wish to steer clear of him.

Daughter of Shanghai (Paramount, 1938): Philip Ahn, Anna May Wong

Importer Quan Lin is waiting on one of his best customers, Mrs. Hunt, when two of the smugglers approach him. They make him an offer to sell cheap labor. He knows who they are, however, and refuses to deal with them. He tells Mrs. Hunt about them and she offers assistance. She tells him and his daughter, Lan Ying, to be at her house that night to meet with an immigration agent. Quan Lin has a file of information on the smugglers to show him. He mentions a man named Hartmann to his daughter as they ride in a cab to Mrs. Hunt's place. Lan Ying suddenly realizes that they are not taking the proper route to Mrs. Hunt's. The cab is driven into the back of a truck; the driver is one of the smugglers. A gang member shoots Quan Lin and Lan Ying falls atop him as she is fired at, feigning death. Quan Lin's papers are taken and the cab is dumped into the bay, but not before Lan Ying is able to climb out and hide under a tarpaulin. As the gang watches the cab sink, she escapes. She goes to Mrs. Hunt with her story and meets the immigration agent and Kim Lee. The latter tells the agent to report Lin's death as an accident so that the smugglers will not suspect they know the truth. Mrs. Hunt again offers aid as Lan

Ying leaves. She then goes to her study where the smugglers await — she is "the boss." She reprimands them, but they show her Lin's file. "Go through all this, see who's been talking, then burn it," she orders. She then informs them that Lan Ying just left; they are very surprised, thinking her at the bottom of the bay. "Now she may be able to identify you," says Hunt. The smuggler shows her papers taken from Lin's safe as appeasement.

Kim Lee is suspicious of Mrs. Hunt and asks Lan Ying how long she's known the woman. Lan Ying tells him of Hartmann; Lee says he's been running a clearing house for aliens somewhere.

Lan Ying goes to her family lawyer and asks him to handle her affairs for a while, as she is going away. She asks if he knows about Hartmann and he tells her the same thing Lee did, adding that he is somewhere in the Caribbean. Lee phones then; Lan Ying tells the lawyer not to tell Lee she is there. He tells Lee that she is going away. Lan Ying says she can find out things Lee could not, that she's tired of government inefficiency.

After traveling around the Caribbean, Lan Ying finds Hartmann in Port O'Juan, where he runs a club. There she asks for a job as a dancer. She is told to see Olga, who tells her that Hartmann does not need any new dancers. She goes to Hartmann's office; he is in another room dealing with men wishing to go to America. One of them gives him a hard time and Hartmann knocks him down and takes his money. Hartmann gives Lan Ying a job, saying he needs something new. That night Lan Ying slips out of bed and goes to Hartmann's office. Almost caught snooping by him, she grabs a glass and tells him that he had invited her for a drink. She gets him to open up — he tells her he wishes he was in San Francisco instead, that the boss makes the real money. Olga suddenly appears; Lan Ying leaves and Olga and Hartmann fight.

Kim Lee turns up in Port O'Juan as a supercargo on one of the smuggler's ships. At Hartmann's club, he recognizes Lan Ying as she dances; she also spots him. He goes to the dressing room afterwards and asks what she's doing there, for she's in danger. She tells him of Hartmann's book; Lee says he'll get it; she must take the first boat she can. They agree to meet in San Francisco. Lan Ying disguises herself as a man before leaving.

Hartmann catches Lee in his office just after the agent has stolen the book; they fight. As Hartmann is about to hit Lee, he is shot in the back by the man he had mistreated earlier. Lee hides the book, then helps with the crew count. Seeing Lan Ying in disguise, he covers for her and she goes aboard.

On the ship Lan Ying's hair falls below her hat and she is revealed as a female. She is attacked by the crew; Lee and a few sailors come to her aid before the captain breaks up the melee. Told about the girl, he tells her all she had to do was ask to come aboard; now she can travel in style, he says leeringly. Hartmann's book falls out of Lee's pocket and the captain sees it. He has Lee locked in a room and suspects the girl as being his accomplice. Two of the smugglers arrive in a seaplane to pick them up. The two are tied up and taken over the ocean in the plane. Lan Ying manages to undo her bonds and frees Lee. When the hatch is opened, they hold on to the side of the plane until the hatch is closed. When the plane lands, Lan Ying and Lee wait for the smugglers to leave in a boat before they swim to shore.

Seeing lights on in the nearest house, they suspect it may be the smugglers' hideout. They go to the garage to steal a car, but are caught by Kelly, Mrs. Hunt's chauffeur, for it is her home. As the smugglers tell of the pair's death, Lan Ying is heard calling to Mrs. Hunt. "The boss" orders smugglers into a back room and goes to Lan Ying. Lee asks to use the phone; Mrs. Hunt tells her butler to take him to the phone room and "see that he is well taken care of." The butler knocks out Lee and ties him up. In the living room, Lan Ying spots Hartmann's book on a table and realizes the truth. She is locked in a room and Kelly is watched by a gang man, for he is not in on the crimes. Kelly, a former boxer, takes his man and overhears Hunt's plan to kill Lan Ying and Lee. Meanwhile, Lee manages to manipulate the phone so that he can speak into it. He tells the operator to call his captain and tell him to send help immediately. Kelly then frees Lan Ying and they in turn untie Lee just as gangmen come to take him to Mrs. Hunt. Kelly and Lee battle the smugglers until the police arrive. Hunt and the others are taken away. Lan Ying and Lee are driven home; in the car, Lee proposes marriage to Lan Ying, but that's as far as it goes, for there the picture ends.

Print status: Available on video.

In her first American starring role since *Daughter of the Dragon*, Anna May Wong was finally given a sympathetic character to portray. Her first feature film in two years was directed by Robert Florey, who made the picture in three weeks in October 1937. He favored Anna May with numerous closeups, none really gratuitous. Miss Wong danced for the last time in this film, foretelling another change in image; never again would she conceal daggers in her sleeve nor slink about in smoke-filled dives. Her subsequent characterizations, except for her next, would all be those of "good" women. This film did well enough to justify the three-picture contract which Anna May signed in November 1937. As entertaining as it is, *Daughter of Shanghai* marked the beginning of the long road downward for Anna May Wong's career. She would no longer star in "A" pictures. In fact she would appear in only one, and that was to be her last film.

This was the first of two films the actress made with Korean-American actor Philip Ahn (1905–1978), with whom she was romantically linked off screen, but it seems only in the press. Also born in Los Angeles, Ahn has been mentioned as having attended high school with Anna May, which is possible, given they were the same age.

It was both interesting and sad to see such former bright lights of the silent screen as Evelyn Brent (1894–1975) and Mae Busch (1891–1946) as two of "the girls" in the waterfront dive. Though both had dialogue, their roles are of little import. *Daughter of Shanghai* marked the first appearance of Anthony Quinn (1915–2001) in an Anna May Wong vehicle. Still at the beginning of his long and distinguished career, he would support her in three more films at Paramount. Twenty years later she would support him in her final picture.

Missing from the on-screen credits is Ching Wah Lee (1902–1980), who played Quan Lin. This is inexplicable, as he had a major role in the early part of the picture, as the father of Anna May's character.

Dangerous to Know

Paramount; Released March 11, 1938; 70 minutes

Director: Robert Florey; *Producer*: Edward T. Lowe; *Screenplay*: William R. Lipman and Horace McCoy, based on a play by Edgar Wallace; *Cinematography*: Theodor Sparkuhl; *Art Directors*: Hans Dreier and John Goodman; *Music*: Boris Morros; *Editor*: Arthur Schmidt; *Costumes*: Edith Head; *Interior Decorations*: A.E. Freudeman; *Sound Recording*: Harry Lindgren and Richard Olson

Cast: Anna May Wong (Madame Lan Ying), Akim Tamiroff (Stephen Recka), Gail Patrick (Margaret Van Kase), Lloyd Nolan (Inspector Brandon), Harvey Stephens (Philip Easton), Anthony Quinn (Nicholai Kusnoff), Roscoe Karns (Duncan), Porter Hall (Mayor Bradley), Barlowe Borland (Butler), Hedda Hopper (Mrs. Carson), Hugh Sothern (Harvey Greggson), Edward Pawley (John

Rance), Eddie Marr (Crouch), Harry Worth (Hanley), Robert Brister (Councilman Murkil), Pierre Watkin (Senator Carson), Garry Owen (Mike Tookey), John Hart (Man), Donald Brian (Judge Hart), Stanley Blystone (Motorcycle Cop), Terry Ray (Secretary), Rita La Roy (Mrs. Barnett), Harvey Clark (Mr. Barnett), Jack Knoche (Messenger), Gino Corrado (Headwaiter).

Motion Picture Exhibitor, March 1, 1938: "Wong as gangster Tamiroff's mistress offers an exotic element ... this is repetitious claptrap...."

The New York Times, March 12, 1938: "In her strange, oriental way, Miss Wong reaches his [Tamiroff's] artistic soul ... is second-rate melodrama, hardly worthy of the talents of its generally capable cast."

Synopsis: Racketeer and art patron Steve Recka, the power behind the throne in politics, runs his town and his beautiful Oriental friend and hostess, Madame Lan Ying, with a hand of iron. He longs for social acceptance, denied him due to his underworld connection.

One day his secretary, Nicky, visits the mayor, informing him that he has just installed a bugging device in the office of Councilman Murkil, who that day is meeting with Recka's lieutenant, John Rance. The two overhear Rance and Murkil plotting for the latter to be the next mayor. Murkil tells Rance, "Nobody can be mayor unless Recka elects him." Rance assures him he can throw a monkey wrench into the political machine now that he is Recka's right-hand man. He adds that he will know everything Recka does before he does it and will keep Murkil informed. Murkil wants to drive out Recka so that he can get some of the city treasury money Recka had been stealing.

It is the boss's birthday, however, and a large party is in progress at his home. Senator Carson and his stuffy wife arrive; he wants to invite Recka to dinner to stay in the gangster's good graces, and be re-elected. His wife will not have it. Lan Ying is introduced by the senator to his wife as Recka's hostess. "Hostess?" asks his wife, eyebrow raised. "Yes, hostess," replies Lan Ying, emphasizing the last word. She goes to get Recka, who is listening to Bach in his den. She reminds him that his guests are waiting, naming three V.I.P.s. Recka says to let them wait; there are many real people in the city; why don't they come to his home? Lan Ying responds: "Perhaps they don't want to know you." Nicky arrives then, and Lan Ying is sent back downstairs to tell the guests that he will be down soon. Nicky tells Recka what he overheard.

Beautiful young socialite Margaret Van Kase crashes the party. She tells the Carsons she would like to meet Recka, to which Mrs. Carson adds that she is sure Recka would like to meet her, too. When Recka finally makes his appearance, he is introduced to Mrs. Carson, then notices Van Kase standing by a window. He introduces himself and says he recognized her from the society pages. She acts coyly, her interest aroused. Lan Ying notices this and drops the tea cup she is holding. Mrs. Carson says she knew Van Kase would find Recka interesting. Lan Ying says coldly, "I'm sure she will." The socialite informs Recka that her neighborhood has been rezoned, so that her stately old home may soon be razed. Noticing the organ player, Van Kase expresses a love of music, which is shared by Recka. He tells her that he plays and would like to play for her after the others have left. The Carsons say good night and Mrs. Carson invites Recka to dinner the next night. As Recka plays for Van Kase, Lan Ying watches quietly. The young woman tells Recka that he should have been a musician. "But I am a musician," he assures her. She recalls the stories of Steve Recka the gangster. "Yes, but not the musician," he sighs. "One who talks like a poet," she adds. He begins to play louder, and Van Kase slips out past Lan Ying without a word. Lan Ying goes over to Recka: "Don't waste your talent,

Steve — she's gone." He continues playing; she leaves.

Recka goes to Rance's office one night. When Rance goes to get a drink, Recka puts note paper on the desk and opens the window. Rance tells Recka he missed the party because he was at the dentist. Recka asks him if he saw Murkil there; Rance knows that Recka knows about him and Murkil, says he can explain. Recka feels he was tempted by Murkil. He understands but the boys would not. Rance begs Recka not to turn him over to the gang. Recka says he will not if Rance follows orders. Recka dictates a letter to Rance which could be construed as a suicide note, then pulls out a gun and advances on Rance, who backs away toward the window and falls out of it to his death.

Inspector Brandon, an old nemesis of Recka's, gets the news and immediately suspects the gang boss. Meanwhile, Recka is meeting with the mayor, getting him to change the zoning laws so that the Van Kase home will be spared. The mayor says it will be no problem, especially with Councilman Murkil on a long trip. Recka says he is sorry to hear that the councilman is not well. Just then police sirens are heard. The mayor leaves the back way as Lan Ying welcomes Brandon. The detective tells her she is the only honest thing in the house. In Recka's den, Brandon and the gangster spar verbally about Rance's death and having the same birthday. Brandon returns a check Recka had sent him and gives him a present of a pair of chocolate handcuffs. Nicky arrives and Brandon leaves. Nicky is worried that Brandon suspects; Recka assures him that Brandon knows, and has for five years. Recka is given some personal information about Margaret Van Kase, including the fact that

Dangerous to Know (Parmount, 1938): Anthony Quinn, Akim Tamiroff, Anna May Wong

she has a boyfriend named Philip Easton, an aristocratic but penniless young bond salesman. Recka orders Nicky to have Easton sell him $20,000 worth of bonds and have him come to the house that evening. Lan Ying learns about Easton and looks knowingly at Recka. Mrs. Carson phones, asking Lan Ying to have Recka pick up Van Kase on his way to dinner. She catches Recka at the door and gives him the message with the warning that Van Kase sees him only as a novelty, that she belongs to a world he can never enter. She tells him to stay where he belongs. He storms out without a word.

At lunch with Margaret one day, Recka learns that Easton has proposed to her; she shows him the ring. He does not congratulate her: "Phil is only a boy; you deserve a man." "But I love Phil," she replies. She tells Recka that he can never have her. At another table, Brandon notices the pair and tells his colleague that Recka is making his first mistake.

Nicky brings an expensive package to Recka's house; when asked by Lan Ying what it is, he tells her that Recka hopes to marry Margaret; if not her then someone else. Recka appears then and tells Nicky he is supposed to be at the airport to meet someone, that they will know him. Seeing Lan Ying staring at him, he asks her if she wants anything. She replies in the affirmative, then says, "Nothing." "You're a strange person, Lan Ying. You want nothing. I've never before met anyone who wants nothing." She reminds him of his mistake, then warns him, "You've reached too far, Steve."

Recka later meets with the two men Nicky met at the airport, Hanley and Crouch, and gives them orders for a job. One dons a fake beard and moustache and goes to Easton with cash to buy a large sum of bonds. Easton recommends keeping them in a safe deposit box, to which the man agrees. As Easton fills out the necessary form, the man pulls a gun and his accomplice enters the back way and stuffs the bonds into a bag. They take Easton with them. When Easton disappears, the newspapers brand him as a runaway thief.

Recka has a tip phoned in to Brandon to check out #7 Eden Apartments. There the detective finds Easton in a stupor, but without the bonds. Nicky phones Recka to tell him that Easton has been picked up. The boss tells him to pick up the bonds and have the two men leave town by car. Nicky is then to go to headquarters and watch for developments.

Recka has van Kase come to his place and tells her that Easton has been found, but that he is under arrest. Van Kase reminds Recka that he has the power to have Easton freed, but the gangster says it is not always so easy to fix things. Van Kase realizes then that Recka planned to have Easton disgraced and jailed. She says no one would believe it, but she and Recka know it is true. Recka tells her there is no way she can expose him. She knows Recka still wants her; she says she will go through a wedding ceremony and be his wife in name, but will do everything in her power to get him for what he has done to Easton and herself. She asks Recka if he loves her; receiving an affirmative reply, she states that it will make it easier for her; she will take but not give, and will show him what living in contempt really means. Van Kase adds that she will fix Recka good, then go back to the man she loves, if he will still have her. Recka tells her to pack and meet him at the airport at seven o'clock. He also promises to have Easton freed immediately. Van Kase asks to see Easton once more, but is denied by the gang boss.

Easton is being questioned by Brandon; he gets a phone call ordering him to book Easton now so that Recka's lawyer can free him on bail. Brandon informs Easton that he is not through with either him or Recka. Out in the hall, Hanley and

Crouch are being brought in for running a red light and having two guns in their car.

At Recka's home, his butler is placing two bags by the door. Lan Ying looks quizzically at them; a messenger brings two plane tickets for Recka; she signs for them and learns of Recka's plans. Nicky runs in and gives Recka the news about Hanley and Crouch. He is worried that they will be identified by Easton. Recka says they would need the bonds too. Nicky opens the bag the pair gave him, only to find that they switched bags; all Recka has is newspaper with a few bonds on the outsides of the bundles. Nicky swears his innocence, saying that he just then opened the bag; Recka berates him for not checking on the two men. They realize the police now have the bonds and that Hanley and Crouch will talk to save themselves.

Easton arrives at Recka's looking for Margaret; Lan Ying goes to the den and sees the bonds and finds out from Nicky what happened. She goes into the hall and overhears Recka telling Easton he must identify Hanley and Crouch as the ones who held him up, that Nicky is waiting for him with the cops at a certain garage. All will be well when he meets Nicky, says Recka. Lan Ying sneaks out then. After Easton leaves, Recka orders Nicky to go after him and kill him, but Brandon is waiting outside for him and forces him into a car.

Inside, Recka finds Lan Ying mixing drinks and is surprised since neither one of them drinks. Lan Ying asks Recka to join her just this once, then offers a toast, something else neither one likes. She says music is much better and puts on a recording of "Thanks for the Memories." She look sorrowfully at Recka, tears falling down her cheeks. Recka asks Lan Ying if she knows whether or not he will return. "Won't you?" He replies that he does not know and gives her money to keep for him until he returns. Recka adds that he trusts her better than himself, that he knows she will be there because she is a real friend. Brandon is watching them through a window. Recka sits at the organ and begins to play; Lan Ying takes a small knife from her purse and stands behind Recka. She touches him tenderly on the shoulder, listens for a second, then plunges the knife into her stomach and drops to the floor, dead. When she does not respond to his next question, Recka sees Lan Ying on the floor and drops beside her, picking up the knife. Brandon bursts in then and tells the gangster to drop the knife. Recka says he could never kill Lan Ying. As Brandon puts handcuffs on Recka, he gloats, "Eight men you've killed — now you're gonna hang for something you didn't do." On the way out, Recka tells his butler to make arrangements for a beautiful funeral for Lan Ying. Later, Nicky settles in Recka's house and Easton and Margaret are together on a plane; the former explaining that Lan Ying gave him the tickets.

Print status: Available on video.

Although unnamed in the credits, *On the Spot* [q.v.], the play in which Anna May Wong made her American stage debut in 1930, was the work adapted for the screen as *Dangerous to Know*. While the character names are all different, the basic plot was retained. One major difference is in the climactic scene. In the play Minn Lee had her back to the audience as she stabs herself. When Tony goes to her, he picks up the bloody knife just as the police enter. In the film, Lan Ying stabs herself in full view of the audience as she stands behind Recka, although the knife is not visible. The emphasis on Lan Ying being Recka's "hostess" rather than "mistress" is due to the Hays Office, which by his time had been making its power felt for about four years. Other than some caring looks by Lan Ying, there is no affection shown between the two. Though it had been several years

When Were You Born (Warner Bros., 1938): Frank Jacquet, Anna May Wong

since she played the role, Anna May brought her character to the screen with the experience of hundreds of prior performances. She makes the part her own, with what must surely be the definitive interpretation.

Anna May got to wear some eye-catching Edith Head gowns, all of which she wore with her trademark grace, as befitted a woman named on the Ten Best Dressed list for a number of years.

Russian-born Akim Tamiroff (1899–1972) came with years of stage and screen experience to this, his first of two films with Miss Wong. He arrived in America in 1923 after training at the drama school of the Moscow Art Theatre. He received an Oscar nomination for his work in *The General Died at Dawn* (1936) and would receive another for his role in *For Whom the Bell Tolls* (1943).

When Were You Born

Warner Bros.; Released June 18, 1938; 65 minutes

Producer: Brian Foy; *Director*: William McGann; *Screenplay*: Anthony Coldeway, based on a story by Coldeway and Manley P. Hall; *Cinematography*: Lewis William O'Connell; *Editor*: Douglas Gould; *Costumes*: Howard Shoup

Cast: Margaret Lindsay (Doris Kane), Anna May Wong (Mei Lee Ling), Lola Lane (Nita Kenton), Anthony Averill (Larry Camp), Charles Wilson (Inspector Gregg), Frank Jacquet (Sgt. Kelly), Eric Stanley (Shields), James Stephenson (Philip Corey), Jeffrey Lynn (Davis), Leonard Mudie (Fred Gow), Maurice Cass (Dr. Merton), Jack Moore (Asst. District Attorney).

Variety, June 15, 1938: "Picture has a reasonably intriguing story and several clean-cut performances. Anna May Wong ... does fairly well though monotone voice tires on listeners."

Motion Picture Exhibitor, June 15, 1938 "…is unusual in departure from form, in appeal to one audience category, while retaining

When Were You Born (Warner Bros., 1938): Anna May Wong

enough suspense as murder mystery to satisfy most average audiences."

Synopsis: The film opens with a lecture on astrology, with the signs of the leading players discussed. As each leading player is introduced, his or her sign and birth date are given; all three leading ladies' dates are erroneous.

Aboard a cruise ship, astrologer Mei Lee Ling predicts the death of a fellow passenger in forty-eight hours. The man, an importer of Chinese art, is found dead two days later and his death called a suicide. The police soon realize it was murder. Ling's prediction is noted and she is called in by the police. She clears herself and offers her services in questioning the suspects in the case. After a number of suspects are introduced, it is discovered that the importer was blackmailing the mother of one of them. It is also revealed that the man's partner was smuggling narcotics. The police, along with Miss Ling, surround the partner's house. She enters the house with them and is grabbed by the partner and led through a secret passageway. The dead man's valet, who had been cheated by the partner, finds them and kills the partner in the same manner that he killed his employer, revealing himself as the murderer.

Print status: Shown on Turner Classic Movies.

Back at Warner Bros. for the first time since she made *The Crimson City* a decade earlier, Anna May found herself with a meatier role, reams of dialogue, and no white females in yellowface to support. *When Were You Born* is the only film of Miss Wong's wherein her ethnicity had no bearing on her character; anyone could have played an astrologer. Although Margaret Lindsay got top billing, Anna May had much more screen time. She makes her entrance on the cruise ship looking very chic with a long cape and a pet monkey on her shoulder. Approaching her role with great elan, she becomes somewhat irritating as she asks each character she meets his or her birth date and begins rambling about the attributes of his or her sign. Then again, she was not responsible for the script. The level of comic relief is not very high, being concerned mainly with puns based on Miss Wong's character analyses.

British actor Leonard Mudie (1884–1965) is completely unconvincing as a Chinese, from his makeup to his accent; he sounds like Sidney Toler after a bad night. Lola Lane (1909–1981) adds some spark in her few scenes, while Margaret Lindsay (1910–1981) brings an extra touch of class to the proceedings.

King of Chinatown

Paramount; Released March 17, 1939; 60 minutes

Producer: Harold Hurley; *Director*: Nick Grinde; *Screenplay*: Lillie Hayward and Irving Reis; *Story*: Herbert Biberman; *Cinematography*: Leo Tover; *Art Directors*: Hans Dreier and Robert Odell; *Music Director*: Boris Morros; *Editor*: Eda Warren; *Costumes*: Edith Head; *Interior Decorations*: A.E. Freudeman; *Sound Recording*: Charles Hisserich and Glenn Rominger

Cast: Anna May Wong (Dr. Mary Ling), Akim Tamiroff (Frank Baturin), J. Carrol Naish (The Professor), Sidney Toler (Dr. Chang Ling), Philip Ahn (Robert "Bob" Li), Anthony Quinn (Mike Gordon), Bernadene Hayes (Dolly Warren), Roscoe Karns (Rep Harrigan), Ray Mayer (Potatoes), Richard Denning (Intern), Archie Twitchell (Second Intern), Edward Marr (Bert), George Anderson (Detective), Charles B. Wood (First Gangster), George Magrill (Second Gang-

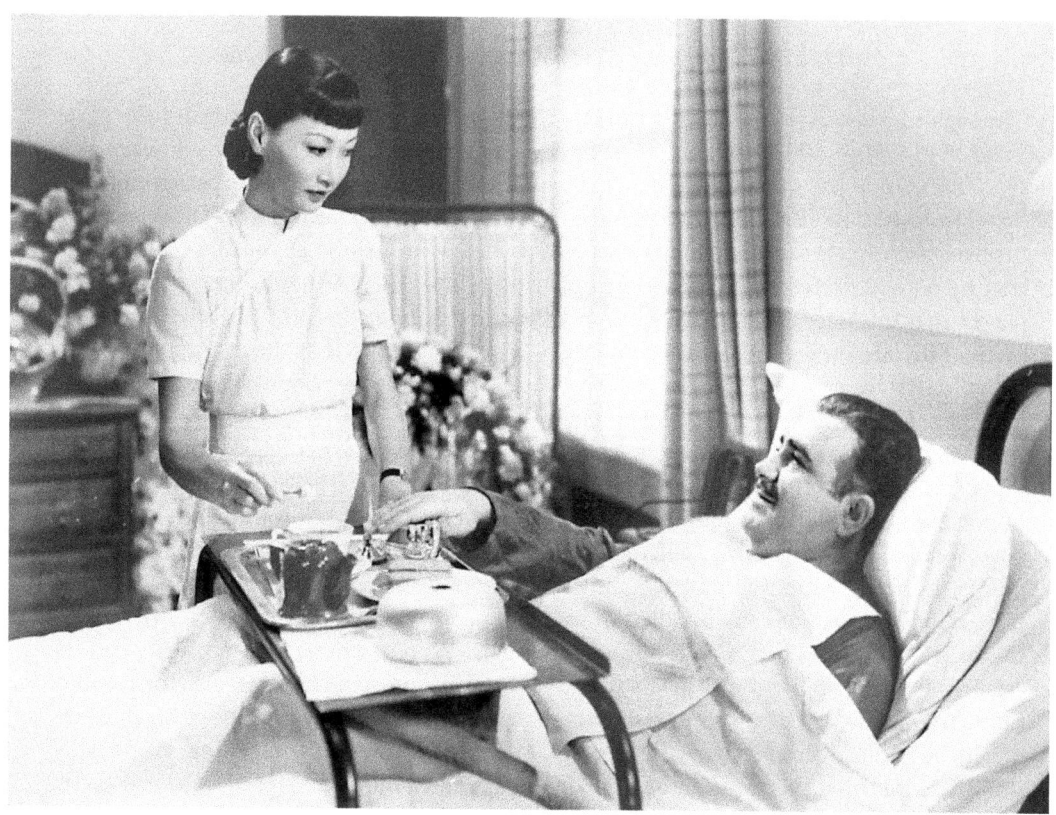

King of Chinatown (Paramount, 1939): Anna May Wong, Akim Tamiroff

ster), Charles Trowbridge (Dr. Jones), Lily King (Chinese Woman), Wong Chong (Chinese Man), Chester Gann (Mr. Foo), Pat West (Fight Announcer), Guy Usher (Investigator), Pierre Watkin (District Attorney Phillips), Sam Ash (Barber), Jimmy Vaughn (Slugger Grady), Alex Pollard (Heath).

The New York Times, March 16, 1939: "…is so microscopic a melodrama that it appears to be kicking around in odd corners of the screen rather than filling it."

Variety, March 22, 1939 : "Miss Wong provides a nice portrayal of the Chinese girl turned doctor."

Synopsis: Frank Baturin, known as "The King of Chinatown," meets Chinese lawyer Bob Li at the Silver Club one evening during the Chinese New Year. Li expresses his concern over the protection racket currently operating in Chinatown. Knowing that Baturin has influence, Li asks him to do something; Baturin says he will try. Later in his office, Baturin discusses the matter with his business manager, known as "The Professor." The latter informs his boss that there will be difficulty if the eminent Chang Ling refuses to buy into their protection scheme. Baturin goes to see Ling that night, but is told by Ling that he needs no protection.

Meanwhile, in the local hospital, Ling's daughter, Dr. Mary Ling, talks with her superior about leaving the hospital to set up a Red Cross unit in China. He offers her a residency and she agrees to think it over. She leaves with two friends from the hospital to have dinner with her father. Afterwards, they all go to a boxing match, where Baturin makes a speech before the main event. He thanks everyone who came, for the money will go to Chinatown charities. Mary is impressed by his speech, but Bob Li and her father denigrate the man. She accuses them both of prejudice. "So prejudiced, that if I were a violent man—but I am not a violent man," responds Chang Ling. One of Baturin's men tells him during the fight that the bout will be thrown by the boxer backed by Mike Gordon, a rival. Baturin tells his man to wait outside. Mike Gordon signals his trainer, who throws in the towel, giving the decision to the other boxer. Baturin and Gordon leave the arena together, expressing surprise at the man who lost. Gordon states that he did not think the King of Chinatown could be fooled. "He can't," replies the King. In the parking lot, Baturin orders the Professor to have a man ambush Gordon later that night. The Professor changes the order when he gives it, so that Baturin will become the victim. Later he and his boss argue over using Gordon's plan for making money. Baturin leaves alone; the Professor calls Gordon and tells him everything is set.

At Chang Ling's, Mary and Bob talk of Baturin's loss; Chang Ling interrupts, saying, "If I had my choice, there would be no Frank Baturin." Mary is taken aback when he adds, "There is also the matter of a small debt I must take care of," and goes out.

Meanwhile, in a Chinatown street replete with New Year's celebrants, Mike Gordon hides in a stairwell. When Baturin drives by, Gordon throws some firecrackers onto the sidewalk to add to the din and mask the reports of his gun. He ambushes Baturin, whose car crashes into the storefront next to Chang Ling's. Mary and Bob rush outside and check Baturin, finding him still alive. They both notice her father among the gathering crowd and fear he may be the assassin, given his earlier statements. Li phones for an ambulance and Mary rides with him. Mary knows she must save Baturin, for if he dies, she fears her father will be accused of murder. At the hospital she begs her superior to let her operate on Baturin. That worthy says he has only one chance in a thousand, but accedes.

Mary operates successfully, but

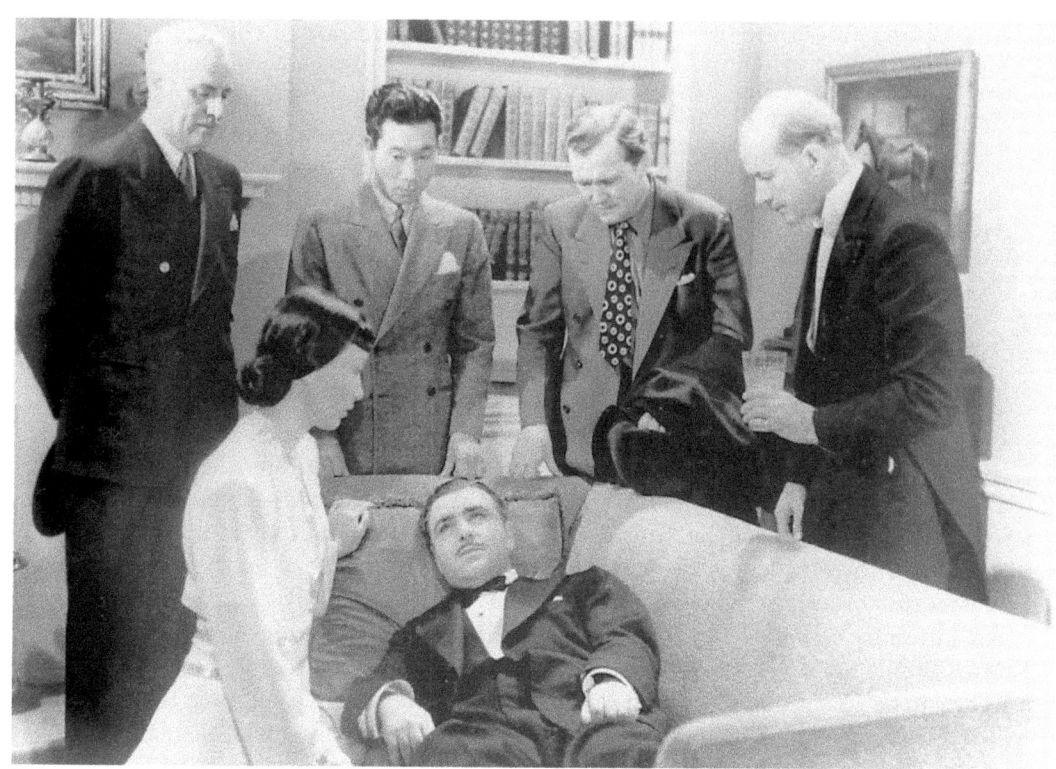

King of Chinatown (Paramount, 1939): Pierre Watkin, Anna May Wong, Philip Ahn, Akim Tamiroff, Ray Mayer, Alex Pollard

Baturin remains unconscious. The Professor goes to see him, but Mary will not allow visitors. She asks if he has any idea who the shooter is; he does not, nor does she. Back at Baturin's office, the Professor finds Gordon waiting for him. Gordon states that he is taking over from Baturin, but the Professor informs him that the gang will only take orders from him in Baturin's absence. Gordon allows the Professor a cut, but the manager says he does not need Gordon. The latter reveals knowledge of the Professor's prison escape seven years before, so the Professor agrees to a partnership.

The district attorney goes to see Baturin, but is put off by Dr. Ling. Next one of Baturin's men decides to stand guard outside his boss's room. Just then Dr. Ling is told that Baturin needs a blood transplant and his man volunteers.

One week later, Baturin regains consciousness and learns that it was Dr. Mary Ling who saved his life. He thanks her and says he owes her. She replies that he has already paid her by remaining alive.

Gordon and the Professor are still scheming; when they learn that he is still alive, they determine to put him away for good.

In Chinatown meanwhile, the protection racket meets resistance and the gang responds by property destruction and murder. When Baturin's man tries to tell his boss about this, he is told by Dr. Ling that such a shock could prove fatal at this point. Baturin wants to see the Professor, but is refused by Mary. He then learns from a nurse that Dr. Ling is leaving for China the next day. He asks if he may be moved home; Mary agrees, but says he will still need care. Baturin makes her a generous offer to tend him at home. She agrees to speak with her father. He says the mobster can get another doctor. She reminds him of her need for money quickly, that this is the fastest way, as it will only be about a month.

Gordon is worried now, but the Professor says that as long as Baturin is out of circulation, there is no need for worry. Realizing that Baturin will not be laid up indefinitely, the Professor goes to Chang Ling and asks if he will order Mary to see that Baturin does not improve. Ling tells him that his daughter is first and foremost a doctor, and loyal to her professional oath. The Professor makes a veiled threat; Ling goes to the district attorney, saying he wants his daughter out of Baturin's house. The D.A. says no, that the Professor is just a front for Baturin, who is the man they really want. Two gangsters who had been following Chang Ling inform the professor and Gordon of his visit. The Professor is unruffled, stating that it is Ling's word against his. Gordon reminds him of his past, saying it will come out. The Professor reaches for a gun, but Gordon dissuades him from killing Ling. At Baturin's, Mary Ling is called to the phone. Baturin tells his man to phone the Professor; he refuses, but agrees to go to the club to talk to him. Baturin tells him to tell the Professor that Chang Ling is not to be molested. Mary is on the phone with the Professor and tells him it will be okay to visit Baturin in a day or two. The Professor and Gordon decide to wait for Baturin to come to them. "And when he does, we'll give him a real nice welcome," promises Gordon.

As Baturin's man arrives at the club, he sees Gordon leaving; he rushes back to Baturin's to tell him that Gordon is still alive. He runs into Mary on the stairs; she will not let him up to see Baturin. He stammers on about Gordon; Mary learns who he is and that he is the one who shot Baturin and why.

The D.A. meets with the Professor to put pressure on him, though he knows the Professor has an alibi for the night of the shooting. The Professor asks if the attorney has bothered to check on Gordon's whereabouts that night. Gordon is soon arrested and his gang rounded up. Gordon confesses and the D.A. sets out to arrest Baturin that night.

Baturin is now up and about; he asks Mary that she not go to China, but send someone in her place. He offers to build a clinic for her, but she declines. The Professor and Chang Ling arrive at Baturin's home simultaneously at different points. The Professor sees Ling, but the Chinese man does not see him. Baturin now offers to give up crime for Mary. Her father appears then, saying he has come to take her home. She asks that he speak with Baturin first. The gang leader is on the phone with one of his men, who informs him that Gordon is alive, that the Professor ordered Ling to be harmed and is on his way to get Baturin. The Professor is waiting in Baturin's den with a gun; his former boss tells him to drop it while advancing toward him. They struggle, the gun goes off and a bullet enters Baturin's chest. As the Professor flees, he is caught outside by police. Inside, Baturin lies on a sofa and assures Mary that all will be well in Chinatown now. He tells her to buy the finest ambulance, then dies. The last scene shows Mary and Bob Li on a plane bound for China.

Print status: Available on video.

For once the reviews are accurate; there is little action or suspense in this picture. Apparently major changes were made in the story, for an early synopsis contains more interesting angles, including a more logical reason for the female doctor to keep the gangster alive. This one is strictly for Anna May Wong fans.

Anna May is as lovely as ever, and again gets to wear some very attractive

Edith Head creations. The actress did some research before essaying the part of a surgeon and seems completely at ease in her medical surroundings.

Island of Lost Men

Paramount; Released July 28, 1939; 64 minutes
Director: Kurt Neumann; *Associate Producer*: Eugene Zukor; *Screenplay*: William R. Lipman and Horace McCoy, based on the play *Hangman's Whip* by Norman Reilly Raine and Frank Butler; *Cinematography*: Karl Struss; *Art Directors*: Hans Dreier and Franz Bachelin; *Music Director*: Boris Morros; *Editor*: Ellsworth Hoagland; *Interior Decorations*: A.E. Freudeman; *Sound Recording*: George Cutton and Don Johnson; *Assistant Director*: Joseph Lefert
Cast: Anna May Wong (Kim Ling), J. Carrol Naish (Gregory Prin), Anthony Quinn (Chang Tai), Eric Blore (Herbert), Broderick Crawford (Tex Bannister), Ernest Truex (Frobenius), Rudolf Forster (Prof. Sen), William Haade (Hambly), Richard Loo (Gen. Ahn Ling), Philip Ahn (Sam Ring), Torben Meyer (Cafe Manager), Lal Chand Mehra (Hindu), George Kirby (Waiter), Vivian Oakland (Blonde), Jack Parry (Blonde's Escort), Ruth Rickaby (First Tourist), Ethyl May Halls (Second Tourist), Bruce Mitchell (Ship's Officer).
Working titles: *North of Singapore*; *King of the River*.
Previously filmed by Paramount as *White Woman* (1933).
The New York Times, August 17, 1939: "…the whole adventure smacks amusingly of a burlesque on the portentous 'Sanders of the River' theme…."
Variety, August 23, 1939: "Anna May Wong and Anthony Quinn turn in dignified, capable

Island of Lost Men (Paramount, 1939): Lobby card

performances.... Setting and artistic dressing of production and scenic highlights achieve high excellence."

Synopsis: Kim Ling, the daughter of a Chinese army general who has been accused of absconding with government funds, is searching for him so that she can clear him of the charge. Kim becomes a singer known as "China Lily" in a bar in Singapore. There she meets Gregory Prin, a self-styled "King of the River," who controls a large stretch of territory along the river north of Singapore. He is supremely contemptuous of everyone and full of himself. Introduced to Lily, he says, "You are honored and please to meet me, yes?" He shows Lily a map of the region he rules, then shows his matchless charm by stating, "Oh, I forgot — your singing. You have a terrible voice." With lines like that, it's no wonder there is no "Queen of the River." The singer notices a medal he is wearing and asks about it. "Something I picked up; a little knick-knack." Lily says nothing, but seems to know exactly what it is. An American named Bannister appears, flaunting money in Prin's face and declaring his independence from him. Lily says she is running from the law; impressed, Prin takes her to his trading post upriver.

There she meets a group of castoffs under Prin's iron-fisted rule. Among them is a Chinese named Chang Tai, who is surprised to see Lily and whom she seems to know, but neither lets on to knowing the other. Another is a Briton named Herbert

Island of Lost Men (Paramount, 1939): Eric Blore, J. Carrol Naish, Anthony Quinn, Anna May Wong, Broderick Crawford, Rudolph Forester

who owns a pet monkey. The Briton acts as a combination butler-valet to Prin. When his monkey takes to Lily immediately, he knows she is a decent sort. Later at dinner, when Lily admires the flowers on the table, Prin orders Herbert to go into the jungle for more. When he shows fear at doing so, Lily threatens to leave if Herbert is made to go into the jungle at night. Prin relents and Herbert swears eternal loyalty to Lily.

Lily and Chang Tai meet secretly. Lily tells of the medal as belonging to her house, figuring her father must be somewhere in Prin's territory. Spying on Prin in his room, Lily discovered where he keeps his valuables. When he is away, she goes to his room and finds the money her father had been accused of stealing. She again meets with Chang and they surmise that the general is at Takwack, Prin's post forty miles upriver. Prin had just appointed another man to take over that post, but Chang Tai gets him to believe he is making a play for Lily, so he is sent instead. That way he can rescue the general if he is there.

Meanwhile, Bannister appears at the post, having found out about the money, and threatens Prin with blackmail unless he gets half the loot. He also tells Prin that a secret service agent named Chang Tai was in Singapore looking for the general some time earlier. Prin orders Tai and the general killed. Prof. Sen overhears this order, however, and has some natives follow the killer to dispose of him first. Prin's operative in Singapore radios him that Lily is being sought by the police because she is really Gen. Ling's daughter, Kim.

Prof. Sen then brings to Prin the head of Frobenius, the man sent to murder Tai and the general. Bannister tells Prin his days are numbered, but Prin decides to take care of things himself.

At Takwack, Tai finds the general and apprises him of the situation, then takes him away.

Back at the post, Prin gets the drop on Bannister and knocks him over the head with a gun butt and throws him into a water-filled pit. He is found in time by Herbert and the professor.

Prin takes Lily for a boat ride where he reveals that he knows her true identity so that she must die. Just then they are overtaken by Bannister and Sen in another boat. At the post, Bannister tells Prin to give him the money, but the money is gone. Kim Ling confesses to having stolen it, but refuses to tell where she hid it. Word gets to Prin that the police are on their way, believing the general and his daughter to be at the post. Prin and Bannister agree to join forces. When he finds out it was the monkey that revealed Bannister's earlier plight, Prin shoots it. Tai then shows up with the news of the general's death. Alone with Kim in her room, however, he tells her that he lives and is nearby.

Prin allows Tai and Kim to leave in one of his boats, along with the money, so that there will be no evidence against him when the police arrive. After they leave, he tells Bannister that there was only enough gas in the boat to get them to the river bend, where the hostile natives would be waiting. All they would have to do is go pick up the money later.

As the natives prepare to attack the post, Sen tells Prin that he had checked the gas in the boat and filled the tank. Prin shoots him and then discovers that all the guns in the place have been thrown in the river by Herbert in revenge for his pet monkey's death. There is only one revolver with one bullet remaining. Bannister grabs it, but Prin talks him into playing a hand of cards to see who gets to leave and who stays. Prin wins the hand, but Bannister backs down as the natives attack. He shoots himself in the head, leaving Prin defenseless. Prin goes mad, shouting, "I am your king!" as he steps outside and receives a spear in his chest.

Print status: Available on video.

Better direction could have made this a much more exciting film; little real action is depicted, though the promise of it is almost constant. The acting is of a high level, however, since all concerned were proven character actors. Comic relief is supplied by the inimitable Eric Blore (1887–1959), he of the twisted sneer, who never needed a monkey as support, and does quite well without "the little nipper" in several scenes. The photography by Karl Struss (1891–1981), the veteran of Germany's golden age of the 1920s, is appropriately gloomy. The final shot depicting Prin's death shows only his shadow on the building wall as a spear strikes him. Anna May, as usual, stands out in all her scenes, though she has little to do or say once she arrives at Prin's dwelling. With her beauty and fine clothes, she is well-named "Lily," for she looks like one in a field of weeds compared to the dregs who populate Prin's trading post. This was the last time she sang in a film, and her final picture for Paramount, with whom she was most associated in the thirties.

Chinese Garden Festival

Republic; Released December 24, 1940; 10 minutes
Meet the Stars Number One. *Director/Producer*: Harriet Parsons
Cast: Rosalind Russell, John Garfield, Anna May Wong, Mary Pickford, Jane Withers, Dolores Del Rio, Patricia Morison, the Brewster Twins, Gertrude Neisen, Kay Aldridge, Buddy Rogers, Mary Beth Hughes, Maria Ouspenskaya, Walter Pidgeon, Georgia Carroll, Dorothy Lamour, Cesar Romero, Mary Martin, Ona Munson, William Bakewell, Rita Hayworth, Beulah Bondi, Charles Coburn, King Kennedy, Vera Vague, Herta Margot, Cliff Nazarro, Ann Hunter.
The Exhibitor, December 25, 1940: "It packs the usual amount of audience appeal and should prove an entertaining adjunct to any theatre's program."

Synopsis: Cliff Navarro directs Vera Vague to Pickfair, where a Chinese benefit party is in progress. It is attended by many screen personalities.

Print status: Copy extant.

Her Paramount contract over, Anna May began freelancing.

Anna May Wong officiated at the festival along with noted Chinese author Lin Yutang, Rosalind Russell and John Garfield. She appeared before a giant Buddha during the opening ceremony and later modeled a Chinese ceremonial costume. She also appeared at a tea booth run by the American Committee for Chinese War Orphans. While Harriet Parsons, the show's producer/director, was also the narrator, Anna May had no dialogue.

Ellery Queen's Penthouse Mystery

Columbia; Released March 24, 1941; 69 minutes
Director: James Hogan; *Producer*: Larry Darmour; *Screenplay*: Eric Taylor, from a story by Ellery Queen; *Camera*: James S. Brown, Jr.; *Editor*: Dwight Caldwell; *Music*: Lee Zahler
Cast: Ralph Bellamy (Ellery Queen), Margaret Lindsay (Nikki Porter), Charley Grapewin (Inspector Queen), Anna May Wong (Lois Ling), James Burke (Sgt. Velie), Eduardo Ciannelli (Count Brett), Frank Albertson (Sanders), Ann Doran (Sheila Cobb), Noel Madison (Gordon Cobb), Charles Lane (Doc Prouty), Russell Hicks (Walsh), Tom Dugan (McGrath), Mantan Moreland (Roy), Theodore Von Eltz (Jim Ritter), Richard Loo (Tuan Yen Sun).
The New York Times, March 7, 1941: "…a flimsily fabricated affair of dubious ventriloquist and Chinese treasures…."
Variety, March 19, 1941: "…Anna May Wong handles a minor role with ease."

Synopsis: An American ventriloquist named Cobb is entrusted by a group of Chinese with taking some gems to New York to sell to get money for needed supplies. He arrives there two days early and

Ellery Queen's Penthouse Mystery (Columbia, 1941): Margaret Lindsay, Charles Lane, unidentified actor, Anna May Wong, unidentified actor

phones Miss Ling, the Chinese representative there, to tell of his arrival.

Two days later, Sheila Cobb, his daughter, goes to Ellery Queen to tell him her father has disappeared. She has two letters which were sent to him. One says "Appointed Place — Serpent;" the other, "Appointed Place — Pig." The three go to Cobb's penthouse suite. While they are there, three men come to take Cobb's trunk to Chicago, so they believe Cobb had sudden business there, until the trunk is opened and his body found inside. They call police. No jewels are found among his belongings, so they feel robbery was the motive behind his murder. They speak with Cobb's agent, Walsh, who tells them that the ventriloquist was also a soldier of fortune performing odd jobs on the side. Ellery notices the notes were written with a brush; only an Asian would do that, so he seeks a Chinese man. Walsh says he knows of no Asian friends of Cobb's in New York.

Later, Walsh meets with one Count Brett and tells him what has happened. Each blames the other for Cobb's death. They figure the gems must still be in the penthouse, so Brett goes there to search for them.

Ellery and his secretary Nikki quarrel and she quits. She goes to Sheila, who has the hotel bellboy, who is really a reporter, tell her of following Cobb from China. He saw two other people interested in Cobb aboard ship — a woman and Brett. The woman is an old friend of Cobb's, but no one knows Count Brett. Nikki goes to the penthouse; Brett is already there searching for the gems. When the medical examiner comes for the body, Nikki hides outside. Miss Ling is also out there; she grabs Nikki and a catfight ensues. The men separate them and Nikki calls the police. Brett leaves the back way. Inspector Queen, Ellery's father, is told by Ling to arrest Nikki as a thief. When Ling refuses to answer questions without counsel present, she is taken to police headquarters. She is cleared by the Chinese embassy and consulate. Told she should not have gone to the penthouse, she replies that she was sworn to secrecy in the matter. The gems Cobb brought were to be left at the customs house in San Francisco because the duty on them would be $300,000. He was to bring her the receipt and collect the money from her. Inspector Queen thinks Cobb may have sold the jewels elsewhere and still hoped to collect the money from Ling. Queen tells Ling to give him a list of the jewels so that he can pass it around. Anyone trying to sell any of them will then be caught. When another note arrives for Cobb, Ellery has police put a phony ad in the Chinese daily saying that the appointed place has been forgotten; meet at the penthouse tomorrow afternoon.

Meanwhile, Ritter, a card sharp associate of Walsh's, overhears him and Brett talking of their scheme. He concocts his own plot for getting the jewels, but is killed by an unknown assailant at Brett's place. When cops arrive, one of them feels he knows the man; he finally recognizes him as "Corey the Magician," a one-time headliner.

Ellery visits Walsh and asks if he knew Corey; Walsh says he has not seen him in years. Queen tells him to be at the penthouse that afternoon. As Ellery leaves, Walsh refers to the dead man as "Ritter," giving himself away, but Queen says nothing. He phones Inspector Queen and tells him of Walsh's slip and to have him followed in case he realizes it and flees.

Nikki discovers that the hotel bellboy is really a reporter; at police headquarters, he reveals that he had killed Ritter in self defense when the latter caught him snooping around Count Brett's apartment.

Brett and Walsh's black servant are brought in by Sgt. Velie and put in a back room while the others — Miss Ling, Sheila Cobb and Nikki — gather in the main room. When the Chinese man arrives, Ling admits him. Inside, Queen tells him that Cobb is dead and wants to know about the jewels. The man says they are still at the customs house in San Francisco and produces a receipt.

Print status: Available on video.

Although given featured billing, Anna May does not have a lot of screen time in this entertaining "B" movie. Seen mainly in the first half of the film, she adds the necessary exotic touch and performs capably as usual, even getting to speak some Chinese in her final scene. For the second and last time, she shares scenes with Margaret Lindsay.

The Ellery Queen series of "B" pictures was mildly successful. Prior to the four films in which Ralph Bellamy (1904–1991) portrayed the character, there had been but two unrelated films. After Bellamy left the series, William Gargan (1905–1979) took over the role for three more pictures.

Picture People #8

RKO; Released March 28, 1941; 10 minutes
Cast: Ginny Sims, Kay Kyser, Jimmy Durante, Victor McLaglen, Lupe Velez, Anna May Wong, Irving Cobb, Tex Ritter, Dick Foran, "Big Boy" Williams, Bill Elliott, Rosemary Lane.

Anna May is seen playing Chinese checkers with one of her younger brothers and showing her Chinese garden.

Print status: unknown

Bombs Over Burma

Producers Releasing Corporation; Released June 5, 1942; 67 minutes

Director: Joseph H. Lewis; *Producers*: Alfred Stevens and Arthur Alexander; *Screenplay*: Milton Raison and Joseph H. Lewis, based on a story by Milton Raison; *Photography*: Robert Cline; *Settings*: Fred Prea; *Editor*: Charles Henkel, Jr.; *Sound Engineer*: Corson Jowett; *Makeup*: Harry Ross; *Assistant Director*: Seymour Ross; *Musical Director*: Lee Zahler

Cast: Anna May Wong (Lin Ying), Noel Madison (Mehoi), Leslie Dennison (Sir Roger Howe), Nedrick Young (Slim Jenkins), Dan Seymour (Pete Braganza), Frank Lackteen (Hallam), Judith Gibson (Lucy Dell), Dennis Moore (Tom Whitley), Connie Leon (Ma Sing), Hayward Soo Hoo (Ling Sing), Richard Loo (Col. Kim), Paul Fung (Toy Vendor).

Re-released in 1948.

Harrison's Reports July 18, 1942: "The formula story is one of espionage, with a smattering of mystery."

The New York Times, August 10, 1942: "...the producers have spliced in the ancient plot device used in 'Shanghai Express' ... with contemporary overtones of war ... and Anna May Wong stare suspiciously at each other and tell the audience what it already knew three reels before."

Synopsis: Lin Ying works for the Chinese Resistance while masquerading as a teacher in an elementary school in Chungking during World War II. She is about to be reassigned to another district when bombs start falling. The class is rushed out, but one of the children remains behind playing games. Lin Ying notices the child missing and comes back to find him. The little boy is strafed with bullets before Lin Ying can reach him. While holding his body, she is given orders for her next assignment. In Lashio, she boards a bus driven by an American. The passengers range in character from suave

Bombs Over Burma (PRC, 1942): Nedrick Young, Anna May Wong

to seedy, looking like a "Casablanca" on wheels.

Driving through the countryside, they get waved on by workers in the field, in a show of patriotism. A bridge washes out and they are forced to stay in a monastery. During dinner, it is announced that the distributor is missing, and they might be there a while. Bombs start to drop, destroying the bridge, but unscathed, they go back to dinner. Sabotage is announced as they all recline in the evening. The head monk mentions how important the next shipment to Chungking is as Sir Roger listens and comments. Lin Ying makes attempts to work out rhyme and reason with the bus driver. They become casual acquaintances as he professes his heart is for the Chinese cause. Later, when all are sleeping, the head monk goes into a secret room with a radio transmitter. He suspects people in the party of being the enemy. Waking Lin Ying, he places a finger over her lips to be quiet, and then he shows her to the room. They are being watched. It is in the room that Lin Ying is informed that the cargo shipment is a decoy, and that the word was spread intentionally. Sir Roger, claiming to be a representative of his government, hid his dispatch case and cries foul that it is missing. One of the passengers is about to expose the spy to the driver when he is knifed in the back. The decoy convoy rolls closer to its destination, as the guests in the monastery try to figure out who is responsible for the killing. Sir

Bombs Over Burma (PRC, 1942): Anna May Wong, Hayward Soo Hoo

Roger and his assistant catch the monk coming out of the secret room, and then plan to cast suspicion on him. The assistant brings Lin Ying to the room, showing her the radio and accusing the police. When she tries to run, Sir Roger grabs her and orders them both tied up. Slim, the driver, comes looking for breakfast, but finds Lin Ying and the monk tied up and accused of being spies. Lin Ying tries to convince him that he is wrong, while Sir Roger is heard sending messages with an electric razor. Slim unties the pair and faces Sir Roger, explaining Lin Ying's accusations. Lin Ying challenges Sir Roger, saying that she will give her life by riding in the first truck of the convoy. Sir Roger agrees to go also.

The two, along with Slim, meet up with the convoy and take over the first truck. Lin Ying offers to take the wheel so Slim can save himself, but he informs her that he is in it till the end. Sir Roger jumps out as the bombers fly overhead, and Lin Ying tells Slim that he has been watched for some time, and that he is working for German intelligence. Fleeing over the hill, Sir Roger becomes surrounded by local field workers wielding the tools of their trade. He cowers as he sees the seriousness in the faces of those around him. He kneels on the ground as if to plead for mercy, but the laborers begin to hack at him with their tools. When no bombs are dropped, Lin Ying informs Slim that the planes were American planes, and they were warned of the attack the opposing forces diverted. The movie ends with the monk telling Lin Ying that there will always be a road into the heart of China.

Print status: Available on video.

The war footage with people running in chaos could have been taken from Vietnam War footage. It is short, but realistic. When Anna holds the dead child, her facial expressions move from shaken to sorrow and back again, in a realistic way. She had not lost the magic of her silent film days, being able to tell a story in her face. To say this is typical Poverty Row fare from P.R.C. does this justice, in that it is a nice tight little story that one would enjoy watching in the middle of the night. On the bus, Anna says that China will never be conquered. Though this may have been put in to support the Chinese, it showed truth in that no matter how downtrodden China may have been, it is too big to take over.

Lady from Chungking

Producers Releasing Corporation; Released December 21, 1942; 71 minutes

Director: William Nigh; *Producers*: Alfred Stern and Arthur Alexander; *Screenplay*: Sam Robins, based on a story by Sam Robins and Milton Raison; *Photography*: Marcel LePicard, A.S.C.; *Settings By*: James Autwied; *Sound Engineer*: Corson Jowett; *Makeup*: Harry Ross; *Editor*: Charles Henkel, Jr.; *Assistant Director*: Lou Perloff; *Master of Properties*: George Bahr; *Musical Director*: Lee Zahler

Cast: Anna May Wong (Madame Kwan Mei), Harold Huber (General Kaimura), Mae Clarke (Lavara), Rick Vallin (Rodney Carr), Paul Bryar (Pat O'Rourke), Ted Hecht (Lt. Shimoto), Louis [Ludwig] Donath (Hans Gruber), James Leong (Chen), Archie Got (Mochow), Walter Soo Hoo (Lu-Chi).

Re-released in 1948 as *Guerrilla Command*.

Harrison's Reports, December 5, 1942: " The film is slow-paced and void of virile action, but it manages to maintain the interest fairly well, despite the familiarity of the plot."

Variety, January 20, 1943: "This is just grist for the grinds."

Synopsis: Madame Kwan Mei works with the Chinese underground against occupying Japanese forces. She is working in the rice fields one day when a boy is mistreated by a Japanese soldier. Kwan Mei intervenes so that the boy is not harmed further. As the coolies line up for water, weapons are surreptitiously passed to them by the man at the water trough. Kwan Mei cautions that the weapons are to be used later, not now.

In the village, General Kaimura arrives at the hotel and is welcomed by the German owner, Hans Gruber. Just then an American plane appears, chased by three Japanese planes. The American shoots down a Japanese plane before being hit. One flier parachutes safely, the other is wounded by the Japanese overseer with a rifle. The overseer is killed by a coolie and his body hidden in a ditch. The coolies get to the flier first, but the Japanese are close behind. The flier turns to shoot at them, but Kwan Mei deflects his hand. It pleases the Japanese that a Chinese is so wise; Kwan Mei plays up to them as the flier is

Lady from Chungking (PRC, 1942): Magazine ad

taken away. The lieutenant tells Kwan Mei that Gen. Kaimura is attracted to women of intelligence and breeding. Looking at her hands, he sees they are not those of a worker. Kwan Mei says she is a noblewoman who lost her family and property in the invasion. "Perhaps a little scrubbing around the neck and even a general might see possibilities," says the officer.

In the town, a singer from the hotel takes a pilot's cap from a little Chinese boy and puts it in her bag as soldiers pass by. Asking where he got the cap, the boy merely spouts some Japanese propaganda he has been taught. Later in the hotel she sees the American flier being brought in under guard and knows the cap to be his.

Kaimura interviews the flier and gets the usual flippant wartime wisecracks for answers. After he is taken out, Kaimura asks the officer about his arrangements and the other flier. The lieutenant says he will take care of the matter. Concerning companionship for the general, he says, "I think I have a surprise for you."

Meeting Kwan Mei in the street, the officer is told she is Lady Kwan Tai; the officer is pleased and suggests some better clothes to wear for the general.

The singer finds the Chinese guerrilla hideout and returns the flier's cap. Kwan Mei tells her the boy got it in the rice fields; it belongs to the flier who was killed. The singer says she took the cap so that the child would not be harmed. Kwan Mei understands that the singer did not want the Japanese to learn anything: "I've seen them torture these kids before." She is pre-

Lady from Chungking (PRC, 1942): Anna May Wong, Harold Huber

vented from leaving by one of the men who wants to be sure she will not tell the Japanese what she has seen. "I'm no one's ally; I work alone," she assures him. Kwan Mei lets her go; the men feel she will go to the enemy. Kwan Mei says her intuition tells her that she will not. Kwan Mei is sure that Kaimura is there for an important reason and cautions the guerrillas to carry on but to be more cautious. She then tends to the wounded flier in another room.

The singer goes to the window of the imprisoned flier's cell. She gives him cigarettes and they chat. He is amazed to learn that she has never been to the U.S.; she says she learned English "out of a sailor's manual." When he asks about his buddy, she says she does not know, "But if he's anything like you, he can take care of himself."

She sings for Kaimura in the hotel restaurant and he invites her to sit with him. After several drinks, they go to the general's room. Kwan Mei is there; the singer, in her cups, recognizes her and begins to spout about the flier's hat. Kwan Mei corrects her and says she means the coolie hat worn earlier by Kwan Mei. She begins to play on the general's vanity; the singer leaves. Kaimura says Kwan Mei's face reminds him of the Great Wall of China with its fragile but durable beauty. He goes on about the New Order being spread by Japan: "Your destiny, madam, will be linked with mine." He kisses her hand; the officer interrupts with news that a coolie has talked and the overseer's body has been found in a ditch in the field. The general says he will handle that tomorrow; Kwan Mei tries to get military information from him, but he is tipsy and not clear in his answer. Gruber takes Kwan Mei back to her room, where he says she is playing with fire. She replies that he cares only for himself and reminds him of their deal—he is to supply arms and ammunition for the guerrillas and be paid in American money. He is afraid and tells her to leave immediately; she calms his fears by saying she will be careful so that he leads a long life.

After he leaves, the Japanese lieutenant threatens Kwan Mei, knowing she was in the rice fields when the overseer was killed. When she refuses to reveal the killer, he says he can return her to the fields or have her shot. "Would you disillusion the general?" she asks. The officer backs off.

The next day several coolies are led out to be executed by a firing squad. Kwan Mei cleverly manages to save the lives of the young ones, but three old men are shot. As the rescued ones depart, Kwan Mei whispers to one, "Meeting tonight."

At dinner with the general, Kwan Mei pours a sleeping potion in his drink after learning of the troop movements. While he sleeps, she goes to the guerrilla hideout, where one young man is questioning her loyalty. On her way out, Kwan Mei meets the singer and asks for her aid in freeing the American flier. The singer says she would like to live, but is reminded that the future is all that matters. Kwan Mei departs without getting a real commitment. She goes to the window of the flier's cell and reveals her true identity to him. She also tells of the troop train due the next night and says his escape has been arranged. He will go and organize a Flying Tigers attack on the Japanese.

The singer goes to Gruber, threatening to tell Kaimura of his deal with the guerrillas. He still refuses to help, so she pulls a gun on him and forces him to open the door of the flier's cell. As soon as he does, he says he will tell the general and is decked by the flier, who flees with the woman. Gruber calls for the guards; one hits the singer, but she is carried off by the flier. The other guard is dispatched by a guerrilla outside the hotel. A man waiting in a jeep takes the flier and woman to safety.

At the guerrilla hideout Kwan Mei defends her actions as the only way to get information from Kaimura; a guard calls out that some Japanese are approaching. Kwan Mei proves her loyalty by going out and killing one with a knife as the others watch. With all satisfied, she tells them to go ahead with their plan to blow up a bridge and get the fliers to their base so that they can return with air support.

Returning to Kaimura's room, Kwan Mei tells the general she has been waiting all the time when he awakens. The general kisses Kwan Mei. The officer appears and tells of the flier's escape and is ordered to find him. Later the lieutenant tells Kaimura that Gruber was seen in the cellar at the time of the flier's escape. The general orders that Gruber be eliminated. The lieutenant adds that there was a woman also present and holds up a bracelet, which Kwan Mei immediately claims as hers, saying it was a gift from the general, which she would hate to lose. Kaimura embraces Kwan Mei when an explosion is heard. She says it may be guerrillas; the general says he can handle them by wiping out the village. When planes are heard, he calls out that they are Japanese. Kwan Mei responds that they are Flying Tigers. Another explosion causes the lady to remark that it is Kaimura's troop train being blown up. "How do you know all this?" "I am Madame Kwan Mei." Kaimura's jaw drops; he knows her to be one of China's foremost patriots. Kwan Mei shoots him, but is grabbed by the officer as she exits the room. The general introduces her to the lieutenant and orders him to take her to the courtyard and shoot her; he himself will give the order to fire. When the officer returns with the report that all is ready, Kaimura muses, "Sometimes I wonder what I would do without you!" and promptly shoots him dead.

He goes to the window to order Kwan Mei's execution. She stands defiantly, preaching that many more will rise to replace her; after she is shot her spirit continues the speech. Up above, the general finally succumbs to his wound.

Print status: Available on video.

This is the last time Anna May's character died in a film, and the second and last time she was kissed by a Caucasian, albeit one masquerading as an Asian. The actress brought the requisite degree of class needed for her character, lifting this production a notch above most of the studio's productions, despite the use of stock footage.

Veteran director William Nigh (1881–1955) directed Anna May for the third and last time. New York–born Harold Huber (1910–1959), capable of playing heavies or humorous policemen, here fails to convince as a Japanese; his accent is inaccurate. He had appeared in yellowface before, but as Chinese characters, in *The Good Earth* (1937) and *The Adventures of Marco Polo* (1938).

Impact

United Artists; Released September 26, 1949; 111 minutes

Director: Arthur Lubin; *Producer*: Leo C. Popkin; *Screenplay*: Dorothy Reid and Jay Dratler; *Original Story*: Jay Dratler; *Cinematography*: Ernest Lazslo; *Art Director*: Rudi Feld; *Editor*: Arthur H. Nadel; *Musical Score*: Michel Michelet; *Costumes*: Maria P. Donovan; *Orchestrations Conducted By*: Michel Perriere; *Orchestrations*: Herschel Gilbert; *Song*: "It Can't Be" Lyrics and Music by Leo C. Popkin and Chuck Gould; *Makeup*: Lee Greenway; *Assistant Director*: Maurice M. Suess

Cast: Brian Donlevy (Walter Williams), Ella Raines (Marsha Peters), Charles Coburn (Lt. Quincy), Helen Walker (Irene Williams), Anna May Wong (Su Lin), Mae Marsh (Mrs. Peters), Tony Barrett (Jim Torrance), William Wright (District Attorney), Robert Warwick (Capt. Callahan), Philip Ahn (Ah Sing), Art Baker (Eldredge), Erskine Sanford (Dr. Bender), Jason Robards (Judge), Glenn Vernon (Ed), Linda Johnson (Telephone Operator), Ruth Robinson (Apartment Manager), Lucius Cooke (Burke), Tom

Greenway (Moving Van Driver), Ben Welden (Moving Van Driver), Hans Herbert (Station Master), Joel Friedkin (Uncle Ben), Joe Kirk (Hotel Clerk), Bill Ruhl (Fingerprint Expert), Mary Landa (Della), Harry Cheshire (Irene's Attorney).

Harrison's Reports, March 19, 1949: "Well produced and acted ... is hampered by a long drawn-out story.... Ella ... with the aid of Coburn, locates Anna May Wong ... who furnishes them with positive proof that Helen and Barrett had plotted Donlevy's murder."

The New York Times, March 21, 1949: "...Brian Donlevy has all the animation and charm of an automaton.... And Ella Raines' performance as the Idaho small-town girl who makes him believe again in women reminds one of that state's most famous crop ... let's label 'Impact' a dull thud."

Synopsis: Walter Williams, auto magnate, has the world by the tail. His expertise in production gives him a full rein with the Board. At home he feels the same confidence, but that is where similarities end. He comes home to find his wife in bed with a toothache. She perks up at his gift of jewelry, and asks how his board meeting went. While explaining what happened, he knocks over a vase and is heard by the maid, Su Lin, repeating what he told his associates. Su Lin hears only the noise and the seeming threat, but not the innocent meaning. Williams convinces his wife to go to Denver with him. She agrees, but sends him on ahead to complete his errand for the company first, offering to go by cab and meet him in Sausalito.

When she does not show up at the appointed time, Walter calls home to find that she is still not well, but would like him to give her Aunt Margaret's favorite nephew a lift to Denver. He then calls his secretary, Della, and gives her instructions to have roses sent to his wife, Irene, every day, along with a note. That would also play into the twisted plot later.

The nephew, Jim Torrance, steps out of a cab, and asks the driver to take his luggage ahead to the Airport Hotel under the name of Jack Burns. Walking towards his car, Williams spots Jim and asks him along. Hours later, at a roadside inn, Walter gets out and asks Jim if he wants something to eat. Jim says no, he will wait in the car. Inside, Walter orders a sandwich and Coke, then calls home to no answer. Calling down to the front desk, he leaves another innocuous message for his wife which would work against him later. In the meantime, Torrance gets out of the car, puts a slow leak into a tire and climbs into the driver's seat. Walt returns and offers to let Jim drive. When the tire runs low, Jim pulls over and tells Walt about the tire. After the tire is changed, Jim tells Walter he lost something on the ground. As Williams bends over, Jim hits him over the head with a tire iron, then pushes him down an embankment. He throws Williams' briefcase after him, but has to go down to retrieve the keys to the car. As he is getting ready to leave, a moving van pulls over and the drivers ask him if he needs help. Frenzied, Jim speeds off and runs into an oncoming truck. The car explodes into flames. Meanwhile, Williams awakens and climbs up the embankment with his briefcase and climbs onto the back on the van.

Western Union wires the news that Walter Williams is dead. It is up to Lt. Quincy to inform Irene Williams of her husband's death. She takes it very hard, though almost slipping with a detail of which she could not have been aware.

Williams gets off the van in a stop in Nevada, and sees a newspaper headline telling of his death. He walks away, leaving his briefcase on the van, which pulls away.

Mrs. Williams, believing her lover to be still alive, tries to locate him. Su Lin informs her that telegrams of sympathy are arriving, and then announces the arrival of Lt. Quincy again, who is there to ask some routine questions.

Impact (United Artists, 1949): Lobby card

Williams walks to a train station and asks how soon the next train to San Francisco will arrive. He is told it will be the next morning. On a hunch, he calls Aunt Margaret, pretending to be Jim. His suspicions become solid now; his wife tried to have him killed.

In Kansas City, the moving van drivers find the briefcase and call the police. Torrance's fingerprints turn up, and now Quincy believes Williams was murdered. He begins to suspect a tie to Mrs. Williams and lays the groundwork to trap her.

Williams winds up in Larkspur, Idaho, whose sign proudly boasts a population of 4,501. He takes a drink at a gas station water fountain and hears banging in the background. After telling the mechanic that is no way to treat an engine, he discovers the mechanic to be a woman. He challenges her to let him look at the car and fixes it with the turn of a screw. Finding out that she is a soldier's widow, he takes a job there and begins a new life as Bill. He takes a room with the woman, Marsha, and her mom, and settles down to a peaceful anonymous life.

Sheila Graham breaks in with a radio news flash that Irene Williams is to stand trial in the death of her husband, while the police look for Torrance. Marsha's mother finds out that Bill is Walter Williams and hints very strongly that he needs to go back to San Francisco in an attempt to explain the truth to Lt. Quincy and the police. He does so; in the courtroom, his wife is brought in, and seeing Walter alive, points an accusing finger at him, saying that he killed Torrance out of jealousy. The police hold Williams on suspicion of murder; Irene is eventually released.

Marsha and Quincy visit Walter in prison, trying to get him to admit everything. Seeing the hope in Marsha's eyes, Walter relents. The lieutenant and Marsha go on a fact finding mission that leads them to the scene of the crime off of the highway, and then back to San Francisco to the Immigration Dept. to look at Su Lin's alien card. They head to Chinatown and come to the home of Ah Sing, the maid's uncle. He denies that she is there, when all the while she is listening in the other room. After the pair leaves, Ah Sing chastises his niece for harboring a secret. Williams stands trial as his wife looks on. All of his innocuous notes and deeds come back to haunt him as he sits hopelessly in the witness stand.

Su Lin, sitting in the courtroom, sees Marsha looking at her and runs out. Marsha follows her; both get into cabs and a chase ensues. They leave their cabs and the chase resumes on foot through the streets of Chinatown. They wind up at the home of Ah Sing. This time he promises to produce his niece, who is afraid she can only hurt Williams' case, not help it. Upon revealing all she knows about Irene Williams, Quincy is able to tie Irene to Torrance, but must also tie her to his alias, Jack Burns. Going through luggage left at the Airport Hotel, the connection is made, and Mrs. Williams is called to the stand. With aggressive questioning by Walter's attorney, her proud and defiant attitude melts and she is confronted with her role in the whole affair. The prosecution asks for a dismissal of the charges brought against Williams and asks that charges of conspiracy to commit murder be brought against Irene. Walter is congratulated by his business associate and he asks Marsha if she could be happy living in Denver.

Print status: Shown on American television.

Ching Wah Lee was the uncredited technical director on this film and certainly provided valuable information. His antique shop was in Chinatown through the sixties, and he is remembered as Chinatown's noted historian. He is also listed among those who remembered the 1906 Earthquake, and is still remembered by those who grew up in Chinatown. The details in this movie, whether by his direction or others, are accurate in every detail.

This was Anna May Wong's first character role and first supporting role since *Shanghai Express*. The part originally called for a Swedish maid, as the story was set in New York. When the locale was changed to San Francisco, the character's nationality was altered to take advantage of that city's famed Chinatown. Anna May was kidded about playing a Swede, but recalled Swedish native Warner Oland's many roles as a Chinese.

Taking realism a step further, signs pop up for Pabst Blue Ribbon Beer, Exide Batteries, Borden's Ice Cream, and United Air Lines. Coca Cola machines and Mobilgas pumps are also used. Brian Donlevy hitched a ride on Bekins Van and Storage, which has been around for over 100 years. On the truck can be seen "Since '91" (1891). Apparently, little or no disguising was used on location, though the town of Larkspur, Idaho does not exist, at least at this late date. The movie, though noir, has a happy ending. Anna May's part, though small and filled with artificially broken English, is key to the movie.

Brian Donlevy (1899–1972) was best known as a heavy, most notably as Sgt. Markoff in *Beau Geste* (1939) for which he received a Best Supporting Actor nomination. He showed his versatility with several good guy parts and some comedies.

Portrait in Black

Universal Pictures; Released June 6, 1960; 112 minutes; Color

Portrait in Black (1960)

Director: Michael Gordon; *Producer*: Ross Hunter; *Screenplay*: Ivan Goff and Ben Roberts, based on their play; *Cinematography*: Russell Metty; *Music*: Frank Skinner; *Costumes*: Jean Louis; *Art Director*: Richard H. Riedel; *Editor*: Miton Carruth; *Set Decorator*: Julia Heron; *Makeup*: Bud Westmore; *Musical Supervisor*: Joseph Gershenson

Cast: Lana Turner (Sheila Cabot), Anthony Quinn (Dr. David Rivera), Sandra Dee (Catherine Cabot), John Saxon (Blake Richards), Richard Basehart (Howard Mason), Lloyd Nolan (Matthew Cabot), Ray Walston (Cob O'Brien), Virginia Grey (Miss Lee), Anna May Wong (Tani), Dennis Kohler (Peter Cabot), Paul Birch (Detective), John Wengraf (Dr. Kessler), Richard Norris (Mr. Corbin), James Nolan, Robert Lieb (Detectives), John McNamara (Minister), Charles Thompson (Sid), George Womack (Foreman), Henry Quan (Headwaiter), Elizabeth Chan (Chinese Dancer), Harold Goodwin, Jack Ryan (Patrolmen).

Variety, June 8, 1960: "…is a contrived murder melodrama with psychological character interplay that is more psycho than logical. Anna May Wong … has chosen a thankless vehicle … the unnecessary part of a suspicious housekeeper."

The New York Times, July 28, 1960: "…its glossy, manufactured figures dulled by anguished infidelity, superficial suspense and dialogue reminiscent of the confession magazines…. Miss Wong is merely inscrutable as the suspicious housekeeper."

Synopsis: Matthew Cabot, a San Francisco shipping magnate, is bedridden and in great pain most of the time and very bitter about it. His wife Sheila has been having an affair with Dr. Rivera, the family physician. When she suddenly gets a driver's permit, her husband wants to know why, since she has a chauffeur. She can give no good reason.

Dr. Rivera gets an good opportunity in Zurich; he cannot decide but is afraid of what he will do if he stays. He tells Sheila that the drug which he administers to her husband can be fatal in overdose, but also undetectable in an autopsy. They look at each other. Cut to Cathy, Sheila's stepdaughter, who has just learned from her boyfriend that he has gotten a contract from her father. He owns some tugboats which are needed to guide Cabot's large ships into the bay.

Cabot dies and no foul play is suspected. The night after, Sheila is awakened by the noise of her late husband's electric bed moving. She finds a cat in the room and figures it somehow hit the switch. As she chases the cat downstairs, she meets Tani, her housekeeper, coming up. Tani says the phone from Mr. Cabot's rang. Sheila's eyes widen; Tani's narrow.

Howard Mason, Cabot's business manager, visits Sheila and confesses his love for her, proposing marriage. She refuses him; he says he is confident and can wait. Meanwhile, he gives the towing contract to another firm, incurring the enmity of Blake Richards, Cathy's boyfriend. Mason has his secretary lie to Blake about the contract. He also tells the young man that Cabot and he knew all along that he was using Cabot's daughter; that was why he was rejected. Blake threatens Mason; he feels that Cabot was responsible for his father's ruin and now this.

Among the sympathy letters received by Sheila is an anonymous printed one which reads: "Dear Mrs. Cabot—Congratulations on the success of your murder." She shows it to Rivera; they cannot figure out who sent it, as the postmark is their only lead. They figure that the writer will give himself away somehow; when they find him, he must be killed.

Mason's secretary meets with Cathy and Blake at a restaurant. Wishing to atone for her lie, which she did under threat of losing her job, she gives Blake some letters proving it was Mason, not Cabot, who ruined his father.

Meanwhile, Cobb and Tani continue their red herring roles.

At Rivera's office one day, Sheila gets an urgent phone call from Mason. Rivera listens on an extension as Sheila finds out

Portrait in Black (Universal, 1960): Magazine ad

that Tani told Mason of her whereabouts and that her proxy is needed for a big company meeting later that week. Mason's tone makes Rivera suspicious. Sheila tells him of Mason's proposal. Sheila mentions that Mason plays golf regularly at a course near where the note was mailed. Rivera tells her to go home and call Mason and have him bring the proxy to her the night of the meeting. Sheila makes sure no one is home that night, but does not know that Cathy's date with Blake is postponed as he has to work. He tells Cathy to go home and he will call her later. She goes to the Yacht Club instead.

Mason gets the proxy from Sheila, and she signals Rivera as planned. The doctor rigged a traffic light and ambushes Mason. Hearing a loud knock at her door shortly afterward, Sheila opens it to find Mason, unharmed. He tells her of the shooting and that he got a partial license plate number. He tells her to call the cops. As she is about to do so, the phone rings. It is Rivera, but Sheila pretends it is Cathy and tips off the doctor. He tells her not to phone the police and to keep Mason there. She tells Mason that Cathy is near a police station and will alert them. A few minutes later, Cathy really calls and Mason takes the call. Realizing the truth, he accuses Sheila of sending the assassin and forces her to tell who called earlier. Mason says that Rivera will not find either of them there, and raises a poker to Sheila, but is shot dead by Rivera. Sheila's little son appears, awakened by the shot; Sheila tells him it was a dream and he returns to bed. Rivera says the only way to get rid of the body is by putting it in a car and pushing it off a cliff. To do so, Sheila must drive, as Rivera needs a way to get back. He gives her a crash course in driving and she follows him to the cliff. At one point they are separated at a railroad crossing and almost discovered, but manage to continue. Rivera gets in Sheila's car and pushes Mason's over a cliff. Blake Richards is blamed for Mason's death because there is a recording of the threat he made to Mason. He shows police the papers incriminating Mason in his father's death, but they do not believe him. Blake admits he hated Mason and threatened him, but only meant to beat him up. He was outside the meeting hall the night of Mason's murder, but has no witnesses.

When the police question Sheila at home, Cathy comes in and tells of hearing from Mason at a later time than Sheila stated. Sheila covers for this error and the police leave. Sheila's son tells Cathy of his "dream"; that Mason and mom were yelling at each other and there was a loud shot after he awoke, but mom told him it was a dream. Cathy asks Tani about this and learns that the housekeeper was given the night off. Cathy makes an appointment with Dr. Rivera and reveals that Sheila is the killer. Rivera tries to confuse her and then they determine that it took two people to move the body, and that they would have needed two cars to do the deed. Rivera reminds Cathy that Sheila does not drive and Cathy leaves.

His nerves on edge, Rivera hears the Hippocratic oath repeated in his mind. He goes to Sheila and tells her he has given up his practice and is going away. Sheila's son comes running in to tell his mother that Cobb just drove back from Seal Rock in twelve-and-a-half minutes; he also has a letter, which he reads aloud: "Congratulations on the success of your second venture." She and Rivera are taken aback; Sheila gives her son over to Tani. While discussing the situation, Rivera looks out a window and sees Cobb putting packed bags into a car trunk. He tells Sheila to call Cobb to the room without letting him know he was seen. She questions the chauffeur and finds he was leaving to avoid some bookies to whom he owed money. He resigns his position and says he is going to Los Angeles. Rivera allows Sheila to write him a reference letter. He then asks Cobb for his Los Angeles address as he has friends who could use a driver and says to print it so it will be legible. Cobb realizes he has no place yet and will send it along later. Under questioning from Rivera, Cobb reveals he was in the town where the first letter was mailed the night of the postmark. Rivera grabs him and asks what he was doing there and finds that he was driving Mrs. Cabot. Rivera throws him out. Sheila confesses to writing the notes; she felt she was losing Rivera and the notes was a way to keep him. Rivera is stunned at first; when he cools off he states that no one knows about them, that they are free to go. He begins kissing Sheila. Cathy suddenly appears and is shocked by what she sees; she reaches for a phone; in a pathetic display of gutlessness, Rivera begs her not to call anyone, explaining that Mason had to be killed. Cathy slowly moves up the stairs and Rivera slowly follows. She locks herself in her room and then climbs through the gabled window onto the roof. Rivera breaks through the door and continues after her. She sees Blake leaving in his car and calls after him. He returns as Rivera gets closer to Cathy. As Cathy is about to climb in another window, Sheila appears at the first one and calls to Rivera; he loses his balance and falls to his death. Sheila's fate is to be freeze-framed and turned into a negative image as the title looms upward on the screen and the studio orchestra hits yet another crescendo.

Print status: Shown on American Movie Classics.

Anna's character has nothing to do except look mysterious before disappearing. She appears in nine scenes and can be seen in the background of another. Critics at least noticed her and sympathized with her plight. For her last film, Anna May seemed to have regained the warm smile of her earlier movies. The pained look that

Portrait in Black (Universal, 1960): Anna May Wong

was obvious in some of her TV appearances was gone. While well-produced, *Portrait in Black* suffers from banal dialogue and unsympathetic characters.

Leading World War II pinup girl Lana Turner (1920–1995) was at the peak of her career, having been nominated for an Academy Award for Best Actress in *Peyton Place* (1957). She would continue appearing in films through the seventies, but only sporadically in that decade. Here she looks wonderful, but struggles with the exigencies of the script along with the rest of the cast.

Addenda

Herlock Shomes in Be-a-Live Crook (U.S.: The Limejuice Mystery, Or, Who Spat in Grandfather's Porridge?) Associated Sound Film Industries (Great Britain); Little People Burlesques No. 5 ;

The Limejuice Mystery (Associated Sound Film Industries, 1930): Anna Went Wrong, Herlock Shomes

Released February 1930; 8 minutes; Silent, with music and sound effects
Director: Jack Harrison; *Music*: Phillip Braham; Presented by Joseph Seiden
Cast: Ottorino Gorno's Marionettes as Herlock Shomes and Anna Went Wrong.

A parody of *The Return of Sherlock Holmes* (Paramount, 1929) starring Clive Brook as Holmes.

Print status: Reference print held by Library of Congress, Washington, D.C.

Proof of Anna May Wong's popularity in Britain is the female character in this curio, whose name is a pun on hers. Her costume was obviously inspired by the one the actress wore in *The Flame of Love*.

In the late 1950s–early 1960s, a Chinese-British actress emerged with the name Anna May Wong. She had parts in a few British films and television shows, then seems to have vanished. It was she who appeared in *The Savage Innocents* (1959), causing much confusion among film historians, who believe it was the American star. Author Leibfried has viewed the film at the Library of Congress and noted that the actress playing the role listed for Anna May Wong is a woman in her twenties; the original Anna May was 54 at the time. The old woman in the film sent off on an ice flow to die, whom some think was Anna May, was a Chinese actress named Marie Yang.

One silent film that is almost certainly one of Miss Wong's uncredited roles is *After Midnight*, released in September

1921 by Selznick/Select. Author Leibfried has a copy of a still, unfortunately lacking an identifying number, showing Miss Wong with Conway Tearle. A check of Tearle's filmography reveals *After Midnight* as his only vehicle containing Chinese characters. Reviews mention a Chinese girl (unbilled) who is befriended by Tearle's character and later informs him that he has been lured from his lodgings so that his sister-in-law can be kidnapped.

V

Stage Work

It was ten full years from Anna May Wong's first uncredited film role to her initial legitimate stage appearance. Even then, the choice was not hers; her agent was approached by British stage impresario Basil Dean (1888–1978) and offered a deal. Dean had acquired the rights to a play entitled *The Circle of Chalk*, which had been adapted from *Der Kreidekreis*, a 1925 German play which in turn had been based upon a 13th-century Chinese drama. Needing an actress with an Asian look, the producer chanced upon Anna's photo in a press release for *Piccadilly* [q.v.], then being filmed in London. Struck by her great beauty, he contacted her agent, who agreed to terms after some haggling. For her leading man, Dean obtained the services of a twenty-two-year-old actor from Dorking, Surrey, by way of the Central School of Speech and Drama, named Laurence Olivier (1907–1989), not yet the consummate Shakespearean interpreter known the world over.

The plot of the play concerns a tea-house girl bought by a wealthy Mandarin who outbids a young prince named Pao for her. The Mandarin is later poisoned by his wife. The girl, now a mother, is accused of the crime and condemned to death by a corrupt judge. She is saved at the last moment by Pao, now Emperor, who is the real father of the child. Dean initially faced censorship problems for failing to properly disguise a brothel as a tea-house; no easy task. It was several months before he was granted permission to produce the play.

In volume two of his autobiography, *Mind's Eye*, published in 1973, Basil Dean recalled Anna May Wong was "…lovely to look at … intelligent, anxious to learn and possessed a natural instinct for drama…" and said that she "…possessed natural grace of movement." He did not like her California accent, however, a point which was brought home on opening night, when her voice not only sounded flat to an audience used to "BBC" English, but failed to reach those in the gallery seats. Though she performed the Lotus Dance flawlessly, Dean was still regretful that he had selected a silent screen actress for the role. With 20–20 hindsight he wrote: "…any attractive English *ingénue* with good voice and gesture might well have carried the production to success.…"

The play received mixed reviews, the most hurtful being that of the *Daily Express*, which stated that neither Olivier nor Miss Wong should be allowed to sing. Others were much more kind. Alan Parsons of the *Daily Mail* wrote: "Miss Anna May Wong proved that she is an actress of deep sincerity; she has a beautiful singing voice, and even if her intonations are a little — shall we say, Californian, they are always soft and pleasant." Of the play itself, he added: "A strange, fantastic, elusive affair, whose delicate and colorful beauty is perfectly interpreted by Mr. Aubrey Hammond's exquisite setting, and the slightly Westernized Chinese music of Mr. Ernest Irving." S.R.L. of the *Morning Post* went even further:

> Not only is "The Circle of Chalk" a success that does credit to everyone concerned, but it is also a peculiarly personal one to Miss Anna May Wong, the little Chinese film star ... Miss Wong shows herself—in spite of a frank but pretty American accent—a perfect little artist—graceful, appealing, intelligent—so good that the fact of her being genuinely Chinese is the least thing.
>
> Her reception was tremendous, and her little speech of thanks in Chinese captured the more an audience that was already won. She sings, too, as beautifully as could be, and dances "such a way!"

Hubert Griffith of the *Evening Standard* devoted almost his entire review to the lead actress:

> Last night Miss Anna May Wong, the Chinese film star, came forward at the New Theatre ... as a star of the stage, in a very modern and westernized adaptation of an old Chinese play, "The Circle of Chalk," and the lesson chiefly to be learnt from the event was that an artist, however supreme in one line of business, is not necessarily supreme in another, and that acting is a trade not easily learnt.
>
> There was one moment in the evening when Miss Wong touched perfection—when she goes back to her own art, that of movement ... and gets up and silently does a long, slow dance.
>
> I have rarely seen anything more completely beautiful. Rhythm, gesture, the expressiveness of motion—she is mistress of them all. One could sit back and watch the lithe, little figure moving across the stage and see how in all the complicated movements of the dance never as much as a finger-tip departed from patterns of the highest grace of felicity.
>
> The dance was a miracle, a masterpiece. And once again, at the end of the evening, when she at first refused to make a speech at the curtain fall, the actress did so in a gesture that was again arresting in its expressiveness and beauty.
>
> Unfortunately, acting a long part was another matter. It was at first a shock to hear that the accent that falls from Celestial lips is a highly Americanized one, and then, when one gets over this as unimportant, to find that it is further an undistinguished one, clipping words leaving many of them almost inaudible. She got no variety into the long speeches, and, generally, if I may so say without unpardonable rudeness, was at her most effective when silent. I return in memory to the dance, which I thank her for as a real experience.

Opening at the New Theatre in London on March 14, 1929, *The Circle of Chalk* closed after a five-week run, on April 20. Others in the cast included George Curzon, Frank Cochrane, Marie Ault, and a Eurasian actress named Rose Quong.

The producers assured audiences of the lengths to which they went to make this work authentic with the following addition to the program:

> **The Music**
> The Chinese scale of five notes has been preserved in the music, most of which is based on the genuine Chinese tunes of antiquity. A certain amount of Western harmonic color has been added in adapting the latter to Western ears.
>
> The old Chinese plays were accompanied by continuous music—mostly on percussion instruments—in fact the plays might almost be regarded as operettes. This tradition has been upheld in the present production of "The Circle of Chalk," although a certain leniency has been exercised towards listeners, for the Chinese Theatre is a very noisy affair indeed!

Despite the mixed reviews, Anna May scored a personal triumph, as young men and women gathered outside the stage door each night to catch a glimpse of the exotic beauty. Taking the critiques seriously, she also spent £200 (about $1,000 then) on elocution lessons, forever after speaking with a broad "a."

Later that year, Anna May was contacted by noted operetta composer Franz Lehar, who wanted her to portray the role of Princess Mi in his latest work, *Das Land des Lachelns*. She regretfully declined, being otherwise occupied with her film work. She did see the play eventually, and noted this fact on the cover of her program.

Moving on to Vienna in the late summer of 1930, the busy actress starred in *Tschun-Tschi (Springtime)* at the Neues Wiener Schauspielhaus. Anna's command of German had her public eating out of the palm of her hand; the musical drama was presented daily for five consecutive weeks.

Back in New York that fall, the popular performer made her Broadway debut on October 29 at Edgar Wallace's Forrest Theatre in that celebrated British mystery writer's hugely successful gangster melodrama, *On the Spot*. Wallace (1875–1932), a former news correspondent for Reuters, was noted for the speed with which he wrote; *On the Spot* was dictated to his secretary on a ship traveling from New York to London in four days. He had spent exactly one day in Chicago, visiting crime landmarks like Al Capone's headquarters and the garage where the St. Valentine's Day Massacre had occurred. Anna May had met the famous author while in London, where they attended a performance of the play, which featured Charles Laughton as the star and one Gillian Lind in the role of the Chinese mistress. Obviously, England had no one of Anna May's uniqueness to play the part. Miss Wong was intrigued with the thought of playing the female lead in the American run, and was quick to sign a contract when offered the role upon her return from Britain. She was paid $800 per week for the first two weeks, and $1000 per week thereafter, and received co-star billing. (In March, 1931,

Anna May Wong, Jacob Feldhammer in *Tschun-Tschi*, 1930

with the widening Depression and a decrease in receipts, she agreed to a cut to $750 per week. However, it was also agreed that should receipts reach $12,500, she would receive an additional $125, and if they reached $15,000, she would again receive her $1,000 per week salary.)

Anna's co-star was none other than Crane Wilbur (1886–1973), her idol from her earliest film-going days. Wilbur was a noted playwright himself, as well as a screenwriter and director. Throughout his long and distinguished career he interspersed his acting with these other skills. Curiously, Wilbur received only $500 per week, making Anna May the highest paid member in the cast. Perhaps Mr. Wilbur should have retained her agent.

Directed by Lee Ephraim and Carol Reed, *On the Spot* proved to be as big a hit as *The Circle of Chalk* was a flop. It was a triumph with the critics as well as audiences as witnessed by the following reviews: Percy Hammond of *The New York Herald-Tribune* wrote: "A trim though gorgeous goose-flesher — ingenious — audience was enraptured." Charles Darnton of *The Evening World* enthused: "...the most fascinating of gangster melodramas ... Anna May Wong was most decorative and sympathetic as Minn Lee...."; Robert Garland of the *Telegram* raved: "A good all-around melodrama — tremendously exciting — violently emotional — taut and thrilling — a hair-raising dialogic concoction." Brooks Atkinson of *The New York Times* was somewhat more reserved in his appraisal, stating: "It has remained for an Englishman to see through the sham of American racketeering — it is refreshingly amusing."

Anna May Wong in *On the Spot*, 1930

After running for 167 performances on Broadway, the play moved to the Majestic Theatre in Brooklyn on March 23, 1931, and from there to Philadelphia, Pittsburgh, Chicago, San Francisco, and Los Angeles, where it had two runs at the Belasco Theatre, in August and September 1931.

Anna May played Minn Lee, mistress of mob boss Tony Perrelli, the role essayed by Crane Wilbur. Wallace modeled the latter character after Al Capone, based on his trip to Chicago, where he soaked up the atmosphere of that gangster-ridden metro-

Anna May Wong in top hat and dress coat for her cabaret act.

atre commencing on October 16. She was billed last on the program of *Variety Fair* as "The World Famous Chinese Film Star—ANNA MAY WONG—in tuneful songs and intriguing costumes." She was accompanied by Australian pianist Gordon Whelan and backed by the Palace Orchestra conducted by Tom Lear.

The program continued: "Her act is composed of singing a Chinese number or two in magnificent Oriental costumes, going by vivid contrast to ultra-modern number in cabaret fashion, in top hat and dress coat, concluding with an impressive character study inspired by the role she played in *Shanghai Express*."

The following year found the busy performer on the continent in Spain, France, Italy and Switzerland, where she performed her cabaret act in a number of major cities.

In early 1935 Anna May Wong headed north to the cooler clime and fjords of polis. The result was the story of a gang leader who cannot leave the ladies alone and is eventually betrayed by his Chinese mistress. Along the way he puts a number of people "on the spot" and disposes of them very neatly. Wallace took a tongue-in-cheek approach to the serious goings-on and Crane Wilbur responded with his own details, such as touching himself with perfume when about to meet a lady. Miss Wong showed her versatility by designing the costumes she wore in the first and second acts.

When *On the Spot* was filmed by Paramount in 1938 as *Dangerous to Know* [q.v.], all the character names were changed; Min Lee became Madame Lan Ying.

While filming *Tiger Bay* [q.v.] in the fall of 1933, Anna May found herself with some free time. Never one to remain idle, she rushed up to Blackpool and began a one-week engagement at the Palace The-

Anna May Wong arriving in Copenhagen, 1935

Scandinavia. She stopped first in the Danish capital of Copenhagen, where she appeared at the National Scala for two weeks, from February 1 to February 14. On opening night, which was attended by many prominent members of the Chinese community there, the actress won over her audience immediately by speaking the introduction to her act in Danish. She solidified their approval when she stopped in the midst of a melody she was singing in Danish and cried "Help me!" After the show she was given a dinner reception by the theater director.

Her performance consisted of six songs, a Chinese mime piece and a Chinese dance. One of the songs, which had lyrics and music by Paul Girard Smith and Warburton Gilbert, respectively, was altered to fit the venue in which she appeared, so that in Copenhagen it was known as *A Danish Girl*. Anna also sang *Street Girl*, *Ingenue*, and *Half-Caste Woman*, the latter a Noel Coward creation which had its premier in Cochrane's Review of 1931 at the London Pavilion. In addition to these, she sang a French song, *Parlez Moi d'Amour* (*Speak, My Love*), and one in Danish, *Før Vi Skilles* (*Before We Part*), which she delivered phonetically, since Danish was not one of her languages. This song was specially written for her by Flemming Geill (lyrics) and Henry Willum (music). Newspaper clippings show Miss Wong visiting and being feted at many locations in that small country.

Proceeding on to Oslo, Norway, the popular celebrity brought her act to the Røde Mølle for thirteen nights, from February 16–28. There *A Danish Girl* became *A Norwegian Girl*, for obvious reasons.

In Sweden, Anna May appeared in both Stockholm and Goteborg. She began her stay in the capital city at the Kon-

Anna May Wong on stage at the National Scala, Copenhagen, 1935

154 • Stage Work

Sheet music for the stage song sung by Anna May Wong in Copenhagen

serthusets from March 2–4, where she did one show daily, at 8 P.M. In Goteborg she did two shows daily, at 7 P.M. and 9 P.M., at the Folkteatern from March 8–10. In both locales her show-stopper was *A Swedish Girl*. Apparently, interest in the actress extended beyond her profession, for there were newspaper articles concerned with her clothing, including her silk pajamas, undoubtedly an unheard-of commodity in that northern region.

In May 1935 it was reported in the *New York Herald-Tribune* that Miss Wong would be appearing on Broadway that fall in a musical version of Don Byrne's novel *Messer Marco Polo*. This never materialized. Neither did *Lady Precious Stream*, a classical Chinese drama in which Miss Wong was to star in late 1935, though it was produced in London.

Upon her return from China in September 1936, Anna May Wong wasted little time in continuing her career, both on the screen and on the stage. She signed with her old studio, Paramount (see "American Sound Films"). The following year she appeared on the boards in a play written especially for her by John Gerard and Lawrence Langer. A friend of the latter, who had founded the Theatre Guild in 1918, Anna May had requested a piece tailored to her talents. Langer immediately thought of the 1762 Carlo Gozzi work *Turandot*, which had been the inspiration for operas by Busoni and Puccini. Retitled *Princess Turandot*, it was presented at the Westchester County Playhouse in Mt. Kisco, New York, for six days beginning on August 2, 1937.

The plot is concerned with a princess of ancient China who, out of revenge for a slain ancestor, makes life difficult for her suitors. They must answer three riddles or die. One Prince Calaf takes up the challenge and correctly answers the three riddles. Turandot begs her father, the emperor, not to let the stranger have her,

Anna May Wong in *Princess Turandot*, 1937

but he is adamant. However, Calaf magnanimously offers his life if Turandot can guess his name by dawn. Calaf's father and a loyal slave girl are discovered; Calaf assures all that these two do not know his secret. When Turandot appears and orders Calaf's father to speak, the slave girl, Liu, states that she alone knows Calaf's name. When the girl remains silent under torture, Turandot asks her the secret of her endurance. "Love," replies the girl. Liu then grabs a dagger from a soldier and kills herself. Turandot confronts Calaf, who forces her to kiss him. Feeling physical passion for the first time, the princess weeps. Convinced of his victory, Calaf tells her his name. Turandot then goes to her father and reveals the stranger's name as "Love."

The August 3 edition of the White Plains Reporter said of her performance: "Miss Wong is, of course, delightful in the natural role of the Princess. Her breeding ... lends a touch to the portrayal which no American actress [sic] could ever hope to duplicate." The Greenburgh News stated on August 6:

> Miss Wong, as Princess Turandot ... was lovely to look at. Her costumes were magnificent and her gestures beguiling. There was, however, a certain toneless quality about her reading that made her seem ... a figure cut from some Chinese print, lacking third dimensional virtues. From a box-office point of view there's too much in a name like Anna May Wong coupled with a Chinese play to worry much whether some other actress would not have given the part just a little more body.

From there the play moved to the Westport Country Playhouse in Westport, Connecticut for the week beginning August 9. Opening night was attended by several luminaries of the theater, including Eva LaGallienne, Ethel Barrymore, Ina Claire and Alla Nazimova. According to Langer, Anna May heard of their presence while backstage and became nervous and overacted badly. Due to this unfortunate occurrence, Langer wrote that he had little hope of ever reviving the play.

The much-travelled actress found herself half a world away from home when she visited Australia in the early summer of 1939. In Melbourne she opened at the Tivoli Theatre, a former music hall and opera house, on June 12. Besides the act which she had performed throughout the British Isles and Europe, Miss Wong added some current songs and comedy material that was written for her radio appearances with Bing Crosby, Edgar Bergen and others. One reviewer stated: "She proved a first-rate entertainer...There is an atmosphere of brightness about her 'turn,' which is easy to look at and to hear. A song number in Chinese, a French chansant [sic], and a dramatic monologue showed her versatility and met with hearty approval. Her presentation is original and 'colour' is added by the many beautiful Chinese costumes she wears." In its various incarnations, the theater had seen the likes of W.C. Fields, Harry Houdini and Lillie Langtry among its many attractions. *King of Chinatown* [q.v.] was playing at the Capitol Theatre at the time, only three months after its U.S. release, and Anna May made a personal appearance at a matinee screening on June 14. Her film was the second half of a double bill, the other feature being a Madeleine Carroll vehicle entitled *Cafe Society*. The remainder of her time Down Under was spent giving lectures and heading subscription campaigns for Chinese War Relief. After visiting New Zealand, she returned to the U.S. on September 4.

Miss Wong was to appear on the legitimate stage but one more time. That was during World War II, when she was the featured player in a production of *The Willow Tree* at the Cambridge Summer Theatre in August 1943. This opus, by J. Harry Benrimo and Harrison Rhodes, had first been performed in 1917 and subtitled "A Fantasy of Japan." (For obvious reasons, it was altered to "A Fantasy of China" for this version.) Fay Bainter (1892–1968) portrayed the Image. The production was

Opposite: Program page from Anna May Wong's appearance at the Tivoli Theatre in Melbourne, Australia, 1939

THE TIVOLI THEATRE PROGRAMME

FRANK NEIL

Announces with Pride
the Personal Appearance of the
WORLD FAMOUS
STAGE AND SCREEN
STAR

Anna May Wong

Opening at THIS THEATRE,

Monday, June 12th

At the Matinee.

A RED LETTER DAY
IN TIVOLI VARIETY

called "Quaint, full of rare charm…" by *The New York Times* critic. Screen Classics made a six-reel film version, which was released in January 1920 and distributed by Metro Pictures. Directed by Henry Otto, it featured a scenario by June Mathis. Viola Dana (1897–1987) played the role later essayed by Anna May.

The authors reworked an old Japanese legend, chiefly by substituting British characters for the Japanese ones. A young Briton, unable to provide for his lady, journeys to Japan, where he buys an image of the Princess of the Willow Tree, the cherished possession of an old wood carver. The latter agrees to the sale in order to obtain money to send his modern son to Cornell University in America. The Englishman places it in his garden. The Image comes to life and dwells for ten days in the garden house. Reminiscent of all that was fair and good in the woman left behind by her new owner, she falls in love and learns the lessons of life, including coquetry and the fear of old age. She is told and believes that all of us have come into the world for happiness. The Image came alive only because the man wished it; when she learns sympathy and self-sacrifice, she renounces her life so that the man may return to his homeland after he is called there.

One reviewer stated: "There isn't much to the story, but the symbolism is exquisite, the Chinese settings an artistic success and the acting sensitive. Miss Wong isn't quite at ease in her part, but her loveliness is effective." A. E. Watt wrote: "…Miss Wong … strove hard to be the elfin-like creature who comes down from her pedestal … to delight with naive speeches about the world she finds herself in. At times she succeeded. At all times she succeeded in being a delight to the eye."

The Plays

The Circle of Chalk
(from the Ancient Chinese)
By Klabund [Alfred Henschke]. English Version by James Laver. Opened March 14, 1929, at the New Theatre, London, England. Ran for 48 performances. Licensed by the Lord Chamberlain to Lady Wyndham (Miss Mary Moore). Scenery and costume design by Aubrey Hammond. Scenery built by Loveday and Higson. Music and musical direction by Ernest Irving. Presented by Basil Dean by arrangement with Miss Mary Moore.

The characters in order of their appearance:

Tong	Mr. Bruce Winston
Yo	Miss Joan Carr
Yu	Miss Louise Merrill
Yow	Miss May Elton
Chang Hi-Tang	Miss Anna May Wong
Mrs. Chang	Miss Marie Ault
Chang-Ling	Mr. George Curzon
Prince Pao	Mr. Laurence Olivier
Mr. Ma	Mr. Frank Cochrane
Yu-Pi	Miss Rose Quong
Chow	Mr. Wilson Blake
The Officer of Patrol	Mr. Peter Ridgeway
Chu-Chu	Mr. Bruce Winston
A Midwife	Miss Marie Ault
The Brothers Sang	Messrs. Oswald R. Roberts and Richard Coke
A Courier	Mr. Lawrence Edgley
1st Soldier	Mr. Huntley Gifford
2nd Soldier	Mr. Frank R. Robertson
The Innkeeper	Mr. Frank Cochrane
A Poet	Mr. Lawrence Edgely
The Master of Ceremonies	Mr. Gordon Lennox

Tschun Tschi
(*Springtime*)
Opened August 14, 1930 at the Neues Wiener Schauspielhaus, Vienna.

Played daily running through September 18, 1930. A play with music in eight tableaux by W. Clifforde. German translation by Fritz Grünbaum and Leopold Jacobson. Produced by Jacob Feldhammer.

Directed by Bernd Hofmann. Dances by Karl Schreiber. Sets designed by Otto Riedermoser. Music by John Gardener. Music and lyrics for Chinese songs by Anna May Wong.

The Cast

Tschun Tschi	Anna May Wong
Annabell Elyde	Ilse Schally
Syd Fokker	Jacob Feldhammer
Hopkins, stage director	Reinhold Bernt
Trapp, General Director	Karl Kneidinger
Tschao, a servant	Alfred Lipschütz
Miss Rubby	Annie Horat
A Pianist	Franz Fox
Li Peng	Joseph Bechell
Pierre d'Anjou	Grif Radolf
Mac Macton	Walter Barndal
Tao Tai	Hans Fontana
First Sailor	Kurt Lieck
Second Sailor	Karl Kalwoda
Third Sailor	Karl Schrieber
Chambermaid	Gerta Landers
Cafe Proprietor	Fritz Gambertt
Tschun Yen	Konrad Streda
Female Dancers:	Landers, Fahringer, Leibensrost, Lizzett, Meeuws, Berdahelny
Male Dancers:	Werberg, Schreiber

On the Spot

Opened October 29, 1930. Ran for 167 performances.

A melodrama in a prologue and three acts by Edgar Wallace. Presented by Lee and J.J. Shubert at the Forrest Theatre, New York. Staged by Carol Reed. Settings designed by Rollo Wayne.

The Cast

A Priest	John Wheeler
Interne	John Adair
Shaun O'Donnell	Mike Sullivan
Officer Ryan	George Spelvin
Capt. Harrigan	Stanley Wood
A Nurse	Jeanne Winters
Tony Perrelli	Crane Wilbur
Minn Lee	Anna May Wong
Keriki	Suezo Tokoro
Angelo	John Gallaudet
Con O'Hara	George Drury Hart
Marie Pouliski	Glenda Farrell
Jimmy McGarth	Alan Ward
Detective Commissioner Kelly	John M. Kline
Mike Feeney	Arthur R. Vinton

Princess Turandot

By John Gerard and Lawrence Langer. Presented at the Westchester Playhouse, Lawrence Farms, Mt. Kisco, New York, from August 2 through August 7, 1937, and at Westport County Playhouse, Westport, Connecticut, August 9 through August 14, 1937.

Presented by Day and Skinner under the direction of Day Tuttle.

The Cast

Pantaloon	Frederic Tozere
Fr. Ricci	Ted Tenley
Bombardon	St. Clair Bayfield
Harlequin	Jack Cole
Columbine	Virginia Miller
Yuan	Jules Schmidt
Executioner	Ray Dennis
Altoum, Emperor of China	McKay Morris
Turandot, his daughter	ANNA MAY WONG
Zelima	Phyllis Langner
Adelma	Anga Kuczak
Calaf	Vincent Price
Barach	Clarence Derwent
Schirina	Rachel Sewall
Priest	Lamar Clark
Guards	William Browning, Fred Honsha
Astrologers	G. Ogsburg, P. Klavun

The Willow Tree

Presented at Brattle Hall, Cambridge Summer Theatre the week of August 2, 1943 by Louise Falk and John Huntington. A Chinese fantasy in three acts by J. Harry Benrimo and Harrison Rhodes. Staged by William Mendrek. Setting by Andrew Mack.

The Cast
in order of appearance

Chen Erh	James Lee
Lu Yi	Allan Tower
Godfrey Fuller	Ernest Woodward
Edward Hamilton	Richard Hart

John Charles Lao	William Weyse
Lao Ta	William Jeffrey
The Image	Anna May Wong
A Bird Seller	Ofelia Cornejo
A Fish Seller	John Gerstad
A Street Singer	Elaine Goodell
Mary Temple	Louise Valery

Special make-up for Miss Wong by Charles of the Ritz.

Chinese costumes assembled by Miss Tsing-Ying Tsang.

Other Appearances

Europe

France — 3 weeks in Paris 1934

Italy — Naples, Rome and Venice — November 1934, Florence — December 1934 at Cinema Teatro Galleria

Spain — Barcelona — 1934

Switzerland — Lucerne, Zurich — 1934

United Kingdom

Southampton — May 1933; London — May, June, September 1933; Liverpool — August 1933; Birmingham and Nottingham — August 1933; Harrowgate — August 1933; Manchester — September 1933; Newcastle and Edinburgh — September 1933; Glasgow — October 1933; Sunderland [Empire] — October 1933; Holl on Holl — November 1933; Leeds — November 1933; Swansea (Wales) — November 1933.

United States

Brooklyn Paramount Theater, New York — one week beginning April 13, 1932; Metropolitan Theater, Boston — one week beginning April 29, 1932; Palace Theater, Chicago — one week beginning July 28, 1935; Michigan Theatre, Detroit — Aug. 16, 1935; Loew's State Theater, New York — one week beginning May 20, 1937 (an original dramatic sketch titled "Harmonizing East with West"); Philadelphia — one week June 1937; State Theater, Hartford, CT — one week beginning April 21, 1939; Palace Theater, New York — July 1960, Trans-Lux 85th St. Theater, New York — July 1960.

VI

Radio and Television

Radio Appearances

Radio was the medium upon which Anna May Wong had the least impact, most of her appearances being those of a guest star. Her two dramatic efforts seem to indicate that she was less than comfortable doing radio work.

San Francisco Veterans War Memorial Fete—Feb. 22, 1933—Anna May acted as hostess.

Rudy Vallee Show—July 11, 1935; May 27, 1937—Anna May was a guest star on both shows.

Royal Gelatine Hour—June 1, 1937; WEAF-NBC, New York; Host: Rudy Vallee—Dramatic sketch with Florence Reed and Anna May Wong, written by Arch Oboler.

Synopsis: A Chinese girl returns to her native land after spending much of her life in the United States.

Variety June 2, 1937: "...a fairly moving yarn on the blood-will-tell motif, scripted liberally with hoke by Arch Oboler.... Miss Wong's performance tended to be expressionless and without depth, faltered slightly on one or two lines." Coincidentally, both actresses had played the role of Zahrat in *Chu Chin Chow*—Miss Reed in the 1917 stage version in New York, and Miss Wong in the 1934 British film version.

The Lifebuoy Program—November 9, 1937; KNX; 8:30 P.M.—Anna May was a guest star and sings in Chinese.

Hollywood Hotel—February 11, 1938. "Dangerous to Know"—Lloyd Nolan, Anna May Wong, Gail Patrick, Akim Tamiroff, Louella O. Parsons—Host Ken Murray—Master of ceremonies Ken Niles—Announcer. Also appearing: Frances Langford, Jerry Cooper, Raymond Paige and his orchestra, Ann Jamison. *Hollywood Hotel* was a program that showcased movies that were soon to be released by broadcasting a short radio adaptation of the film.

Kraft Music Hall—March 31, 1938—Anna May was a guest star.

Edgar Bergen—Charlie McCarthy Show—Nov. 20, 1938—Anna May was a guest star.

Campbell Playhouse—April 14, 1939; CBS; 55 minutes; *Producer*: Orson Welles

The Patriot by Pearl Buck. *Announcer*: Ernest Chappell; Music arranged and conducted by Bernard Hermann; With Orson Welles (I-Wan), Anna May Wong (Peony), Ray Collins (Wu), Myron McCormick (En-Lan), Margaret Curtis (Tama), Edgar Barrier (Muraki), Elliott Reid (Bunji), Everett Sloane (Broker; Chiang Kai-Shek).

Synopsis: I-Wan, the son of the banker Wu in Shanghai China, describes in detail what is going through his mind as he decides to join Chang Kai Shek's forces. He confides in his maid, Peony, who unlike him, thinks the right goes to the mightier.

His father finds his name on a list of revolutionaries and comes to wake him up to warn him that Chang has betrayed them by making an agreement with the leaders of Shanghai. The father tells his son that he is sending him to Japan, fearing for his safety. In Japan, I-Wan stays with his father's friend, Mr. Muraki, noting how beautiful the new surroundings are. He is taken into the family firm. He pays more and more attention to the patriarch's daughter, Tama, and makes an attempt to keep her from marrying an older man. Conditions change, and Mr. Muraki decides to send him to the Yokohama branch of his firm. Distressed, I-Wan tells Tama the news and asks her not to marry, to which she relents.

After a year in Yokohama, he goes to a matchmaker to have him propose a marriage with Tama to her father, Mr. Muraki. With difficulties, an agreement is reached. I-Wan's father writes, blessing the marriage, but warns the son not to bring her back to China, due to the times.

Tama wants to see her new family in China after she becomes pregnant, but war between Japan and China comes between I-Wan and Tama. He discovers the importance of dying for one's country from an old man. Missing his old life, I-Wan tells Tama he must go home to take up arms. Tama understands that he is not leaving her, but doing what he has to do. She promises to keep his memory alive for his children.

He returns home to find that General Chang can use him, and now Chang is considered a great man. He finds out from one of his former revolutionaries that Peony became his bride. Peony describes her troubles on the Long March, giving away one of her children.

Ordered by Chang to go to another city, he asks for time to see his father. Chang confronts him about his marriage to a Japanese, asking him how he can be sure I-Wan is faithful to him. He asks him to give up his wife, and I-Wan refuses. Chang, convinced, grants him a week with orders to return to his duty when done. With a few thoughts about war, the story ends.

Anna has a small role in this play and has some trouble with her lines. The story itself reads like a book, much less a play, and most is told from the person of I-Wan.

After the play Orson Welles introduces Pearl Buck and Anna May Wong, speaking Anna's name, Wong Liu Tsong, in Chinese and translating to English (Frosted Yellow Willows[sic]). Anna expresses interest in Miss Buck's books and the author describes the times in China and Japan, and the commonness of this story. She goes on to explain how China is hastening the unification of the continent.

Fred Allen Show— Nov. 12, 1941— Anna May was a guest star.

Television Appearances

Television was another matter. Still in its infancy in 1951, it became a training ground for fledgling thespians, as well as a source of employment for film stars who had a career choice to make. A 1948 Supreme Court ruling had stated that the major film studios were guilty of monopolistic practices by their block-booking of films and the fixing of admission prices. Forced to reduce costs after selling off their theater chains, the studios reduced their player rosters by cutting the fat, namely the contracts of the stars who no longer brought in the audiences. Their contracts were either not renewed or bought out by those performers who refused severe pay reductions. While Anna May Wong did not fit under either heading, she was still a proven performer. Accepting the starring role in a series offered by Dumont, she became the first Asian-American entertainer to have her own television series. The title was *The Egyptian Idol* (Anna's Chinese name); Miss Wong played the owner of an art gallery who becomes involved in international intrigue in the art world.

Dumont was the fourth network in those early days of live television, but the second to become part of the business, closely following NBC. In 1945, it established a link between its Washington, D.C. and New York stations, broadcasting over Channel 5 in both cities. Only those cities received Dumont's entire lineup of programs; WABD in New York and WTTG in Washington. Developed by DuMont Laboratories, which had been founded by the inventor Dr. Allen B. DuMont, it eventually folded in 1956, having failed to capture a large enough segment of the viewing audience to be profitable. Part of the problem was funds for decent production values, one of the factors which doomed Anna May's series. The story goes that all remaining Dumont kinescopes were dumped into one of New York's rivers in the 1970s after it was determined that it would be too expensive to preserve them. In the late 1990s one of the *Gallery* episodes on 16mm was advertised for sale, according to noted early TV expert Ed Hurley. It is not known which one, however, but it is good to know at least one episode of this pioneering series has survived.

The Gallery of Mme. Liu-Tsong

30 min.; Mondays 8-8:30 P.M. EST; Dumont, from New York.

The Egyptian Idol
Air date: August 27, 1951
Director: William Marceau; Writer: Iris Marion
Cast: Anna May Wong, Natalie Priest, Cliff Carpenter, Jean Pearson, John Stanley, Ralph Stantley, Winifred Cushing.
Variety August 29, 1951: "...strictly out of the pulp mill ... neither the acting nor the direction contributed toward its enhancement as a major TV contender."
The Golden Women—Air date: September 3, 1951
Spreading Oak—Air date: September 10, 1951
The Man with a Thousand Eyes Air date: September 17, 1951
Burning Sands—Air date: September 24, 1951
Shadow of the Sun God—Air date: October 1, 1951
Golden Caravan—Air date: October 8, 1951
Message from Beyond—Air date: October 15, 1951
The Prodigal Stepson—Air date: October 22, 1951
Tinder Box—Air date: October 31, 1951
The House of Quiet Dignity—Air date: November 7, 1951
Boomerang— Air date: November 14, 1951
The Face of Evil—Air date: November 21, 1951

With the October 8 episode, the title was changed to *Mme. Liu Tsong*.

Producer's Showcase

The Letter
Air Date: October 15, 1956; NBC; Color
Director/Producer: William Wyler; Executive Producer: Mort Abrahams; Associate Producer: Leo Davis; Director: Kirk Browning; Adaptation: Joseph Schrank, from the play by Somerset Maugham; Music: George Bassman; Settings: Otis Riggs; Costumes: Dorothy Jeakins; Costume Supervisor: Robert Fletcher; Casting Director: Joan MacDonald; Associate Director: Dean Whitmore; Technical Director: Jack Coffey; Graphic Art: Guy Frauneni; Associate Producer: Leo Davis; Production Stage Manager: George Lawrence; Production Supervisor: Shelley Hull; Unit Manager: Warren Burmeister; Film Technical Director: Edward Hoffmeister ; Lighting Director: Jack Fitzpatrick; W. Somerset Maugham Story Rights Arranged by: Ann Marlowe
Cast: Siobhan McKenna (Leslie Crosbie), Michael Rennie (Howard Joyce), John Mills (Robert Crosbie), Anna May Wong (the Woman), John Irving (John Withers), Cathleen Cordell (Mrs. Joyce), Aki Aleong (Ong Chi Seng), Margaretta Warwick (Mrs. Parker), Kaie Deei (Chung Hi).

The New York World-Telegram October 16, 1956: "As in the old days, Miss Wong was beautiful—and savage! Her eyes were dagger points and her silken shoulders quivered with hate."

The New York Daily News October 17, 1956: "Anna May Wong shone ... as the native mistress of the murder victim."

Synopsis: The wife of a British rubber plantation owner shoots a man to death in the opening scene. She tells her husband and their lawyer that he got drunk and attempted to rape her in her home (her husband being away). She is to be tried for murder, but her lawyer is sure she will be acquitted, until a certain letter surfaces. The lawyer's clerk acts as a go-between for the person who has the original. It was written by the woman; in it she asks the victim to come see her that night as her husband will be away. She denies she ever wrote it, but the lawyer feels he should secure the original, as it is very incriminating. He gets the husband's permission to do so without revealing the cost or the contents of the letter. He and the woman meet with the Chinese woman, who has the letter. After the trial and the woman's acquittal, her husband discovers the truth when he is told his entire fortune was used to purchase the letter. The woman confesses that she and the man she killed had been lovers for some time, then admits she still loves the dead man.

A live production from television's Golden Age, this version of *The Letter* holds up rather well, despite two instances worthy of a blooper tape. One occurs off screen, but is very audible—the crash of an overturned cart in the club scene. The other is verbal: when asked by lawyer Joyce what the person holding the incriminating letter wants for it, his clerk replies, "Two thousand dollars." The lawyer then says: "*Ten* thousand dollars is a lot of money..." Later the clerk states that his cut in the deal is two thousand dollars. Apparently the

The Letter (NBC, 1956): Anna May Wong

actor could not get that figure out of his mind, only his mouth.

Anna May has only two scenes, but makes the most of them, utilizing her marvelously expressive eyes to portray her feelings. She has several closeups and her entrance at the merchant's shop is right out of one of her early films—her shadow precedes her behind a beaded curtain. She speaks only two lines, both in "Malay Chinese." When Mrs. Crosbie approaches her to receive the letter, the contempt and hatred in the Chinese woman's eyes blaze forth as she drops the letter, rather than hand it to her lover's killer.

For the first and only time in her career, Anna May Wong got to play a role for which she had originally been rejected. She had been considered for the part in the 1940 film version, but director Wyler felt she was "too young" for it. She was only thirty-five at the time, but what about make-up? This was clearly a lame excuse for cheating Anna May out of a role in another major production.

Miss McKenna (1923–1986) was appearing in George Bernard Shaw's *Saint Joan* at the time, and seems to have brought some of her theatrical mannerisms with her. Live television was undoubtedly like being on a stage.

Veteran film star John Mills (b. 1908) made his American television debut in this drama.

Climax!

Air date: November 22, 1956; CBS; 60 minutes
The Chinese Game
Director: Buzz Kulik; Screenplay: Charles Larson
Cast: Anna May Wong, MacDonald Carey, Rita Moreno, Constance Ford, Harry Townes.

CBS Photo Division Press Information

Anna May Wong stars in the weird story of a man who walks through a door marked murder in *The Chinese Game* on *Climax!*, Thursday, Nov. 22 (CBS Television, 8:30–9:30 P.M., EST). Program also stars Macdonald Carey, Rita Moreno, Constance Ford and Harry Townes.

Bold Journey

Air date: February 14, 1957; ABC; 30 minutes
Producer: Jack Douglas

Anna May narrated a documentary about China, utilizing footage shot there during her visit in 1936.

Mickey Spillane's Mike Hammer

Air date: 1958 (syndicated); 30 minutes
So That's Who It Was
Director: John English; Teleplay: James Gunn and Fenton Earnshaw; Story: Curt Cannon; Director of Photography: Jack Mackenzie, A.S.C.; Art Director: Don Ament; Sound: Harold Hanks; Supervising Film Editor: Bud Small; Set Decorator: George Sawley; Assistant Director: James Hogan; Casting Supervisor: Irving Levitt; Makeup: Jack Barron
Recorded by Glen Glenn Sound Co.; Filmed in Hollywood.
Cast: Darren McGavin (Mike Hammer), Anna May Wong (Mme. Li Chu), Bart Burns (Pat Chambers), Barbara Luna (Lily Yu), Keye Luke (Sam Wong), Robert Foulk (Gus

The Chinese Game (Climax!, CBS, 1956): Anna May Wong (Courtesy St. Louis Mercantile Library)

Peters), John Harmon, Weaver Levy (Clerk at Chinese Club), William Yip, Charles Horvath (strong arm).

Synopsis: Mike is coming out from undercover in Chinatown. Joey, a junkie that Mike met, comes up to him and gives him a nice tie in hopes that Mike will reciprocate with some cash. Mike gives him five dollars, telling him to use it for some food and to give some to Gus Peters at the hotel where Joey stays and Mike was undercover.

A week later, back at Hammer's office, the phone rings. Joey is very scared and asks to meet him. Mike has to break a date with the pair of legs sitting in front of him. He reluctantly leaves as something is thrown at him.

In the hotel, Gus tells Hammer that Joey was gone, while on the streets of Chinatown, people crowd around the dead body of Joey. Pat Chambers arrives, trying to find out what Hammer knows, only to be given a brush off. Hammer goes back to the hotel where Gus gives him a lay off speech. Hammer tells him to keep talking, and asks if it had something to do with the death of Li Chu. Gus tells him the last thing he heard Joey say was "So that's who it was." Mike asks for the key to Joey's room and when Gus balks, he threatens to kick the door in. Gus gives him the key. Entering the room, Mike is accosted by a couple of strong arms, who knock him out. Gus enters and empties a pitcher of water on Mike to wake him up. Hammer accuses Gus of letting the guys in and beats him around a little until Gus mentions Li Chu's wife.

At Li Chu's apartment, Mme. Chu's servant opens the door for Mike. Mme. Chu seems to know all about Mike, and then expresses sorrow over her loss when Mike brings up the death of her husband. She says that maybe the Tong was responsible for his death, as Li Chu was an important man. She asks why he is so interested and he tells her about Joey. She then asks Mike to investigate her husband's death. She tells him that she is sure he will find the killer.

Mike's next stop is the Chinese Neighborhood Club. He enters, saying "hello" in Cantonese, to which he is answered in English. He asks if Sam Wong is in, and is told to come back around five. Mike tells him that he remembers him as his assailant, twists his arm and knocks him to the floor. Another strong arm comes out from behind the door, and Mike knocks him out the window. He then walks into the private office. Sam Wong greets him in poor English, and Mike asks him about how much Li Chu won at the game. Sam tells him that Li Chu had won four dollars, and that he knew nothing of his death. He then asks Hammer to leave, and as he does, Mike tells him to quit speaking "no-tickee" dialog and asks where he graduated from. Wong answers that he graduated from University of California, Berkeley. Mike knows now that the two murders are connected, but the word had gone around Chinatown not to talk to Mike Hammer. He shows up at Li Chu's business, where the secretary is putting on her lipstick. She asks if he is looking for something, to which he tells her that he is looking at her. She knows of Joey and Gus, but said she never met Joey. She says that Gus told her Joey's words, "So that's who it was." When Mike finds out that she had seen Mrs. Chu the night before, he questions it, and Lily says that they are friends. Mike hints that maybe Lily is jealous of Li Chu and his wife. She denies anything going on between her and Mr. Chu.

At Pat Chamber's office, Mike finds out that Joey was shot with a .22 and had fresh needle marks on his arm. Mike seems to have it figured out. Pat wants him to spill, and Hammer, leaving, says he will call. Back at Mrs. Chu's place, he explains his thoughts to her. He then asks her if she walks through Chinatown without protection. She mentions carrying a gun, and then he asks her about denying having known Joey, also mentioning what Lily said. She explains about going to see where her husband died and running into Joey, who, ridden with guilt, confesses to killing her husband with a knife. She goes on to say that someone gave Joey some money which got him started on the junk again, alluding to that being what killed her husband. Mme. Chu confesses to shooting Joey, asking Mike what he would do. He explains that maybe she should have gone after him, as he gave Joey the five dollars. On their way out the door, he tells her that the police may be understanding.

Climax!
Air date: May 1, 1958; CBS; 60 minutes
Deadly Tattoo
Director: Paul Nickell; *Screenplay*: Oliver Crawford, based on a story by Ed McBain

Cast: Anne Francis, Peter Graves, Anna May Wong, Henry Silva, Olive Deering.
CBS Photo Division Press Information

A slayer who brands his victims with a tattoo before luring them to their deaths comes to Anna May Wong for assistance in *Deadly Tattoo* on *Climax!* Thursday, May 1 (CBS Television Network, 8:30–9:30 P.M., PDT). The program also stars Anne Francis, Peter Graves, Henry Silva and Olive Deering.

Adventures in Paradise
Air date: November 2, 1959; ABC; 60 minutes
The Lady from South Chicago
Director: Paul Stanley; *Written by*: Ken Kolb; *Producer*: Richard Goldstone; *Associate Producer*: Peter Nelson; *Executive Story Editor*: Kenneth L. Evans; *Director of Photography*: Maury Gertsman, A.S.C.; *Musical theme and Supervision*: Lionel Newman; *Assistant Director*: Jack R. Berne; *Editorial Supervisor*: Richard Farrell; *Art Directors*: Duncan Cramer, Charles Myall; *Story editor*: Robert Dillon; *Film Editor*: Thomas Scott; *Music Editor*: Morrie McNaughton; *Set Decorators*: Walter M. Scott, Claude Carpenter
Cast: Gardner McKay (Capt. Adam Troy), Paulette Goddard (Mme. Victorine Reynaud), Suzanne Pleshette (Minette), Simon Oakland (Martin Quirk), Anna May Wong (Madam Lu Yang), Weaver Levy (Oliver Kee), Oscar Beregi (René Duchamp), Nga West (Nani), Brian Roper (Nicky), James B. Leong (Chinese Merchant), Tor Johnson (uncredited) (Doorman/Bouncer).

Synopsis: Victorine Reynaud's shady past comes back to haunt her when Martin Quirk, a crooked former associate from her days in Singapore, escapes from jail and comes seeking money. She was known as Flossie Mulvaney then and dealt in money laundering, among other things. She married and moved to Noumea, but has since been widowed. Victorine's daughter, Minette, is arriving from Paris aboard the *Tiki*, Adam Troy's boat. Quirk arrives aboard ship in Noumea and gets ashore disguised as a sailor. He sees Victorine heading across the dock, and turns

Deadly Tattoo (Climax!, CBS, 1958): Anna May Wong (Courtesy St. Louis Mercantile Library)

away. As she returns with her daughter and Troy, he allows himself to be seen by her. She is taken aback, but says nothing; neither does Quirk.

The local police inspector visits Victorine to ask her about Quirk, for he knows she once knew him. She denies having seen him. Later, Troy asks her what so disturbed her on the dock and she tells him about Quirk. Describing him as very evil, she asks Troy to watch over her daughter. Quirk sneaks into Mme. Reynaud's house one night and demands £2000 so he can return home to Ireland, reminding her of what he knows. Just then Minette enters; Quirk didn't know of her existence, and ups his demand to £5000. Reynaud wants him gone, so agrees.

Quirk is spotted by a policeman one night and chased. Quirk tricks the cop and kills him, taking his gun. Minette tells Troy about Quirk. Troy goes to Victorine and learns of Quirk's demand. He tells Mme. Reynaud to let the police handle it, but she says no, otherwise Quirk would talk and she'd be ruined.

Quirk returns to Reynaud's home, but only Minette is home. He threatens her and tells her where the money is to be left.

Troy sees Mme. Reynaud's point and takes her money to have it exchanged by Madame Lu Yang, who runs an operation covering the entire Pacific. When she learns whom the money is for, she agrees, having been Flossie's friend in the old days.

Minette tells Troy of Quirk's visit and threat, so he takes a package to the address given by the criminal. It turns out to be a warehouse; Troy enters and is jumped by Quirk; they fight. The package opens to reveal tools; Quirk knocks out Troy and goes to Victorine's, where Minette is confronting her mother about Quirk. The latter arrives and slaps Victorine for trying to cheat him. She tells him the money is in her safe; he takes it. Troy arrives; Quirk begins to tell Minette about her father and how her mother got rich running a dive in Singapore. Victorine moves toward Quirk, he shoots her and is jumped by Troy. They struggle; the gun goes off, killing Quirk.

After she recovers, Mme. Reynaud and her daughter board the *Tiki* and head for an airport from where they will fly to Paris.

Adventures in Paradise

Air date: November 23, 1959; ABC; 60 minutes
Mission to Manila
Director: Bernard Girard; *Written by*: Richard Landau; *Producer*: Richard Goldstone; *Executive Producer*: Dominick Dunne; *Associate Producer*: Peter Nelson; *Director of Photography*: Maury Gertsman; *Art Directors*: Duncan Cramer & Lewis H. Creber; *Executive Story Editor*: Kenneth L. Evans; *Musical Theme and Supervision*: Lionel Newman; *Assistant Director*: Joseph E. Kenny; *Editorial Supervisor*: Richard Farrell; *Story Editor*: Robert Dillon; *Film Editor*: William Mace; *Music Editor*: Morrie McNaughton; *Set Directors*: Walter Mascott & Claude Carpenter; Song "The Show Must Go On" by Bobby Troup; Filmed at the Hollywood Studios of Twentieth Century Fox Television, Inc.
Cast: Gardner McKay (Capt. Adam Troy), Julie London (Mrs. Dalisay Lynch), Thomas Gomez (Capt. Bello), Anna May Wong (Madame Lu Yang), Weaver Levy (Oliver Kee), Charles Quinlvan (Joe Lynch), Douglas Dick (Dan Lynch), Steven Marlo (White Suit), Clarence Lung (Bartender), Mario Gallo (Rizai), Tor Johnson (uncredited) (Doorman/Bouncer).

Synopsis: Danny Lynch, disabled artist, is painting a portrait of Adam Troy when he receives a letter from his sister-in-law in Manila, telling him that his brother Joey is dead. He implores Adam to seek out his sister-in-law and her son and to make sure that they are alright, and to bring them back to Honolulu. Adam sets sail in the *Tiki* with his partner Ollie.

In Manila, Adam goes to see his friend, Madam Lu Yang, who knows the entire goings on wherever she is. She asks what brings him to Manila, and he replies that he is looking for cargo, but then adds that he is looking for a woman. He then tells Lu Yang about Joey's death and asks about his widow, Dalisay. She tells him that she will do him no favors as a friend, and that it would be strictly business. He hands her some cash and she tells him that Dalisay is working in a nightclub called the Americano. Dalisay is singing as Adam walks into the nightclub. After the show, Adam goes to her dressing room and tells Dalisay about Danny's concerns and hopes. Adam then asks to visit the grave when she informs him that Joey killed himself and was cremated, so there is no body. Adam leaves, telling her that she and her son, Thomas, are welcome to come to the *Tiki*.

At her apartment, as her son is sleeping, there is a knock on the door. A man in a white suit comes in and hands her an urn, apparently with her husband's ashes, walks over to the sleeping boy, picks him up and walks out, while Dalisay looks on.

Adam steps down in his boat to find the man in the white suit and his partner with him. The two knock out Adam, and when he wakes up, another man in a white suit is looking over him. It is Captain Bello of the police. In the verbal exchange, Bello tells Adam that he is interested in anyone who is interested in Joey Lynch. Adam then finds out that Joey was into the black market and dope. Bello believes that whoever killed Joey is still operating his business and that Dalisay can lead him to them.

Adam comes back to an empty bar to get information from the bartender on where Dalisay is. He goes to her apartment and is turned away. The next day Adam goes back to the Americano, while Dalisay again sings "The Show Must Go On." After the show, she goes back to her room to find the man in the white suit waiting for her. He wants information from Adam, telling her to be kind to him and find out what she can. In a seeming about face, she goes to Adam's table and sits down. She asks why Danny did not come himself, to which Adam tells he that Danny is a paraplegic. After her next song, she is dancing with Adam in an empty nightclub. She tells him that her concern is for her son, but feeling she has said too much, she asks him to take her home.

At home, the phone rings, and the man in the white suit asks what she found out. Telling him nothing, she receives a threat to convey to Adam.

Back on his boat, Captain Bello pays him a visit. Adam tells him that he is not involved anymore, but Bello tells him that Dalisay's son is not with friends, worrying Adam.

Adam starts to get close to Dalisay, taking a nighttime swim on the beach. Just as they are getting cozy, she asks to swim back to the boat. She remarks what a wonderful time she had, but spurns his advances. He tells her that he wants them both out of Manila, but she says that he needs to leave. Upon telling her that it is too late, he kisses her and she leaves.

He goes back to the bar to find that she is nowhere to be found, so he ends up at Lu Yang's again. She explains why she did not tell him about what Joey Lynch was involved in, and Adam asks about Dalisay. Lu Yang says that she, too, is in it up to her neck.

With Dalisay nowhere to be found, Dan and Ollie decide to head out to sea when Captain Bello pays a visit, saying he knows where Dalisay is. Adam goes to Dalisay, asking that she tell the truth. White suit comes in holding a gun and takes them to a small boat. They pull away, as Captain Bello's men keep an eye on them. On the small island, they go into a man-made tunnel to discover that Joe Lynch is still alive. Joe has the boy and when Dalisay asks about him, he turns her away. Throwing a tantrum of anger and sorrow over his brother's concern, he decides to do in Adam and Dalisay. Adam turns out the lights, shots are fired, but both make it to the outside, only to have Dalisay fatally shot by the man in the white suit. Adam carries her away as Joey shoots White Suit, and as he is about to pull the trigger on Adam, Captain Bello shoots Joey, who dies firing stray shots. Dying, Dalisay asks Adam to look out for Joey. Back in Honolulu, the little boy Thomas is brought to the waiting arms of his uncle Danny.

During this period in Anna's career, she had said how happy she was to be taking on character roles on TV. Her brother had helped her prepare for many of the parts. Some of the roles, like Madam Lu Yang, brought about a more natural character in her, rather than the screen star who was forced to speak broken English.

Former wrestler and Ed Wood regular Tor Johnson (1903–1971) appears as her doorman/bouncer in both of the *Adventures in Paradise* stories strictly as decoration.

Anna May Wong boarding plane for promotional tour for *Portrait in Black*, June 1960

The Life and Legend of Wyatt Earp
Air Date: March 15, 1960; ABC; 30 minutes
China Mary
Filmed in Hollywood by Desilu.
Cast: Hugh O'Brian (Wyatt Earp), Morgan Woodward (Shotgun Gibbs), Anna May Wong (China Mary), Aki Aleong (Lee Kung), Carl Benson, Paul McGuire.

Synopsis: As a Chinese parade is going through town, a white man pushes a Chinese man to the ground. Later that night, the white man is beaten. Earp questions the man, who acts very innocent. He investigates and finds a ring with a Chinese character on it. He decides to ask China Mary.

He goes to the door of her business, but is turned away. Earp is greeted again by one of her police. He asks to see her again and is allowed to enter. He looks the other way as gambling is going on. China Mary welcomes him to her ornate office and offers him tea. He shows her the ring, and wants to know if the ring has anything to do with the trouble. She mentions that it may not be a Chinese man. He explains that he does not agree with all of the Chinese justice, but he looks the other way as long as it stays within Chinatown's walls. This has spilled over into the street, so he must uphold the law.

At night, a man is killed by three Chinese men, but a witness comes on and tries to grab one. The man escapes anyway. The witness is sure that the man was Chinese. Wyatt goes back to China Mary's. Mary is at one of the parlor tables, and she says she knows why he was there, and he tells her that he is now sure it was a Chinese culprit. She asks if he doubts that she can control her people, but adds that this was not done by the same individuals. Wyatt demands to know if it is a *tong* or one of the Six Companies. She tells him that she will handle it herself. He warns that her people will be chased out. Mary again says to leave it to her. Wyatt leaves, telling her that he knows a way to solve it.

In disguise, Wyatt walks the streets of Tombstone, to be accosted by three Chinese men. He puts up a fight, and manages to catch one, but his deputy could not catch the others. The witness from the previous crime does not recognize the prisoner, who then gives Earp an excuse as to how he wound up in the same spot as the other two who accosted Wyatt. When he goes on to act like a victim of white society, Wyatt asks him if he wants to be a martyr, and calling him a wet-nosed boy. He then sees a similar ring on the prisoner's finger, and pulls it off. He and Shotgun decide to take him to see China Mary. The prisoner pleads not to be taken there. At China Mary's, Earp shows the prisoner to her. She tells him that he is Lee Kung, and asks how Earp knows it was he. He tells her of going in disguise, and she tells him how brave he was. She then says that she does not control his kind. Lee Kung does not accept her justice. He asks to be taken back to jail. China Mary tries to dissuade Earp, telling him that the mobs of people would turn against the Chinese. He gives him to China Mary. Mary alludes to the fact that she knows the mother, giving indication that it might be her, going on to say that though the mother tried to give her son the things she did not have, it may not be enough.

Later, a Chinese man comes into the Sheriff's office and speaks to Shotgun. He asks to see Marshall Earp, and says that Mary sent him. Lee Kung has escaped and Mary wanted to warn Wyatt.

On the street, Lee Kung waits for Earp, as China Mary looks on from the shadows. As Lee Kung is ready to accost Earp, Mary shoots him, then leaves the scene. Earp asks the dying young man why he wanted to kill him, and is told that he is the only one who knew that China Mary was his mother. Praying before Buddha, Mary speaks to the entering Earp. She says that it is better for one to die than for it to be bad for the whole people. Earp tells her innocently, that he hopes he does not find the killer. He gives Mary the ring, asking her to give it to the boy's mother.

The Life and Legend of Wyatt Earp began its six-year run in 1955, becoming the first "adult" western, airing its premier episode four days before that of *Gunsmoke*.

Hugh O'Brian was kind enough to respond to our queries about the "China Mary" episode, calling Anna May Wong "…very much a lady and I enjoyed having her on the set. A pro!" She has a lot of screen time in this episode, and her acting is inspired.

The Barbara Stanwyck Theatre
Air date: January 30, 1961; NBC; 30 minutes
Josephine Little: Dragon by the Tail
Cast: Barbara Stanwyck (Josephine Little), Anna May Wong (Ah Sing), Philip Ahn (Li Chin).

Synopsis: Josephine Little is an adventuress and a scoundrel. She travels the Far East wheeling and dealing while looking for love. Ah Sing, her servant, does her best trying to keep Little Joe out of trouble, but she keeps finding more. In a mixed up plot, from cheating at cards to fencing pearls, she finds herself trying to get on top of each situation. In Hong Kong, she is accused of having fixed horse races, but she said it was never proved. A Macao casino owner, Nick, asks her to deal blackjack, to which she refuses. A minute later, her boyfriend, Steve, shows up, all hugs and kisses. He asks Ah Sing how things are in Gloccamorra, to which she says that she has never been there. She seems to have his number and looks on as he tells Little Joe about his latest endeavors needing six hundred dollars. He also says he has found an island for them to live on when they are married. She asks him when, and he explains that he has spent the money that they had planned for the island in an investment. Ah Sing calls out "The Day of the Pig" in the background. Steve asks Little Joe for a few more weeks until the deal pays off. He kisses her goodbye. Ah Sing tells Little Joe how she knows her boyfriend is lying. When Little Joe says that she will kill him, Ah Sing takes her seriously, reminding her that she is a lady.

Little Joe moves on, trying to convince someone to front her in selling fake Tang Dynasty vases. She is informed by this man that Steve has just been arrested behind the Bamboo Curtain. She goes to Lee Chin of the police. He tells her of the arrest and that it will cost her ten thousand dollars to help in freeing him. She says it is too high, and he tells her that the prison where her boyfriend is staying is full of rats. She says she will have the money by morning. She goes to Macao, to the casino run by her Nick, and sits down at a card table, putting up some money. She is offered the deal, and immediately sets about cheating. She takes her quick winnings, but it is discovered that there were five aces in the deck. Nick takes care of the pot and asks her why she cheated. She gives him a song and dance about some family trouble, dodging him when he says that she has no family. She claimed to have been married before, and that her husband died in a plane crash. He asks her for his money back, or to stay there and deal blackjack. She says that the money is with Ah Sing who is getting the boat ready. A group of people comes along as Ah Sing comes back in, saying the boat is ready. The two slip out the door, leaving an angry casino owner.

Later, she is offered a deal by Mr. Takamoto to fence pearls at fifty percent of the profit. She tells him that she is leaving for the south seas. When the man leaves, Ah Sing gives her more trouble over her boyfriend, calling her a fool and that there is no island where he claimed it was. She then tells Little Joe that her boyfriend's boat has docked. Josephine sees her boyfriend, and he tells her of his latest deal, involving the pearls that she turned away last night. As soon as he tells her that he profited forty thousand dollars, Nick shows up demanding the ten thousand that he used to cover for her. Steve gladly hands over the money, and says it is no big deal, as they will be married soon. Ah Sing says she will leave Little Joe's employ, feeling she has lost face. Little Joe protests, but Ah Sing leaves. Steve says they will be married after his next trip. Little Joe kisses him goodbye, knowing that there will always be a next trip to wait for. She sees Ah Sing, whom she talks into coming back. Ah Sing reintroduces Mr. Takamoto, who gives her a strand of the pearls as a gift. She gratefully accepts.

This was one of three stories about Josephine Little, but the only one in which Anna May Wong appeared. This one aired less than a week before she died. Had she continued to be a character actor in television, Anna May would have had no problem keeping busy. With the variety shows to come in the 1960s, parts would have been written for her in more abundance than they were in the 1950s. Even in *Green Acres* her name turned up, when Eb Dawson spent a week's allowance for a picture of Anna May Wong. Her second career, unnoticed for many years, should not be forgotten, as it was an important part of television history.

Epilogue

The name Anna May Wong is once again becoming as familiar as it once was, with her memorabilia commanding ever higher prices, and recognition from various Asian-American groups. One of them, the Asian-American Artists Foundation, has instituted The Anna May Wong Award of Excellence, given in recognition of an artist whose work has had a significant impact on the advancement of Asian-Americans in the arts. The first winner was the Chinese actress Ming Wa Nen.

The island nation of Grenada marked the 50th anniversary of the USO in 1991 with a series of postage stamps; Anna May Wong was among the honored celebrities.

In November and December of 1995, the British Film Institute ran a retrospective of Anna May's films at the National Film Theatre in London. Included were most of her European films and three of her American silent films—*The Toll of the Sea* (1922), *The Thief of Bagdad* and *Peter Pan* (both 1924). Under the heading "Anna May Wong—A Touch of Class," a total of 14 of her pictures were screened. Stephen Bourne, who wrote the notes, called Miss Wong "...a tragedienne as great as Lillian Gish." and "...one of the best-loved, charismatic stars of the 20s and 30s." The Museum of the Moving Image in Astoria, Queens in New York ran a combined Anna May Wong/Sessue Hayakawa festival in August 1997 wherein three of Anna's films were screened, including *Daughter of the Dragon*, in which both stars were featured.

In June, 1997, Elizabeth Wong's [no relation] play *China Doll* was first performed at the Ohio Theater in New York. Seen at a number of venues since then, it deals with Anna May Wong's struggle against racism.

A fully restored version of Miss Wong's final silent film, *Piccadilly* (1929), including the sound prologue, was screened at the New York Film Festival on October 4, 2003. Interest was apparently great, as tickets were sold out the first day they went on sale. Given her sterling performance in this picture, a new appreciation of her talent may be in the offing.

Bibliography

Baxter, John. *The Cinema of Josef von Sternberg.* New York: A. S. Barnes, 1971.

Beauchamp, Cari. *Without Lying Down.* Los Angeles: University of California Press, 1997.

Blake, Michael F. *The Films of Lon Chaney.* Lanham, MD: Vestal Press, 1998.

Braff, Richard E. *The Universal Silents.* Jefferson, NC: McFarland, 1999.

Brownlow, Kevin. *Behind the Mask of Innocence.* Los Angeles and Berkeley: University of California Press, 1990.

Bucher, Felix. *Screen Series: Germany.* New York: A. S. Barnes, 1970.

Callow, Simon. *Charles Laughton — A Difficult Actor.* New York: Grove Press, 1987.

Carnes, Mark C., ed. *Past Imperfect — History According to the Movies.* New York: Henry Holt & Co., 1985.

Cary, Diana Serry. *Hollywood's Children.* Dallas: Southern Methodist University Press, 1978.

D'Agostino, Annette M. *Filmmakers in "The Moving Picture World,"* Jefferson, NC: McFarland, 1997.

Dickens, Homer. *The Films of Marlene Dietrich.* Secaucus, NJ: Citadel Press, 1968.

Dong, Stella. *Shanghai — 1842–1999 — The Rise and Fall of a Decadent City.* New York: William Morrow, 2000.

Drabble, Margaret. *Arnold Bennett.* New York: Alfred A. Knopf, 1974.

Ellenberger, Allan R. *Ramon Novarro.* Jefferson NC: McFarland & Co., 1999.

Elsaesser, Thomas, ed. *The BFI Companion to German Cinema.* London: British Film Institute, 1989.

Endres, Stacy, and Robert Cushman. *Hollywood at Your Feet.* Los Angeles: Pomegranate Press, 1992.

Friedrich, Otto. *Before the Deluge: A Portrait of Berlin in the 1920s.* New York: Harper and Row, 1972.

Gifford, Denis. *The British Film Catalogue, 1895–1985, Facts on File.* Oxford: New York, 1986.

Hancock, Ralph, and Letitia Fairbanks. *The Fourth Musketeer.* New York: Henry Holt & Co., 1953.

Hanke, Ken. *Charlie Chan at the Movies.* Jefferson, NC: McFarland, 1989.

Hanson, Bruce K. *The Peter Pan Chronicles.* New York: Birch Lane Press, 1993.

Hoexter, Corinne K. *From Canton to California — The Epic of Chinese Immigration.* New York: Four Winds Press, 1976.

Knight, Arthur. *The Liveliest Art.* New York: New American Library, 1979.

Kobal, John. *Marlene Dietrich.* New York: Dutton, 1968.

Kreimeier, Klaus. T*he UFA Story.* New York: Hill and Wang, 1996.

Lahue, Kalton C. *Gentlemen to the Rescue.* New York: Castle Books, 1972.

_____. *Bound and Gagged.* New York: A. S. Barnes, 1968.

Lambert, Gavin. *Nazimova — A Biography.* New York: Alfred A. Knopf, 1997.

Lane, Margaret. *Edgar Wallace — The Biography of a Phenomenon.* New York: Book League of America, 1939.

Liebman, Roy. *From Silents to Sound.* Jefferson, NC: McFarland, 1992.

Low, Rachel. *The History of the British Film, 1918–1929.* London: George Allen Unwin Ltd., 1971.

Mank, Gregory. *The Hollywood Hissables.* Metuchen, NJ: Scarecrow Press, 1989.

Marill, Alvin H. *The Films of Anthony Quinn.* Secaucus, NJ: Citadel Press, 1975.

Martin, Len D. *The Columbia Checklist.* Jefferson, NC: McFarland, 1991.

Miller, William D. *Pretty Bubbles in the Air — America in 1919.* Urbana, Chicago: University of Illinois Press, 1991.

Munden, Kenneth. *American Film Institute*

Catalog of Feature Films, 1931–1940. Berkeley: University of California Press, 1993.
Paris, Barry. *Louise Brooks,* New York: Alfred A. Knopf, 1989.
Okuda, Ted. *Grand National, PRC and Screen Guild/Lippert.* Jefferson, NC: McFarland, 1989.
Parish, James R. *Prostitution in Hollywood Films.* Jefferson, NC: McFarland, 1992.
Pitts, Michael. *Poverty Row Studios.* Jefferson, NC: McFarland, 1997.
Preston, Diana. *The Boxer Rebellion.* New York: Berkeley Books, 2000.
Ralston, Esther. *Someday We'll Laugh.* Metuchen, NJ: Scarecrow Press, 1985.
Rentschler, Eric. *The Films of G. W. Pabst.* New Brunswick and London: Rutgers University Press, 1990.
Rainey, Buck. *Those Fabulous Serial Heroines.* Waynesville, NC: World of Yesterday Publications, 1990.
Rotha, Paul, and Richard Griffith. *The Film Till Now.* London: Spring Books, 1967.
See, Lisa. *On Gold Mountain.* New York: St. Martin's Press, 1995.
Silver, Charles. *Marlene Dietrich.* New York: Pyramid Publications, 1974.
Skal, David, and Elias Savada. *Dark Carnival.* New York: Anchor Books, 1995.
Slide, Anthony. *The American Film Industry.* New York: Limelight Editions, 1990.
_____. *Early American Cinema.* Metuchen, NJ: Scarecrow Press, 1994.
_____. *Aspects of American Film History Prior to 1920.* Metuchen, NJ: Scarecrow Press, 1978.
Smith, R. Dixon. Ronald Colman, *Gentleman of the Cinema.* Jefferson, NC: McFarland, 1991.
Spoto, Donald. *Laurence Olivier, A Biography.* New York: Harper Collins, 1996.
Stone, Rob. *Laurel or Hardy.* Temecula, CA: Split Reel, 1996.
Taves, Brian. *Robert Florey—The French Expressionist.* Metuchen, NJ: Scarecrow Press, 1987.
Thompson, Richard A. *The Yellow Peril, 1890–1924* (thesis). University of Wisconsin, 1957.
Vazzana, Eugene Michael. *Silent Film Necrology.* Jefferson, NC: McFarland, 1995.
von Sternberg, Josef. *Fun in a Chinese Laundry.* San Francisco: Mercury House, 1988.
Wapshott, Nicholas. *Carol Reed: A Biography.* New York: Alfred A. Knopf, 1994.
Wilson, A. E. *Prime Minister of Mirth—The Biography of Sir George Robey,* C. B. C., London: Odhams Press, 1956.
Wu, William F. *The Yellow Peril—Chinese-Americans in American Fiction, 1850–1940,* Hamden, CT: Archon Books, 1982.
Zhang, Yingjin, ed. *Cinema and Urban Culture in Shanghai, 1922–1943.* Stanford, CA: Stanford University Press, 1999.

Magazine Articles

Bodeen, Dewitt. "Blanche Sweet." *Films in Review.* November 1965.
_____. "Ramon Novarro." *Films in Review.* November 1967.
_____. "Betty Bronson." *Films in Review.* December 1974.
Geltzer, George. "Herbert Brenon." *Films in Review.* March 1955.
Knight, Arthur. "Marlene Dietrich." *Films in Review.* December 1954.
Luft, Herbert G. "Josef von Sternberg." *Films in Review.* June 1981.
Spears, Jack. "Marshall Neilan." *Films in Review.* November 1962.
Uselton, Roi A. "Renée Adorée." *Films in Review.* June–July 1968.

Internet Articles

Cohen, Aaron M. "Tokugo Nogai Takagi—Japan's First Film Actress" *Bright Lights Film Journal.* October 2000. brightlightsfilm.com
Ingram, Clarke The Dumont Television Network. members.aol.com/cingram/television/dumont.htm

Index

Across to Singapore (1928) 61–64
Adorée, Renée 47
Adventures in Paradise (TV) 167–169
The Adventures of Marco Polo (1938) 138
After Midnight (1921) 146, 147
Ahn, Philip 115
The Alaskan (1924) 34, 35
Alien Land Act (1870) 1
Allan, Elizabeth 87
Ames, Adrienne 90
Aoki, Tsuru 3
Art and Archaeology 34
Asche, Oscar 84
Ault, Marie 149

Bainter, Fay 156
Baker, Josephine 13
The Barbara Stanwyck Theatre (TV) 171, 172
Barrie, James M. 38
Barrymore, Ethel 156
Barrymore, John 51
Beau Geste (1926) 41
Beau Geste (1939) 141
Beery, Noah 43
Bellamy, Ralph 131
Bennett, Arnold 72
Benrimo, J. Harry 156
The Big Parade (1925) 48
Bits of Life (1921) 9, 17–19
The Bitter Tea of General Yen (1933) 88
Blore, Eric 129
Bold Journey (TV) 9, 165
Bombs Over Burma (1942) 90, 132–134
Brenon, Herbert 38, 88
Brent, Evelyn 115
British International Pictures (BIP) 65, 73

Bronson, Betty 38
Brook, Clive 99, 146
Brooks, Louise 68
Browning, Tod 12
Buck, Pearl S. 88, 162
Burnell, Helen 77
Busch, Mae 115
Byrne, Don 155

Cafe Society (1939) 156
Calthrop, Donald 76
Campbell Playhouse 161
Capra, Frank 88
Carroll, Madeleine 156
The Cat and the Canary (1927) 53
C. B. C. Film Sales 40
Chadwick Pictures 44
Chan, Charlie 53
Chaney, Lon 17
Chautard, Emile 99
Chinatown Charlie (1928) 60, 61
Chinese Exclusion Act (1882) 1
Chinese Garden Festival (1940) 129
The Chinese Parrot (1927) 51–53
Chinese Theatre 13
Chu Chin Chow (1934) 80–84, 161
The Circle of Chalk 9, 148, 149, 151, 158
The City Butterfly see *Grosstadt Schmetterling*
Claire, Ina 156
Climax! (TV) 166, 167
Cochrane, Frank 149
Cohn, Harry 40
Colman, Ronald 41
Columbia Pictures 40

Comstock, Daniel F. 22
The Cosmics *see* Hollywooders
Costello, Dolores 51
Costello, Helene 51
Costello, Maurice 51
Courtneidge, Cicely 77
Crawford, Joan 64
The Crimson City (1928) 59, 60, 121
Crosland, Alan 51
Cummings, Constance 88
Curzon, George 149

Dana, Viola 158
Dangerous to Know (1938) 115–120, 152, 161
Daugherty, Jack 12
Daughter of Shanghai (1938) 112–115
Daughter of the Dragon (1931) 3, 91–85, 115, 173
Dean, Basil 148
The Desert's Toll (1926) 43, 44
The Devil Dancer (1927) 53–55
Dinehart, Allan 105
Dinty (1920) 14, 15
Disputed Passage (1939) 90
Donlevy, Brian 141
The Dove (1928) 58, 59
The Dragon Horse see *The Silk Bouquet*
Drifting (1923) 25, 26
Driven from Home (1927) 44
Dumont, Dr. Allen B. 163
Dumont Network 163
Dupont, E(wald) A(ndre) 72

Edgar Bergen and Charlie McCarthy Show 161
Eichberg, Richard 65, 68

177

178 • Index

Ellery Queen's Penthouse Mystery (1941) 129–131
Elstree Calling (1930) 76–78
Elstree Story (1952) 72
Elvey, Maurice 48
Ephraim, Lee 151

Fairbanks, Douglas 12, 32
Fifth Avenue (1925) 41, 42
The First Born (1921) 17
The Flame of Love (1930) 77, 146
Flaming Youth (1923) 15
Florey, Robert 104, 115
Flower Drum Song (play) 8; (film 91
Folkteatern (Goteborg) 155
For the Freedom of the East (1918) 3
For Whom the Bell Tolls (1943) 120
The Fortieth Door (1924) 32–34
Forty Winks (1925) 40
Fred Allen Show 162

The Gallery of Mme. Liu-Tsong (TV) 9, 163
Garfield, John 129
Gargan, William 131
Garmes, Lee 99
Geary Act (1892) 2, 4
Geill, Flemming 153
The General Died at Dawn (1933) 120
George, Heinrich 68
Gerard, John 155
Gilbert, John 20
Gilbert, Warburton 153
Goldwyn Picture Corp. 12
The Good Earth (1937) 88, 112, 138
Green Acres (TV) 172
Gregory, Ena 12
Griffith, Raymond 40
Grosstadt Schmetterling (1929) 68–70
The Gulf Between (1917) 22
Gunsmoke (TV) 171
Gwenn, Edmund 87

Hai-Tang (1930) 73–76, 78
Hardy, Oliver 45
Harlan, Kenneth 23
Hawley, Wanda 12

Hayakawa, Sessue 3, 17, 90, 94, 173
Hergesheimer, Joseph 86
Herlock Shomes in Be-A-Live Crook (1930) 145
His Supreme Moment (1925) 41
Hitchcock, Alfred 65
Hollywood Hotel 161
Hollywood on Parade (1932) 100
Hollywood Party (1937) 111, 112
Hollywooders 12, 13
Holmes, Helen 12
The Honorable Mr. Buggs (1927) 44, 45
Hook (1991) 39
The House That Shadows Built (1931) 95
Howe, James Wong 39
Huber, Harold 138

Impact (1949) 138–141
Island of Lost Men (1939) 126–129

Java Head (1935) 9, 84–87
Johnson, Noble 105
Johnson, Tor 169

Kalmus, Herbert T. 22
King of Chinatown (1939) 120–126, 156
A Kiss for Cinderella (1926) 38
Komai, Tetsu 105
Konserthusets (Stockholm) 153, 155
Kortner, Fritz 83
Kraft Music Hal 161
Der Kreidekreis 148

The Lady from Chungking (1942) 90, 134–138
Lady Precious Stream 155
Lady Tsen Mei 3, 43
La Galliene, Eva 156
Lamour, Dorothy 90
Das Land des Lachelns 150
Landis, Cullen 12
Lane, Lola 122
Lang, Matheson 48
Langner, Lawrence 155
Laughton, Charles 72, 150
Lear, Tom 152

Lee, Ching Wah 115
Lee, Gon Toy 5
Lehar, Franz 150
Leni, Paul 52
Leong, James B. 43
The Letter (TV, 1956) 163, 164
The Life and Legend of Wyatt Earp (TV) 170, 171
The Lifebuoy Program 161
Limehouse Blues (1934) 105–109, 111
Lin, Yutang 129
Lind, Gillian 150
Lindsay, Margaret 122, 131
The Little White Bird 38
Loder, John 87
Loew's Inc. 12
Lotus Blossom (1921) 43
Loy, Myrna 13, 60
Lubin Co. 3

Mandarin Film Co. 3
Marin, Edwin L. 105
The Mask of Fu Manchu (1932) 60
Mathis, June 158
McKenna, Siobhan 165
McPherson, Aimee Semple 89, 90
Meighan, Thomas 35
Messer Marco Polo 155
Mickey Spillane's Mike Hammer (TV) 165, 166
Mills, John 165
Milner, Victor 95
Miracle on 34th Street (1947) 87
Mori, Toshia 88
Mudie, Leonard 122

National Origins Act (1924) 2
National Scala (Copenhagen) 153
Nazimova, Alla 12, 14, 156
Neufeld, Sigmund 90
Newfield, Sam 90
Nigh, William 138
Niblo, Fred 55
Novarro, Ramon 64

Oboler, Arch 161
O'Brian, Hugh 171
Oland, Warner 51, 53, 99

Old San Francisco (1927) 48–51
Olivier, Laurence 148
On the Spot 9, 115, 150–152, 159
Otto, Henry 158
Outside the Law (1921) 15–17
Owen, Reginald 105

Pabst, G(eorg) W(ilhelm) 68
Palace Theatre (Blackpool) 152
Panama Patrol (1939) 90
Parker, Jean 111
Parsons, Harriet 129
The Patriot 161, 162
The Pavement Butterfly see *Grosstadt Schmetterling*
The Perfect Flapper (1924) 15
Peter and Wendy 39
Peter Pan (1924) 35–39, 173
Peyton Place (1957) 145
Piccadilly (1929) 70–72, 148
Pickford, Mary 23
Picture People #8 (1941) 131
Portrait in Black (1960) 9, 141–145
Powers, Francis 17
Princess Turandot 155, 156, 159
Producers Releasing Corp. 90

Quinn, Anthony 115
Quong, Rose 149
Quota Act (1927) 80

Raft, George 111
Ralston, Esther 39
Ray, Allene 34
Reboch, Alfred 55
The Red Lantern (1919) 9, 12–14
Reed, Carol 151
Reed, Florence 161
The Return of Sherlock Homes (1929) 146
Rhodes, Harrison 156
Richardson, Ralph 86
Roach, Hal 13
The Road to Dishonour (1930) see *The Flame of Love*
Robey, George 83
Robin Hood (1922) 32
Rock Springs (Wyoming) 2
Røde Mølle (Oslo) 153
Rohmer, Sax 95
Rowland, Richard 12
Royal Gelatine Hour 161
Rudy Vallee Show 161
Russell, Rosalind 129
Russo-Japanese War 3

San Francisco Veterans War Memorial Fete 161
The Savage Innocents (1959) 146
Scott Act (1888) 2
Screen Snapshots 39, 40
Shame (1921) 19, 20
Shanghai Express (1932) 90, 95–100, 141
Sherlock Holmes (1932) 105
Shores, Lynn 55
Sidney, Sylvia 23
The Silk Bouquet (1926) 43
Smith, Paul Girard 153
Sojin 32, 45
Song (1928) 9, 65–67
Stanwyck, Barbara 88, 171
Star Studios 88
Stonehouse, Ruth 12
Streets of Shanghai (1927) 55–58
Struss, Karl 129
A Study in Scarlet 100–105
Sweet, Blanche 41
Swickard, Josef 51

Talmadge, Norma 13
The Taming of the Shrew (1929) 76
Tamiroff, Akim 120
Tearle, Conway 147
Technicolor Motion Picture Co. 22
The Thief of Bagdad (1924) 9, 12, 28–32, 173
Thundering Dawn (1923) 26–28
Tiffany Productions 104
Tiger Bay (1933) 78–80, 152
Tivoli Theatre (Melbourne) 156
Tokagi, Tokuko Nagai 3
Tol'able David (1921) 39
The Toll of the Sea (1922) 9, 12, 20–23, 173
Torrence, Ernest 39, 64
A Trip to Chinatown (1927) 42, 43
Troland, Dr. Leonard T. 22
Tschun-Tschi 9, 150, 158
Turandot 155
Turner, Lana 145
Twentieth Century Pictures 51

Van Dyke, W.S. 88
von Schlettow, Hans Adalbert 68
von Sternberg, Josef 99

Wallace, Edgar 150
Washburn, Bryant 12, 13
Welles, Orson 162
Whelan, Gordon 152
When Were You Born (1938) 120–122
Wherry, Edith 14
Wong, Anna May (Liu Tsong) 4, 5, 7, 9, 11–15, 17, 19, 20, 23, 25, 26, 28, 34, 35, 39, 41, 42, 45, 47, 51, 55, 59–61, 63–65, 68, 70, 72, 73, 76, 78, 80, 83, 86, 88–91, 95, 99, 100, 105, 109, 111, 115, 119, 120, 121, 125, 129, 131, 134, 138, 141, 145, 146, 148–153, 155, 156, 158, 161–165, 167, 169–173
Wong, Liu Ying (Lulu) 5
Wong, Marion E. 3
Wong, Mary 91
Wong, Richard 91
Wong, Sam Sing 5
Wu, Butterfly 89
Wyler, William 164

Yellow Peril 3
Yuen, Lily 89

Zanuck, Darryl F. 51

www.ingramcontent.com/pod-product-compliance
Ingram Content Group UK Ltd.
Pitfield, Milton Keynes, MK11 3LW, UK
UKHW050523150426
5217IPUK00026B/1770